THE EPIC OF THE CID

with Related Texts

THE EPIC OF THE CID

with Related Texts

Translated and Edited,
with an Introduction, by
MICHAEL HARNEY

Hackett Publishing Company, Inc.
Indianapolis/Cambridge

Copyright © 2011 by Hackett Publishing Company, Inc.

15 14 13 12 11   1 2 3 4 5 6 7

For further information, please address
    Hackett Publishing Company, Inc.
    P.O. Box 44937
    Indianapolis, Indiana 46244-0937

    www.hackettpublishing.com

Cover design by Abigail Coyle
Text design by Mary Vasquez and Sara Stevens
Composition by Professional Book Compositors, Inc.
Printed at Sheridan Books, Inc.

Library of Congress Cataloging-in-Publication Data

Cantar de mío Cid. English
    The epic of the Cid, with related texts / translated and edited, with
an introduction, by Michael Harney.
        p. cm.
    Includes bibliographical references and index.
    ISBN 978-1-60384-316-4 (cloth) — ISBN 978-1-60384-315-7 (pbk.)
    1. Cid, ca. 1043-1099—Romances.   2. Epic poetry, Spanish—
Translations into English.   I. Harney, Michael, 1948- II. Title.
    PQ6367.E3H37 2011
    861'.1—dc22   2010028937

In memoriam
Frederic Amory
(1925–2009)

CONTENTS

Introduction   ix

Bibliography   xxv

Maps   xxviii

The Epic of the Cid   1

Related Texts   107

    A. *Treasury of the Excellencies of the Spaniards.*
    Ibn Bassam (Abu l'Hassan Ali ibn Bassam).
    Chronicle composed in Arabic in the early
    twelfth century.   109

    B. *The History of Rodrigo (Historia Roderici).*
    Anonymous. Chronicle composed in Latin,
    sometime between 1102 and 1238 but
    probably after 1144.   115

    C. *The Song of the Campeador (Carmen Campidoctoris).*
    Anonymous. Ode composed in Latin verse,
    sometime between the early 1080s and 1190.   123

    D. *First General Chronicle (Primera crónica general).*
    Alfonso X of Castile. Chronicle composed in
    Old Castilian, late thirteenth century.   127

    E. *The Chronicle of Twenty Kings (Crónica de
    veinte reyes).* Anonymous. Chronicle composed
    in Old Castilian, late thirteenth century.   161

F. *The Youthful Deeds of Rodrigo* (*Mocedades de Rodrigo*). Anonymous. Epic poem composed in Castilian, latter half of the fourteenth century.   165

G. "The Cid and the Moorish King." Anonymous. *Romance* ("ballad") composed in Castilian verse, late fifteenth or early sixteenth century.   175

Compendium of Proper Names   179

Index   207

INTRODUCTION

The Work

The Epic of the Cid (*Cantar de Mio Cid*) is the only medieval Spanish epic to come down to us in more or less complete form. Composed in Old Castilian, possibly some time in the latter part of the twelfth century, it was probably put into written form in the first decade of the thirteenth. It is known to us through a single manuscript, dating from the fourteenth century and housed in the Spanish National Library. The first page of the manuscript, and two others in the middle of the text, are missing. The text gives no indication of any title. English translations have called it the *Song* (*Cantar*), *Poem* (*Poema*), or *Lay of the Cid*. Only one of these terms is justified by evidence from the work itself: *cantar*, "song," is used by the narrator to refer to the work. I have decided on "epic" for reasons that will be explained presently.

The Historical Background

Invaded by Muslim troops from North Africa in 711, Visigothic Spain was soon conquered and subdued by the invaders. Only a zone along the northern coast remained in the hands of Christians. Al-Andalus, as the Muslims called it, was an independent emirate from 756 to 912, then a caliphate in its own right from 912 to 1031, and during its heyday was the most prosperous and advanced civilization in Europe. Its great cities — Toledo, Cordoba, Seville, Malaga, Saragossa, and Valencia — were famous throughout the Muslim and Christian worlds. Its economy, agriculture, science, military organization, and urban sophistication were the envy of medieval Christendom.[1]

---

1. All proper nouns and references to historical figures are identified and explained in the Compendium of Proper Names.

At the collapse of the Cordoban Caliphate in 1031, Al-Andalus broke up into independent city states called *taifas*. These remained relatively more advanced and prosperous than the Christian kingdoms to the north, but at the same time became more vulnerable to attack. This ushered in the era that came to be known as the Reconquest. Throughout most of the earlier years of this period, from the mid-eleventh to the early thirteenth century, the relationship between the two Peninsular civilizations was one of intermittent conflict rather than constant and systematic warfare. Raiding, pillaging, and extorting tribute were the preferred modes of Christian aggression, with outright conquest the exception (as in the case of Toledo, conquered in 1085 by Alfonso VI, the king of the Cid's epic). In order to slow the Christian advance, two Berber dynasties came from across the Strait of Gibraltar to the ostensible aid of the imperiled Spanish Muslims, but stayed on to become de facto invaders and rulers of Muslim Spain. These were the Almoravids (1086–1147) and the Almohads (c. 1160–1248). The Cid confronted the first of these Berber dynasties, while the second was eventually overthrown during the culminating phase of the Reconquest. Notable episodes in that final chapter were the victory of Alfonso VIII and his Christian coalition at the battle of Las Navas de Tolosa (1212), and the campaigns of his grandson Fernando III, conqueror of Cordoba (1236), Seville (1248), and many other Muslim kingdoms of Al-Andalus. Only the mountain kingdom of Granada remained independent, persisting as a tributary state of Castile until its conquest by the Catholic Kings in 1492.

The Cid of History

Rodrigo Díaz de Vivar, known to history and legend as the Cid, was born in the town of Vivar, near Burgos, in the early 1040s, into a family of *infanzones*, or barons of the lesser nobility. Orphaned in 1058, he was taken into the household of Sancho, the eldest son of King Fernando I. Fernando, on his death in 1064, had divided his domains among his five children. To Alfonso, the second son, he left León, at that time the principal kingdom. Sancho received Castile, and García, the youngest son, was given Galicia. Fernando's younger daughter, Elvira, was given the town of Toro, while the eldest of the five siblings, Urraca, was given the city of Zamora.

After the death of their father, Sancho proved unwilling to abide by his father's division of the kingdom. With Alfonso's help, he took over Galicia from their brother García. Then, turning on Alfonso, Sancho defeated him at the battle of Golpejera in 1072. After annexing León and driving Alfonso into exile, Sancho then turned his attention to the domain assigned to his elder sister, Urraca. When she defied him from within her stronghold in Zamora, Sancho laid siege to the city. During the siege, according to some accounts, a Zamoran noble named Vellid Adolfo, pretending to be a deserter, assassinated Sancho. Returning from exile after the murder, Alfonso succeeded to the various realms once controlled by his slain brother.

Rodrigo Díaz had served as Sancho's *alférez* or constable (a post combining the functions of standard-bearer and captain of the royal guard) at Golpejera. One of Sancho's staunchest supporters, Rodrigo was not at first favored by Alfonso. The latter, however, sought to win Rodrigo over, granting him honors and arranging an excellent marriage with Jimena Díaz, a woman of an aristocratic Asturian lineage. But increasing tension between Alfonso and his brother's one-time henchman led to Rodrigo's banishment in 1081. The exiled Rodrigo served the Muslim ruler of Saragossa, Yusuf al-Mu'tamin, under whose banner he obtained victories against Christian Barcelona and the Muslim kingdoms of Lérida, Tortosa, and Denia.

Meanwhile, Alfonso had carried out the conquest of Muslim Toledo (1085). The Almoravids, the Berber dynasty controlling northwestern Africa, invaded Spain and defeated Alfonso at the Battle of Sagrajas (1086). Alfonso then reconciled with the Cid, after which the latter went to assist the Muslim ruler of Valencia, an ally and protégé of Alfonso, in defending that city against attacks from the Muslim towns of Denia, Tortosa, and Lérida. After managing to gain control of Albarracín, Valencia, and other towns, the Cid marched to the aid of Alfonso, who was advancing into Al-Andalus.

Another quarrel between the two men provoked Alfonso's wrath and led him to take the Cid's wife prisoner. In the meantime, a coalition was organized against the Cid, which consisted of the Muslim kingdoms of Saragossa and Lérida, as well as

Christian Barcelona. The ensuing Battle of Tévar was won by the Cid, who took as prisoner Berenguer, the Count of Barcelona.

In 1091, as the Almoravids threatened another invasion, the Cid marched into Al-Andalus, intending to come to Alfonso's aid. After another falling out with the king, the Cid remained in Al-Andalus as Alfonso returned to Castile. The Cid retired to Valencia, where he fortified the city's defenses and formed an alliance with the emir of Saragossa and the Christian king of Aragon. While defending Valencia, the Cid declined to make outright war against Alfonso, even when the latter, allied with Genoa and Pisa, advanced against him. However, the Cid invaded the territories of his Castilian enemies, a number of whom were favored members of Alfonso's court. The king then decided to reconcile with his famous vassal.

In the Cid's absence, meanwhile, the Almoravid party came to power in Valencia. The Cid laid siege to the city and took it in the summer of 1093. As the Almoravids sent reinforcements, their allies within the city again seized power. When the Almoravid forces withdrew, the Cid undertook a second siege, reentering the city in 1094. While granting very favorable conditions of capitulation, the Cid and his Christian forces remained in the city. The Cid moved his family there and welcomed many more Christian knights who came to join him. Another Almoravid force was sent against the city, but, with the help of Castilian reinforcements, the Cid defeated it in December of 1094. He then became the ruler of Valencia, while continuing to acknowledge Alfonso as his liege lord.

Of the Cid's two daughters, Christina married Ramiro, the crown prince of Navarre, and María married Ramón Berenguer, the Count of Barcelona. After the Cid's death by natural causes in 1099, his wife Jimena remained in Valencia until 1103. In that year she returned to Castile with her husband's remains, which she buried in the monastery of San Pedro de Cardeña.[2]

---

2. A famous Benedictine monastery, situated 8 kilometers southeast of Burgos (see Compendium of Proper Names). Historically associated with the Cid, it was a significant shrine in the most important period of the Camino de Santiago (Way of Saint James) and figures prominently in this epic.

The Muslim Perspective

Although the historical Rodrigo Díaz de Vivar had enemies and rivals among the Spanish Christians, the profile of him that emerges from reading Christian authors is mostly a positive one. He is portrayed as a supremely brave warrior, consummate in his martial ability; a clever tactician and astute strategist; a staunch vassal and wise counselor; a shrewd diplomat and inspirational leader of men.

Medieval Muslim historians paint a different portrait. Their perspective with regard to this Christian champion is paradoxically exemplified by the name they apply to him. His Christian nickname, *El Cid,* derived from the Hispano-Arabic dialectal *sid,* and ultimately from the classical Arabic *sayyid,* "lord," is not used by Arab-speaking authors. Their accounts, as the great Arabist Reinhart Dozy (*Le Cid d'après de nouveaux documents,* 62–63; see *TES* in Related Texts) points out, refer to Rodrigo by the term *Campeador,* the term also used by Christian biographers and chroniclers writing in the vernacular (those writing in Latin call him *Campidoctor,* "master of the field"). *El Cid* is apparently used mainly by Christians. The name literally means "lord," but it also may have meant, as Richard Fletcher suggests (*The Quest for El Cid,* 3), something like "The Boss." The seeming Arabism of the epithet *El Cid* may, in other words, have originally expressed a slangy admiration, among Peninsular Christians, for the resolute man of action who gets things done, for the inspiring leader of men in battle and siege, for the equitable redistributor of plunder who gives poor men the chance to escape poverty.

The Spanish Muslims, while recognizing Rodrigo's bravery, energy, and military talents, saw him as a pitiless mercenary, a cunning opportunist, a shameless trickster, a ruthless extortionist, a dangerous terrorist. In the accounts of the Valencian Ibn Alqama (b. 1036–1037) and Ibn Bassam (born in what is now Portugal, latter half of the eleventh and first decades of the twelfth centuries; see Related Texts A, *Treasury of the Excellencies of the Spaniards*), Rodrigo is the scourge of Spanish Islam, a self-interested rogue who wars against Christian and Muslim alike. Crossing religious frontiers as needed, he serves now Christian masters, now Muslim. A man dominated by material greed and lust for power, he is not above the cruelest methods of torture when interrogating or meting out exemplary punishment.

This alternative view of the protagonist must be born in mind as we read the tale of a hero who is shown by the poet to be an exemplary father, vassal, and warlord, but who also leads his men into fierce battle, conducts lightening raids in search of plunder, storms fortresses, besieges towns, levies tribute, and extorts ransom. The narrator does not hide these ugly facts about his hero. He approves of them, even glorifies them, because for him and his audience Rodrigo is their leader, their patriarch, their Cid against the world.

History and Poetry

This historical personage — a virtuosic warrior, a daring tactician, a formidable strategist, and a charismatic leader — deeply impressed his contemporaries, both Christian and Muslim. Already, in the Cid's lifetime, legends, stories, and chronicles were devoted to his exploits. *The Epic of the Cid*, composed about a century after the real Cid's death, shows a detailed awareness of that tradition. The Cid continued to be a character in subsequent Hispanic poetry, balladry, and theater, and has become a Hispanic cultural icon, as evidenced — to mention only two of many possible examples — by Corneille's 1636 play *Le Cid* and the 1963 film *El Cid*, starring Charleton Heston as Rodrigo Díaz de Vivar and Sophia Loren as Jimena.

The Epic of the Cid is a historical narrative, but it is not a work of historiography. It is a poetic narrative that uses historical detail, or embellishes its yarn with details that sound historical, for the purposes of storytelling. Those purposes may not agree with our preconceptions about the Middle Ages. A striking fact about this epic, for instance, is that despite being composed in its present form around the time of the Third Crusade (1187–1192), a famous instance of conflict between civilizations, it shows no sign of a systematic crusading spirit. One of the Cid's best friends is a Muslim; his worst enemies are Christians.

In determining the poet's intentions, and the sympathies and antipathies he wants to elicit in his audience, the text is our main source of information. Despite the essential mystery of the work's original circumstances of composition and performance, the narrative gives clues in many places as to the poet's attitudes regarding ethical, social, and economic questions. Kinship and marriage, money and politics, law and order, status and prestige, honor and dishonor, are all on the mind of the poet and his audience.

An especially important clue is the poem's obsession with the law. The poet uses many legal terms and phrases. The plot of this epic turns on legal issues. The Cid, estranged from his rightful lord, unjustly outlawed and exiled, and separated from his beloved wife and daughters, must make his way in a hostile frontier world. His adventures and vicissitudes culminate in a court case that utterly vindicates him while utterly humiliating his enemies.

This emphasis on legal issues and the poet's frequent use of legal terms and concepts have been cited in arguing that the poet was not only conversant with the law, but may in fact have been a lawyer. Scholars have demonstrated parallels with specific Peninsular charters and law codes. Others have countered that in the era when the poem as we know it was composed, probably in the last decade or two of the twelfth century, law had not been professionalized in the Peninsula. The first Spanish degree-granting universities, Palencia and Salamanca, were not founded until the second decade of the thirteenth century.

The Epic of the Cid shows evidence that its composer knew something of the law and was possibly familiar with some law codes, but to say that he was a man of the law seems unverifiable. If the poet were a secular student of the law, he would presumably have "practiced" it in the generalized, nonadvocating, nonprofessional way of several characters in the poem, including the Cid himself. The laws known to the poet might well have been oral lore written down by scribes, many or most of them clerics. But this common law consisted of phraseologies and precedents accessible to all knowledgeable men in the arguing of cases before judges and peers.

The hero of the Cidian epic and his friends express hatred of those who manipulate the law, written or otherwise. Whether or not the historical Cid and his followers felt that way about such issues is difficult to verify. The epic narrator, however, clearly wants us to side with the Cid and his men. Pedro

Bermúdez, the Cid's nephew and one of his most intimate vassals, insults one of the villains by calling him a "blow-hard" (l. 3328). In the original manuscript, Pedro calls his despicable adversary "a tongue without hands" (*lengua sin manos*). Actions, not words, define manhood. An honorable man may have to argue his case before the law, may argue it without compromising his integrity, but only if regrettably obliged to do so by makers of idle promises, poltroons who hide behind the letter of the law.

The Cid is a skillful and learned litigant, but he is not defined by his words. He is above all a charismatic patriarch. From this status spring all his other roles: father, husband, uncle, father-in-law, comrade, warrior, lord. No matter where he is or what he does, in peace or in war, he lives up to the expectations incumbent on patriarchy.

As the leader of a merry band of loyal vassals, a cheerful besieger of cities and fair-and-square redistributor of wealth, the epic Cid (as opposed to the historical Cid) is a benevolent warlord. He is like his historical counterpart, but the harsher elements of the historical warlord's profile are played down. The epic Cid is mostly truthful, generous, and fair. He is a father to his people. His paternal altruism, however, is reserved for his clansmen, vassals, and subjects; everyone else is fair game. This is why he guiltlessly manipulates the money lenders Raquel and Vidas, slyly engaging to repay an enormous loan using a chest full of sand as collateral. The Cid makes his false assurances to the moneylenders with ethical impunity because they are not his people. The crime of the Scions of Carrión is that they treat their wives, the Cid's daughters, like outsiders. These young men, in other words, behave like greedy moneylenders. Indifferent to all standards of decency, they ignore the ties established by marriage, which make them and the Cid kinsmen.

Like Robin Hood and other robbers and rebels of folklore, figures defined by the historian Eric Hobsbawm as social bandits, the Cid is an Everyman.[3] He personifies the folkloric motif of the unjustly disgraced nobleman who rebels against an unfair regime. In ways specific to the time and place, he is a

---

3. For discussion of the populism of bandits, see Hobsbawm, *Primitive Rebels*, 20–28; and *Bandits*, 41–56.

protector of the common people. The conqueror of Valencia and many other towns, the epic Cid patriarchically nurtures the impoverished, predatory hordes who follow him. The story sides, in other words, with besiegers and invaders in the same way that stories of Robin Hood side with bandits and highway robbers.

Although not exactly the same kind of outlaw as the legendary Robin Hood, the epic Cid is, like the English folk hero, an outsider. Backstabbing courtiers have estranged him from his rightful lord and procured his exile. The plot of the poem is channeled toward the ultimate moral and social vindication of the hero and his family. The outrage committed by wastrel nobles who marry the Cid's daughters for money affords the hero the moral leverage and material opportunity to ensure that his socially superior but morally inferior enemies get their comeuppance. As in much bandit folklore, the eventual chastisement of the effete upper-class miscreants — in this case taking the form of a judicial combat that they lose in shameful fashion — was probably understood as ruggedly humorous. The audience of this epic tale would have consisted of all those who might identify with the hero's vindictive project and cheer for his champions as they teach these miscreants a lesson. This audience might well have included, in addition to commoners, lesser nobles like the Cid and even some of higher status. As with sports figures, movie stars, and politicians, audience identification is not based on actual analogy between literary characters and readers, listeners, and spectators, but on the suitability of bigger-than-life personalities for vicarious projection.

Title, Genre, Language, Style

This is a prose translation. All that is rhythmically poetic in the original — irregular line length, loose stanzaic structure, and assonant rhyme scheme — is lost. I make no attempt to emulate the admirable work of translators like Richard Lattimore and Robert Fagles, whose verse renderings of Homer enable readers to experience something aesthetically analogous to the metrical glory of the original works. On the other hand, I try to convey something like the easy flow and colloquial accessibility of the original. This will enable readers, I hope, to focus on the characters, the setting, the social and psychological tensions, and the episodic buildup of the narrative.

Other translators have called this work the *Poem* or the *Song of the Cid*. By calling it *The Epic of the Cid*, I emphasize its similarities to other works that are also generally called epics, such as the *Iliad, The Odyssey, The Aeneid, Beowulf,* or *The Song of Roland*. Common features defining this genre include the following: a narrative that begins in medias res ("in the middle of things"); a beginning that includes an invocation to a muse or a statement of the central theme; a narrative that focuses on the destiny and exploits of an exemplary hero; heroic actions taking place in the past from the perspective of the poet and his audience; a society and economy dominated by warfare, clan confrontation, and economic predation; the backdrop of a greater world encompassing peoples, nations, far-reaching travels, opposing peoples and civilizations; the use of recurrent epithets and other sorts of formulaic language; simple, even stereotypical characterizations; an emphasis on action rather than introspection, involving intensely dramatic scenes of intimate emotion, alternating with violent, man-to-man confrontations; the tendency of characters to speechify in formal-sounding language; the tendency of narrators to list things, such as names of personages or places; and, of course, divine intervention in the affairs of men.

If we regard scenes in which God could be seen as disposed to intervene on behalf of the hero and his cause (the Cid's dream, Jimena's prayer), the only epic traits omitted by the Cid poet are the invocation to the muse (or its medieval equivalent) and the initial thematic statement. One or both of these features, however, might have been present in the missing first folio of the extant manuscript. Given the poem's inclusion of all the other epic features, it seems generically accurate, then, to call the work *The Epic of the Cid*.

The honor of membership in this august genre, however, comes with several problems of interpretation. To begin with, how do we explain the apparently shared features of works composed in places and eras far removed from one another in space and time, including works from the literary traditions of India, Japan, Germany, and Africa? Some similarities might be explained by assuming that later works imitate earlier works.

However, this notion can only be taken so far. It is hard to imagine, for example, how the Cid poet, composing probably in the latter half of the twelfth century, could know anything of ancient Indian epic, or even of the Homeric epics, the texts of which were probably not directly known to western European readers until much later.

The Cid poet might have known Virgil's *Aeneid*, which was well known throughout the Middle Ages. However, despite some suggestive similarities, there is no irrefutable evidence of such direct knowledge or imitation. Some scholars have thought that this epic imitates the Old French *Song of Roland*, probably composed a century or so before. There are many suggestive similarities between the two works, and between the Cid epic and other French *chansons de geste*. These similarities, on the other hand, might reflect not the Spanish poem's direct imitation of French epic but rather the participation of both French and Spanish epics in a primordial and enduring Romance folksinging tradition that predates by centuries the earliest epic manuscripts.

From an even broader perspective, the analogies that justify our perception of an epic genre could derive, in some cases, from composition in an earlier — that is, more tribal, clanish, and patriarchal — phase in the history of the respective histories of the peoples and nations that have produced epics. According to this concept, so-called folk or primitive epics, such as Homer's works, are called primary. Works that self-consciously imitate them, such as Virgil's *Aeneid* or Milton's *Paradise Lost*, are called secondary.

Such questions have been debated for many years. The issues, including the validity of the primary/secondary classification, remain controversial. The debate intensified in the 1920s, and 1930s, when a new theory of epic composition emerged. Developed by Milman Parry and his then-assistant Albert Lord (who would later write *The Singer of Tales*, the most influential book ever written on the subject), this oral-formulaic theory of epic demonstrated stylistic parallels between the Homeric works and poems composed within a living tradition of oral epic poetry in Yugoslavia. Parry and Lord sought to show how poets trained in a traditional, and very possibly illiterate, singing tradition, and employing extensive repertoires of recombinant, contextually variable metrical formulas along with extensive thematic narrative schemes, could indeed produce lengthy narrative songs that seemed strikingly analogous to the Homeric epics.[4]

The Parry-Lord model, while provoking extensive and on-going debates among scholars of Greek epic, has been applied, also with much controversy, to other epic traditions, including those of medieval France and Spain. Two orientations, roughly speaking, have emerged from this discussion. The oral-traditionalists envision a popular, and possibly illiterate, singer of tales, a folkloric bard who composed his text for performance before a live audience in baronial halls, monastic refectories, taverns, marketplaces, or street corners. An extreme version of this model postulates an illiterate poet who composed not *for* performance but *during* performance. Defenders of this notion point to the remarkable memory and agile improvisation of the folk poet working within an oral-formulaic tradition. Each performance in such a tradition is a variation on the same basic song; no two performances will be exactly alike. The text of a work like *The Epic of the Cid* will thus most likely be the transcription of such a performance.

The other orientation assumes a learned writer, possibly a cleric, who composed in writing. This approach emphasizes the deliberate narrative and metrical artistry of poetic production. More subtle presentations of this concept allow that traditional folk poetry exists, and that the poet might well have imitated certain aspects of that poetry, such as narrative formulas, epithets, stereotypical characterization, and so on. However, although he may adapt or imitate originally oral or folkloric works, the literate poet, according to the individualist model, is like any other author, ancient, medieval, or modern. Even if he imitates oral style, and wants to lend his work a folksy air and archaic setting, he composes in writing. This implies methodical choices as to diction, rhyme scheme, metrical structure, stanza length, and other literary features. Oral folksingers

---

4. The performance and training of the oral singer are discussed in the second chapter of Lord's *The Singer of Tales*. Lord's third and fourth chapters analyze the narrative and metrical intricacies of composition in performance. His sixth chapter describes the complex interaction of oral and written traditions.

within a formulaic tradition perhaps make similar choices. But their choices are severely limited by the narrative and metrical constraints of the tradition. The literate poet, in contrast, has a far broader range of stylistic and thematic possibilities. Even if intended for eventual recitation, or even if influenced by oral tradition, the literate poem, according to the individualist theory, results from the singular labor of an author rather than from the improvisational, public domain give-and-take of an interactive singing performance.

This controversy cannot be rehearsed in any detail here. Many students of the problem decline to align themselves with one side or the other of the issue, pointing to the lack of corroborating documentary evidence as to the practical details of poetic training, methods of composition, and styles and venues of recitation. Lacking such external evidence, debate tends to focus on technical issues of versification, stanzaic structure, rhythm, diction, and so on. Such topics are difficult to discuss in the context of a translation.

We can point out, however, that a nuanced model of the medieval epic singer has to allow for the coexistence of literacy and illiteracy. Reading and writing were probably not conveniently separable regimes in the Middle Ages. A poet could be both bardic and scribal, and be moved by all kinds of motives and influences. Although we cannot definitely confirm the exact circumstances or methods of composition—and thus cannot say for sure whether *The Epic of the Cid* is a primary or a secondary epic—we can point to several features of the poem that suggest it was meant to be performed, and probably was performed, before an audience. These features include the following:

1. Indications that singing and music were involved. The narrator, for example, several times calls the tale a *cantar* ("song").
2. Consistently repetitious language. This makes the work sound like a song, which repeats itself with refrains and catchphrases. This repetitive tendency is especially apparent in the work's use of epithets, a trait with which readers of Homer will be familiar. *The Epic of the Cid* is fond of formulaic repetitions. Thus, Homer's "rosy-fingered dawn," "grey-eyed Athena," and "wily Odysseus" are matched by the Cidian poet's "Campeador" and "man

born in a lucky hour." But the repetition is not always exact. Rather, the poet paraphrases with slight variation. This seems to suggest the almost-but-not-quite-exact repetition of semi-improvisational oral performance, whose dynamics have been studied by present-day folklorists and linguists.

3. Direct address. Throughout the poem, the narrator speaks to his audience. "You see," "You know," and similar phrases are repeated numerous times. This gives the impression of a singer-poet maintaining eye contact, engaging his listeners, working his audience.

4. Disregard of the concordance of verbal tenses. The poet continuously alternates between present and past tenses. This could result from metrical constraints (different syllable counts required for different metrical environments). It could also result from dramatic immediacy. The singer is a storyteller, not a grammarian. He is, in the parlance of method acting, "in the moment" —he tells it like he feels it.

All these factors suggest that this poet was a singer of tales who earned his daily bread by performance. This would probably involve a rowdy and very possibly interactive audience. Two recurring themes confirm the image of a poet performing before a popular audience: one involves kinship, the other social status.

Throughout the poem, characters' motivation in helping or cooperating is expressed by the phrase *por amor de.* Literally this means "for love of." It seems to be used in most cases in the way we use the phrase "for the sake of," and I have translated accordingly when a literal rendering might seem overstated. But a bardic reading assumes boisterous traditionalism, vehement suspicion of outsiders and newfangled ways, and old-fashioned commitment to kith and kin. In some situations, rendering "for love of" as "for the sake of" attenuates the emotional intensity of the characters' declarations. The literal reading in such cases therefore seems best. People do things for each other from love, backed by readiness to risk life and limb in defense of their loved ones and of the group's collective honor.

Another much-repeated term is *cavallero.* This is often translated as "knight." But the epic Cid is not very chivalric, if by that term we mean the amalgam of martial prowess and courtly gallantry that emerged as a literary and social ideal in subsequent centuries. Knighthood as an ethos, order, and lifestyle may have already made its presence felt in some sectors of society in the time of the poet. But this poem scarcely recognizes or understands such developments. Most of the time it uses the word *cavallero* in the rough-and-ready macho sense of "mounted warrior." Only occasionally, when the poet uses *cavallero* to refer to the ancillary functions that later came to define the concept (such as attending a lord at council meetings), or when there is some slight implication that the status of *cavallero* is more privileged and desirable than that of, say, the *peón* ("foot soldier"), does rendering *cavallero* as "knight" seem justified.

Names and Epithets

A great many place names are mentioned in the narrative. I have tried to use modern-day forms that match, as much as possible, the corresponding entries in present-day atlases and geographical dictionaries. Standard English-language versions of Spanish place names are preferred to Spanish forms (e.g., Saragossa instead of Zaragoza). Where there is no standard English form, names are rendered in the modern Spanish spelling. Names of persons with equivalents in modern Spanish have been rendered in the modern forms.

The epithet most frequently applied to the Cid is *Campeador.* The meaning and etymology of this formulaic descriptor have elicited debate. Some derive it from the Latin *campidoctor,* meaning literally "drill instructor," "master of the military arts," and by metaphorical extension, "champion." Another plausible derivation is from the verb *campear,* "to do battle." "Battler" has thus been used by other translators to render this epithet. If we translate the word simply as "he who does battle," the best rendering might be "the Warrior." The Cid is the Warrior, in the same way that Shakespeare is the Bard.

But the epic Cid is more than just a warrior among warriors. He is a charismatic leader of predatory hordes, a strategist and diplomat, a frontier legalist and dispenser of rough justice, a distributor of stolen wealth, a sacker of cities and a conqueror of kingdoms. *Campeador* connotes all these things in the poem.

The most accurate translation is probably "warlord," based on an analogy that could be drawn between the Cid of the poem and similar personages of the modern world. Examples might be found in late-imperial China, revolutionary Mexico, or contemporary Africa. The epic Cid is certainly no friend to the bourgeois city-dwellers who are the closet match in the poem to most of the work's modern readers. But "warlord" is weighed down by a certain political baggage. It might remind the reader of ugly historical realities (predatory violence, poverty and starvation, lawlessness and corruption) that this medieval story overlooks or plays down, realities not too different from those of present-day dystopias in the developing world and elsewhere—the environments that give rise to the politics and economy of warlords.

In short, there may not be a term in contemporary English that exactly conveys what *Campeador* seems to mean in the poem. Accordingly, I have retained the Spanish word, as have other translators before me.

BIBLIOGRAPHY

Spanish-Language Editions

Michael, Ian, ed. *Poema de Mio Cid.* Madrid: Castalia, 1984. Originally published in 1975; also available as facing text of Hamilton and Perry's translation (see below).

Montaner, Alberto, ed. *Cantar de Mio Cid.* Barcelona: Crítica, 1993.

Smith, Colin, ed. *Poema de Mio Cid.* Madrid: Cátedra, 2006. Originally published by Clarendon Press, 1972.

Other Translations into English

Blackburn, Paul, trans. *The Poem of the Cid: A Modern Translation with Notes.* Norman: University of Oklahoma Press, 1998.

Hamilton, Rita, and Janet Perry, trans. *The Poem of the Cid.* Harmondsworth: Penguin Books, 1984.

Huntington, Archer M., trans. *The Poem of the Cid.* Vol. II of 3 vols. New York: Hispanic Society of America, 1901–1908.

Merwin, W. S., trans. *Cantar de Mio Cid.* New York: New American Library, 1975.

Ormsby, John, trans. *The Poem of the Cid.* London: Longmans, Green & Co., 1879.

Raffel, Burton, trans. *The Song of the Cid: A Dual-Language Edition with Parallel Text.* Introduction and notes by María Rosa Menocal. New York: Penguin Books, 2009.

Rose, Robert Selden, and Leonard Bacon, trans. *The Lay of the Cid.* Middlesex, England: The Echo Library, 2007. Originally published by University of California Press, Berkeley, 1919.

Sherwood, Merriam, trans. *The Tale of the Warrior Lord: El cantar de Mio Cid.* New York: Longmans, Green & Co., 1930.

Simpson, Lesley Byrd, trans. *The Poem of the Cid.* Berkeley: University of California Press, 2006. Originally published in 1957.

Such, Peter, and John Hodgkinson, trans. *The Poem of the Cid*. Warminster: Aris & Phillips, 1987.

For Reference and Further Reading

Bailey, Matthew. "Oral Composition in the Medieval Spanish Epic." *PMLA* 118.2 (2003): 254–69.

———, ed. and trans. *Las Mocedades de Rodrigo: The Youthful Deeds of Rodrigo, the Cid*. Toronto: University of Toronto Press, 2007.

Bartlett, Robert, and Angus MacKay, eds. *Medieval Frontier Societies*. Oxford: Clarendon, 1989.

Barton, Simon. *The Aristocracy in Twelfth-Century León and Castile*. Cambridge: Cambridge University Press, 1997.

Barton, Simon, and Richard Fletcher, trans. and ed. *The World of the Cid: Chronicles of the Spanish Reconquest*. Manchester and New York: Manchester University Press, 2000.

Barton, Simon, and Peter Linehan, eds. *Cross, Crescent, and Conversion: Studies on Medieval Spain and Christendom in Memory of Richard Fletcher*. Leiden and Boston: Brill, 2008.

Burke, James F. *Structures from the Trivium in the "Cantar de Mio Cid."* Toronto: University of Toronto Press, 1991.

Collins, Roger, and Anthony Goodman, eds. *Medieval Spain: Culture, Conflict, and Coexistence*. New York: Palgrave Macmillan, 2002.

Deyermond, Alan, ed. *"Mio Cid" Studies*. London: Tamesis, 1977.

Deyermond, Alan, David G. Pattison, and Eric Southworth, eds. *"Mio Cid" Studies: "Some Problems of Diplomatic" Fifty Years On*. Papers of the Medieval Hispanic Research Center, 42. London: Department of Hispanic Studies, Queen Mary, University of London, 2002.

Duggan, Joseph J. *The "Cantar de mio Cid": Poetic Creation in Its Economic and Social Contexts*. Cambridge: Cambridge University Press, 1989.

Fletcher, Richard. *The Quest for El Cid*. Oxford: Oxford University Press, 1991.

Ganshof, F. L. *Feudalism.* Translated by Philip Gierson. Rev. ed. New York: Harper & Row, 1964.

Gies, David T., ed. "The Medieval Period." Part III in *The Cambridge History of Spanish Literature.* Cambridge: Cambridge University Press, 2004.

Glick, Thomas. *Islamic and Christian Spain in the Early Middle Ages.* 2nd rev. ed. London and Leiden: Brill Academic Publishers, 2005.

Harney, Michael. *Kinship and Polity in the "Poema de Mio Cid."* West Lafayette: Purdue University Press, 1993.

Hart, Thomas R. *Studies on the "Cantar de mio Cid."* London: Department of Hispanic Studies, Queen Mary and Westfield College, 2006.

Hobsbawm, Eric. *Primitive Rebels.* New York: W. W. Norton, 1965.

———. *Bandits.* Rev. ed. New York: New Press, 2000.

Lord, Albert B. *The Singer of Tales.* 2nd ed. Cambridge, MA: Harvard University Press, 2000.

Menéndez Pidal, Ramón. *The Cid and His Spain.* Translated by Harold Sunderland. London: F. Cass, 1971. Reprint of 1934 ed.

Michael, Ian. "Geographical Problems in the *Poema de Mio Cid*: I. The Exile Route." In *Medieval Studies Presented to Rita Hamilton,* edited by Alan Deyermond, 117–28. London: Tamesis Books, 1976.

———. "Geographical Problems in the *Poema de Mio Cid*: II. The Corpes Route." In *Mio Cid Studies,* edited by Alan Deyermond, 83–89. London: Tamesis, 1977.

Menocal, María Rosa. *The Ornament of the World: How Muslims, Jews, and Christians Created a Culture of Tolerance in Medieval Spain.* New York: Back Bay Books, 2003.

O'Callaghan, Joseph F. *A History of Medieval Spain.* Ithaca and London: Cornell University Press, 1975.

Reilly, Bernard F. *The Kingdom of León-Castilla under King Alfonso VI, 1065–1109.* Princeton: Princeton University Press, 1988.

Smith, Colin. *The Making of the "Poema de Mio Cid."* Cambridge: Cambridge University Press, 1983.

Spain in the late eleventh century

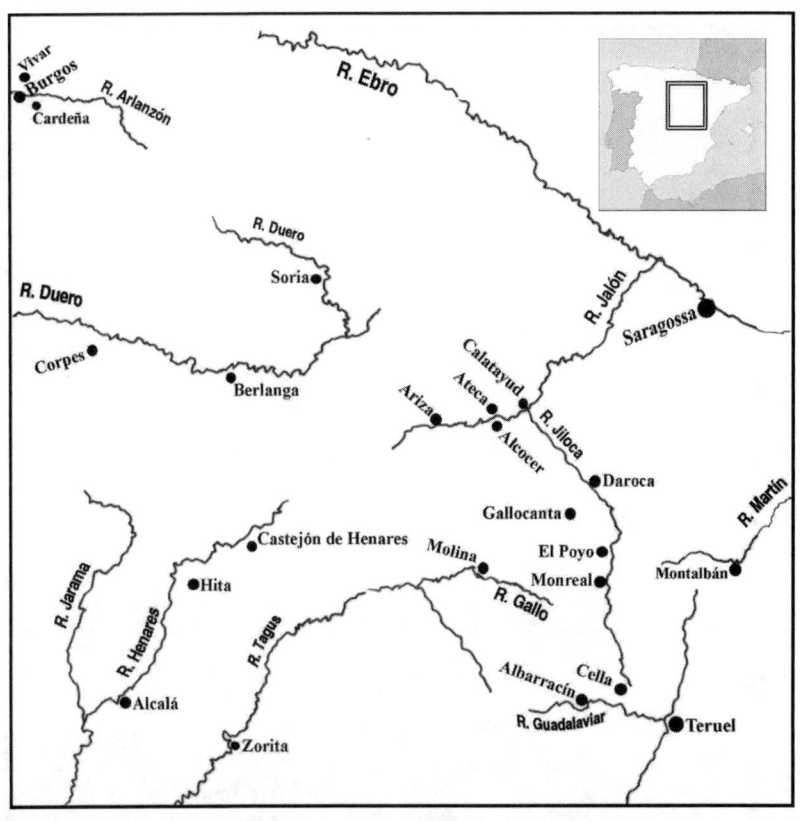

Geographical setting of journeys, Books I & II
(Campaigns in exile; Journey to Carrión)

Setting of the eastern campaigns (Book II)

THE EPIC OF THE CID

First Book: Exile
(Verses 1–1086)

Falsely accused by lying enemies at court, and estranged from his lord, King Alfonso,[1] Rodrigo Díaz de Vivar, known as the Cid, is banished from the land. While his wife and daughters remain in Castile, the Cid, with the help of an ever-growing band of loyal followers, organizes raiding campaigns in Moorish territory. After each victory, he sends a present to the king, seeking to effect a reconciliation.

Weeping bitterly, the tears streaming from his eyes, he turned his head and beheld the empty house: doors left open, shutters without padlocks, empty racks without furs or cloaks, perches with no falcons or molted hawks.[2]

My Cid sighed deeply, for his cares were very great.[3] He spoke clearly, in measured tones:

"Thanks be to thee, Lord Father, Thou who are art on high! This wrong has been done to me by my wicked enemies!"

There and then did they spur their horses, there and then they loosed the reins. On leaving Vivar, they had the crow on

---

1. Proper nouns and references to historical figures are identified and explained in the Compendium of Proper Names.

2. The first page of the only extant manuscript is missing, leaving a gap of about fifty lines. Other works of the time, none of whose versions of the Cid's story exactly correspond to that of the epic's, indicate that the Cid has been accused by his enemies of stealing tribute money meant for Alfonso, and that the king has banished him as a consequence of these accusations. See Related Texts E, *The Chronicle of Twenty Kings*.

3. Throughout the poem, the Cid is referred to by the narrator, and addressed by other characters, as "My Cid." The epithet is fixed and formulaic, like an official title. Even when spoken of in the third person, by a group speaking in the first person plural, the title is used. An example is the scene in which town criers announce the hero's departure: "the criers spread the word: how My Cid Campeador was heading into exile."

3

the right hand, and, on entering Burgos, they had it on the left.[4]
My Cid shrugged his shoulders and shook his head:

"Good luck to us, Álvar Fáñez! Here we go, setting out
into exile!"

My Cid Ruy Díaz entered into Burgos, with sixty pennants
in his company.

Women and men came out to see him—townsfolk, men
and women alike, leaned out their windows, weeping bitterly,
so greatly did they share his sorrow! The same words were on
everyone's lips:

"God, what an excellent vassal, if he only had a good
lord!"[5]

Gladly would they offer him hospitality. But no one dared:
such was the wrath of King Alfonso. Before nightfall, the royal
decree had been proclaimed in Burgos, with great solemnity
and formally sealed: that none shall give shelter to My Cid Ruy
Díaz, and to anyone who might dare do so, be it most certainly
known, that both their property and the very eyes in their heads
would be forfeit—yea, even their very bodies and souls.

Great were the lamentations among the Christian folk; they
hid from My Cid, for none dared speak a word to him.

The Campeador headed toward his residence. Arriving at
the door, he discovered it all locked up. For fear of King Al-
fonso, the townsfolk had done as the king commanded, seeing

---

4. Alert to all kinds of signs and omens, the people of the Cid's
world, including the hero himself, are superstitious. The crow and
its movements are particularly meaningful. The right-hand side is
traditionally seen as favorable and propitious. The left-hand side
is the opposite: dire, adverse, unfavorable, sinister (from the Latin
sinister, meaning "left," "left-hand").

5. Feudalism, in its interpersonal aspect, is a pact and a relation-
ship between two men: a lord and a vassal. The term *vassalage*
refers to the mutual obligations and expectations entailed by the
two roles. The relationship is symbiotic. A lord is nothing without
vassals; a vassal is incomplete unless he serves a lord. In its eco-
nomic and military aspect, feudalism is the conditional granting of
a landed estate, the fief (medieval Latin *feudum*), by a superior lord
to a subordinate vassal. Use of the fief was granted on condition
of the vassal's continued homage and service to the lord, who re-
tained ownership. Inheritance of the fief by a vassal's heirs was
subject to the same feudal obligations.

to it that unless the Cid broke it down by force, no one would open it for him, not on any account.

The Cid's men shout out to those within. The people inside would not answer them.

Spurring his horse, the Cid rode right up to the door, took his foot from the stirrup, and kicked at the door, good and hard.

The door stayed shut; it was securely locked.

All at once a girl, a nine-year old, showed herself.

"Enough, Campeador! Lucky was the hour when you first put on your sword! The king has forbidden us to give you shelter. Last night his decree was proclaimed, with great formality, and most solemnly sealed. We wouldn't dare open the door for you, nor welcome you, not for anything. Otherwise, we would lose our property, our houses, and what's more, the very eyes out of our heads. Cid, you would gain nothing by causing us such grief. But God be with you, and all good things that come from Him."

This the little girl said, then went back into her house.

Now the Cid fully understood that he was really and truly in disgrace with his king. [50] Turning away from the door, he rode through Burgos, spurring his horse. Coming to the church of Santa María, he quickly dismounted. Kneeling, he prayed with all his heart. After he had prayed, he got back on his horse. Going out through the gate, he crossed the Arlanzón, setting up camp on the sandy river bank close to town. Showing where his tent was to be placed, he got down from his horse.

My Cid Ruy Díaz, he who girt on his sword in a lucky hour, camped on the river bank, since no one gave him shelter. A stout company all around him, the Cid camped out as if he were in the wilds. The marketplace had been forbidden to him, anywhere within the town limits of Burgos: they would not dare sell him so much as a farthing's worth of any kind of provision.

Martín Antolínez, the doughty man of Burgos, supplied the Cid and his men with bread and wine. This he did not purchase, for he had it with him, so he could readily provide them with all the necessities. The Cid and all those who served him were very pleased.

Martín Antolínez spoke up—listen to what he said:

"Now then, Campeador, you were born at a lucky hour! Let us camp here tonight and set out tomorrow morning. For I will surely be accused of giving you aid, and will be subject to King Alfonso's wrath. But even if I get away with you now, safe and sound, sooner or later the king will most likely want me back as a friend. And if not, everything I leave behind matters not a fig to me."

My Cid spoke then, he who girt on his sword in a lucky hour:

"Martín Antolínez, you valiant spear-man! If I manage to get out of this alive, I'll double your pay. For the moment I've spent all the gold, all the silver. You can see I've got nothing left. And I'm going to need a lot to provide for all my men. I'll have to get it by force, since nobody will provide it willingly. With your help, I intend to load up two chests. We'll fill them with sand, so they weigh a lot. Two chests covered with embossed leather and finely studded — the leather scarlet-colored, the studs of shiny gold. Go now in secret and pay a visit to Raquel and Vidas. Tell them that since I was forbidden access to the markets in Burgos, and I'm subject to the king's ban, I can't carry all my goods with me, they're much too heavy. I'll pawn it all, for whatever seems reasonable. Tell them to take it away with them by night, so not a Christian soul can see them. By the good Lord and all His saints, I don't see any other way. I do this only because I have no choice."

Martín Antolínez did not wait around. In all haste he went to seek out Raquel and Vidas. Passing through Burgos he entered the inner city, urgently asking for them.

Raquel and Vidas were both together, [100] counting up their goods and earnings, as Martín Antolínez courteously presented himself.

"Where are you, Raquel and Vidas, my dear friends? I wanted to speak to you both in private."

Without delay, all three went aside, conferring in secret.

"Raquel and Vidas, both of you give me your hands. Reveal me to neither Moor nor Christian, and I will make you rich from now on, so you will never know want. The Campeador went to collect the tribute money. It was an important sum he took charge of, a very tidy sum indeed. Of that sum he held on to a large share for himself — that's how he got into this fix, this thing he stands accused of. He has two chests, full of finest gold. As you already know, the king has banished him. The Cid has left behind his whole estate: houses, palaces, everything. He

can't very well take those chests along with him either —
otherwise, people will get wind of it. So the Cid wants to leave
them in your hands. Lend him some money, whatever seems
reasonable. Take charge of the chests, and put them into your
safekeeping. Solemnly swear, both of you give me your word:
that you will not once look into them, in all this coming year!"
  Raquel and Vidas talked it over:
  "In everything we do, we must look to make some profit.
We know the Cid must have acquired some considerable
amount, seeing that he went to Moorish country and must have
brought back a small fortune. As they say, 'Uneasy sleeps the
man who carries cash around.' Let's take charge of these two
chests. We'll put them in a place where nobody will get wind
of them. Now then, Martín Antolínez, tell us about the Cid —
what will he be satisfied with? What interest will he pay us, for
all this coming year?"
  Martín Antolínez shrewdly replied:
  "My Cid will agree to whatever seems reasonable. He
won't ask much of you, to keep his goods safe. From every-
where, poverty-stricken men are flocking to his banner. He
needs six hundred marks."
  Raquel and Vidas replied:
  "We will gladly give him that amount."
  "As you can see, nightfall is upon us, and the Cid is in a
hurry. We need you to get us the money right away."
  Raquel and Vidas replied:
  "That's not the way business is done. First there's the re-
ceiving of collateral, then there's the lending."
  Martín Antolínez answered:
  "That is satisfactory. Both of you come with me now to
meet with the renowned Campeador. We will help you, as is
only proper, to bring away the chests and put them in your
keeping. Meanwhile, let no one, Moor or Christian, hear any-
thing about this."
  "That is satisfactory," said Raquel and Vidas. "When the
chests have been brought to us, you will receive the six hundred
marks."
  Martín Antolínez rode off straightaway, and with him
Raquel and Vidas, ready and willing. He did not go by way of
the bridge, but instead forded the river, [150] so nobody in
Burgos would be aware of his coming.

Presently they found themselves in the tent of the famous Campeador. As soon as they entered, they went to kiss the Cid's hands. Smiling, the Cid said to them:

"Now then, my good Raquel and Vidas, you seem to have forgotten all about me! Here I am, about to go into exile, seeing that I'm in disgrace with the king. It seems to me you are going to get a share of my fortune — as long as you live, you'll never know want."

Don Raquel and Don Vidas kissed the Cid's hands. Martín Antolínez had already prepared the contract: that against those chests they would lend the Cid six hundred marks, while keeping the chests safe until the end of a year's time. Thus did they make their promise, swearing their oath: that if they looked into the chests before that time, they would be committing perjury, and the Cid would not pay them so much as a farthing of interest.

Martín Antolínez said:

"Let the chests be loaded right away. Take them, Raquel and Vidas, and put them under your safekeeping. I will now go with you so we can get the money ready, for My Cid will be setting out before the cock crows."

As they loaded up the chests, you should have seen their joy! They could barely lift them up, even though they were both very strong. The two of them rejoice, Raquel and Vidas, at the enormous sum of cash. Indeed, they thought they were going to be wealthy men for the rest of their lives.

Raquel goes to kiss the Cid's hand.

"Now then, Campeador, you who girt on your sword in a lucky hour! You are setting forth from Castile, going out among foreign folk. As you prosper in all you undertake, I am sure your winnings will be great. A fine, vermilion, fur-lined cloak, of Moorish cut — this, My Cid, I beg of you as a gift."

"Granted," said the Cid. "From this moment consider it yours, if I bring it back from where I'm going; otherwise, you can deduct its cost from the money in the chest."

There in the middle of the hall, they laid out a rug. On it they spread a white linen sheet. First, they dumped out three hundred silver marks. Don Martín counted them, accepting the sum without weighing the coins. Then they paid out to him the remaining three hundred marks in gold.

Don Martín had all five of the squires accompanying him load up the treasure. Once he had done this, hear what he said then:

"Now then, Don Raquel and Don Vidas, the chests are in your hands. Seeing as how I brought you this business, I think you owe me at least a fine pair of breeches."

Raquel and Vidas went aside to discuss the matter.

"Let's give him a nice gift, seeing that he did indeed bring this business our way. Martín Antolínez, you far-famed man of Burgos: you do indeed deserve something. We intend to give you a handsome reward. With this you can get breeches, a fine tunic, a nice cloak: thirty marks we give you, as a gift, free and clear. We owe you this, seeing that you will be the guarantor of this whole arrangement that we have agreed upon with the Cid."

Don Martín thanked them, accepting the thirty marks. Eager to set out, he took his leave of them. [200]

Leaving Burgos and quickly crossing over the Arlanzón, he presently arrived at the tent of the far-famed Campeador.

The Cid welcomed him with open arms:

"You've returned, Martín Antolínez, my loyal vassal! God grant I see the day when I may repay you!"

"I come, Campeador, with the deal all set: you get six hundred marks, and I get thirty into the bargain. Order the camp to be struck, so we can leave right away. We should reach San Pedro de Cardeña by cock-crow. We'll see your wife, that prudent noblewoman. We'll stay there a little while, then leave the kingdom behind us. That's how it's got to be, seeing that the deadline's fast approaching."

No sooner did he speak those words than the tents were struck. My Cid and all his men rode speedily out. The Cid guided his horse toward Santa María. Raising up his hand and crossing himself, he said:

"Thanks be to you, God, you who watch over heaven and earth. And may your virtues stand by me, glorious Holy Mary! From here on, I leave Castile behind, since I am in disgrace with the king. I don't know if I'll ever come back, as long as I live. May your power be with me, glorious Lady, as I set forth, and help and support me, night and day! If you do this, and things turn out for me, I will endow your altar with fine and splendid offerings. This I solemnly promise: that then and there I will order a thousand masses sung in your name."

The intrepid one took his leave, resolute in body and soul; they all loosed the reins and began to give spur to their mounts.

Martín Antolínez spoke:

"I'll go see my wife, who is my only comfort. Then I'll tell my people how they should behave while I'm gone. If the king wants to take everything away from me, I don't care. I'll be back with you before sunrise."

Martín Antolínez set out for Burgos, while My Cid spurred on toward San Pedro de Cardeña, as fast as he could ride, along with those knights who served him right willingly. The cocks were eagerly crowing and dawn was about to break, when the good Campeador arrived at San Pedro. The abbot Don Sancho, a godly Christian man, was saying his matins at break of day. Doña Jimena was present there, and five worthy ladies with her.

She prayed to Saint Peter and to the Creator:

"You who guide us all, Lord, stand by My Cid, the Campeador."

There was a knocking at the door. Throughout the place, news of the Cid's arrival quickly spread. Lord, how the abbot Don Sancho rejoiced! Bearing torches and candles, they all went out into the courtyard. Joyfully they welcomed the renowned Campeador.

"I thank God, My Cid," declared the abbot, Don Sancho. "Now that you have arrived here safe, you must accept my hospitality."

The Cid replied:

"Thank you, sir Abbot. I am much obliged! I need to supply provisions for myself and all my vassals. But, since I am heading into exile, I give you fifty marks [250] for the time being. If I manage to survive a while, I'll double that amount. Meanwhile, I don't want my stay to involve any expenditure at all for the monastery. Please accept these hundred marks for Doña Jimena; take care of her and our daughters, and their ladies-in-waiting, for the coming year. I leave my two little daughters here with you: take them under your protection. I entrust them to your safekeeping, my good abbot. Be sure to look after my daughters and my wife, in every way you can. If this amount is not enough, or you run short of anything, I bid you provide them whatever they need. For every mark you spend, I will donate four to the monastery."

The abbot willingly agreed to the Cid's request.

At this point, Doña Jimena and her daughters arrived. A lady-in-waiting accompanied each girl and led them in to see their father. Doña Jimena knelt down on her knees before the Campeador. Weeping, her eyes full of tears, she made to kiss his hands.

"I pray you, Campeador, you who were born in a lucky hour! Because of evil meddlers you are now banished from the land. I pray you, you of the flowing beard! Behold me here before you, me and your daughters—they are so little, so very young in years. With us are these, my ladies-in-waiting. I can see that you are about to leave, and we must now live apart from you. Say something to raise our spirits, for blessed Mary's sake!"

He of the flowing beard held out his hands, taking his daughters into his arms. He hugged them close, for he loved them dearly. Weeping, the tears filling his eyes, he heaved a deep sigh.

"Lady Jimena, my most constant wife, I have always loved you as I love my very soul! Now you see how we must henceforth live apart. I must go, and you must stay behind. Please God and holy Mary that someday I myself, with my own hands, may give away my daughters in marriage, and that He bring me luck and long life, so that I may serve you, my loving spouse!"

They prepared a great feast for the Campeador. In the monastery of San Pedro the bells resounded. Throughout Castile, the criers spread the word: how My Cid Campeador was heading into exile. Some abandoned their homes, others their estates. On that day, at the Arlanzón Bridge, a hundred and fifteen knights gathered, all asking for My Cid Campeador. Martín Antolínez met with them, and they all went together to San Pedro, where the one born in a lucky hour was waiting.

When My Cid, the man of Vivar, heard that his company was growing, thereby improving his standing, he speedily rode out to meet them. He smiled as they all came forward to kiss his hand. My Cid addressed them with heartfelt words:

"I pray to God, our spiritual Father, [300] that before I die I may be able to reward all you who have left behind your homes and estates—whatever your loss, I will repay it twofold."

My Cid was greatly pleased to see his company increase, and all the men there with him were likewise pleased. Six days of the grace period had already gone by — you know, there were barely three days left, no more. The king, meanwhile, had ordered the Cid to be closely watched. If he should be caught in the royal domain after the deadline was up, neither gold nor silver would avail him — there would be no escape.

Day was done and nightfall was upon them. Ordering all his knights to gather round, the Cid addressed them:

"Listen, good men of mine, don't be dismayed. I don't bring much wealth with me, but I intend to give all of you your fair share. Be careful, as you should be, when the cocks crow tomorrow morning. Don't dawdle, have your horses saddled promptly. In San Pedro, at matins, the good abbot will ring the bell and then say mass for us, the mass of the Holy Trinity. Right after mass, we ride out. The deadline is fast approaching, and we have a long way to go."

Everybody did as the Cid commanded, as they were all bound to do. At the middle watch, when it was still dark and dawn was far off, they made to saddle up. Urgently the bells rang out, summoning everyone to matins.

My Cid and his wife went in to church. Throwing herself on the altar steps, she prayed to the Creator, with all her might, that He might keep My Cid, the Campeador, safe from harm:

"Glorious Father, you who dwell on high, who made heaven, earth, and the sea on the third day, the stars and moon above, and the sun to keep us warm; who were made flesh in the body of Holy Mother Mary and appeared in Bethlehem, to be glorified and praised by shepherds; three kings of Araby did adore you — Melchior, Caspar, and Balthasar — and offered you gold, frankincense, and myrrh, as you willed; you who saved Jonah when he fell into the sea, who saved Daniel from the lions, in the foul dungeon; who saved Saint Sebastian, there in Rome, and Saint Susanna from the lying evildoer; you who walked on earth for thirty-two years, Blessed Lord, performing your miracles for us to marvel at. From water you made wine, and bread from stone, raised Lazarus, by Your will; let the Jews arrest you, in the place they call Calvary, and put you on the cross in the place named Golgotha, two thieves on either side of you, one now in paradise, while the other never entered

there. [350] On the cross you worked a mighty miracle: Longi-
nus—blind, sightless from birth—stabbed you in the side with
his spear, the blood flowed forth, ran down the shaft, drenched
his hands. He raised them up, touched his face, opened his eyes,
looked all around, instantly believed in You, and was thereby
saved from perdition. You rose from the tomb, descended into
hell, as was Your will, broke down the doors and delivered the
Holy Fathers. You are King of Kings, Father to us all—I adore
and believe in you, with all my heart, and pray to Saint Peter
that he help me pray for My Cid, the Campeador: that God
keep him from harm, and that though we go our separate ways
today, He will someday bring us back together."

Her prayer was done, the mass was over. They all came out
from the church, and went to mount their horses. The Cid
hugged Doña Jimena, while she kissed his hands, weeping, her
eyes filled with tears, beside herself with grief. And he looked
again at his daughters:

"To God I commend you, my daughters, and to the Blessed
Father. Now we must leave—God knows when we will see
each other again."

Weeping bitterly, their eyes full of tears—you never saw
such heartache!—they parted from one another, like fingernails
from flesh.

As My Cid and all his vassals made to ride away, he turned
his head, looking back as he waited for the others.

Minaya Álvar Fáñez spoke well-timed words:

"Cid, where's that grit of yours? In a lucky hour were you
born of woman. Let's be on our way and leave all this for some
other time. All these woes will soon turn to rejoicing. God, who
gave us our souls, will surely come to our aid."

Again the abbot Don Sancho is instructed as to how he
might assist Doña Jimena and their daughters, and all the ladies
with them, and reminded that he would be handsomely re-
warded for all he did on their behalf.

As Don Sancho turned to go back, Álvar Fáñez said:

"If people come looking to join our band, sir Abbot, tell them
to ride after us. They are sure to catch up with us somewhere,
whether in open country or in some town along the way."

Loosening the reins, they set out riding, as the deadline
approached for leaving the kingdom.

My Cid and his men stopped to spend the night at Spinaz de Can. That same night, many men, from all over, came to join up with him.

Next day, in the morning, they set out riding. As the loyal Campeador was departing from the land, on the left was San Esteban, a proper town, and on the right the towers of Alilón, held by Moors. He passed Alcobiella—which marks the boundary of Castile—crossed the Quinea Road, [400] then forded the Duero River at Navapalos. As My Cid stopped for the night at Figueruela, more men, from all over, joined his band.

In that place, as My Cid stretched out after dinner, falling into a deep sleep, a pleasant dream came to him. In his dream, the angel Gabriel appeared to him:

"Ride forth, Cid, noble Campeador! For never did any man set out with such promise. As long as you live, things are bound to go your way."

When the Cid awoke, he crossed himself, commending himself to God as he did so. He was much pleased with the dream he had had.

Early next day, they set out riding. They had only that one day more of grace, no more.

They stopped to take lodging in the Miedes Mountains. It was still daylight, the sun had not yet set. My Cid, the Campeador, ordered a review of his troops. Apart from the foot soldiers, brave fellows that they were, he counted three hundred lances, all of them bearing pennons.

"Feed the horses first thing, God keep you! Whether getting something to eat or not, let's ride on from here. We'll soon pass through the mountains, high and wild, and leave behind King Alfonso's land by nightfall. Afterward, anyone looking for us will find us easily enough."

That night, they passed through the mountains, then headed down the far side at daybreak. Amid a forest vast and fearsome, the Cid ordered them to make camp and feed the horses. He told them he wanted to spend the night there. Worthy vassals, they heartily obeyed, willingly carrying out any command of their lord.

Before nightfall they were ready to ride, the Cid making sure that nobody in those parts got wind of their movements. They rode by night, taking no rest.

At the place called Castejón, on the banks of the Henares, My Cid and all his men placed themselves in ambush. All that night they stayed hidden, the one born in a lucky hour and all his troops, just as Minaya Álvar Fáñez had advised.

"Now then, My Cid, you who girt on your sword in a lucky hour! You stay with a hundred of our men and cover us while we draw the men from Castejón into an ambush."

The Cid replied:

"You men go with the two hundred men in the vanguard. Take Álvar Álvarez with you, and Álvar Salvadórez, and Galíndo García, a valiant spearman — let all these brave knights go with Minaya. Ride forth, bold and fearless — overcome everything in your path, from Hita down river, toward Guadalajara. Let the raiding parties advance as far as Alcalá, gathering up all the loot they can, and leave nothing behind for fear of the Moors. Meanwhile, I'll stay back here with these hundred men. We'll hold Castejón, where we can set up fortified positions. [450] If you run into any trouble during the raids, send back word right away — all over Spain, they'll be talking about how I came to the rescue!"

They named the ones assigned to go on the raid, and the ones who were to stay behind with the Cid. The day dawned, morning came, and the sun came out — Lord, how splendidly it shone! In Castejón, everyone got up, opened the gates, and went out to till their croplands and look over their estates. They all went out, leaving the gates wide open behind them, with very few remaining in the town. The people outside the walls were all scattered here and there as the Campeador, coming out from ambush, descended on Castejón in a rush. They captured Moorish folk, men and women, and all the livestock grazing around the town.

My Cid, Don Rodrigo, headed straight for the main gate. Those who held it, seeing the attack, took fright and left the gate unguarded. My Cid Ruy Díaz went through the gates, a naked sword in his hand. Fifteen Moors he killed, of the ones within his reach.

Thus the Cid and his men took Castejón, with all its gold and silver. His knights rode up carrying the loot, and dumped it out on the ground before their lord — it meant nothing to them at all.

Meanwhile, there they were, the two hundred of the vanguard and the three brave knights with them, attacking fearlessly. All the way to Alcalá, Minaya's standard reached. From there, they returned back up river with their loot, up past Henares and Guadalajara. So much booty they brought with them: plenty of livestock, sheep and cattle, and clothing, and other valuable goods. Straight on sped Minaya's standard: none dared attack his rearguard.

With this loot that company returned. There they were, back in Castejón, where the Cid was waiting. The castle now his, the Campeador rode out with his men to meet them. Holding out his arms, he welcomed Minaya:

"There you are, Álvar Fáñez, my brave spearman! Wherever I send you, I expect nothing less! Now then, let that loot be placed with this. To you, Minaya, I award the fifth part, if you want it."

"Many thanks, renowned Campeador. With this fifth that you've granted me, Alfonso the Castilian himself would be most pleased. I give it back to you, free and clear. To God I vow, to Him who dwells on high, that as long as I'm happy fighting on my good horse, against Moors on the battlefield, and hurling the lance and taking sword in hand [500] 'til the blood runs down to the elbow, here beside the renowned warrior, Ruy Díaz, I will not accept so much as a farthing from you. Until I get you something really worthwhile, everything else I'll gladly hand over."

As all this loot was gathered up there, it occurred to My Cid, he who was born in a lucky hour, that King Alfonso and his troops might show up and work some mischief against him and his men. The Cid ordered all that wealth to be divided up then and there, with the paymasters marking down each man's share in writing. His knights made out very well, with one hundred silver marks falling to each. Half that sum went to every foot soldier, without exception, while the Cid received a fifth of all the goods.

Seeing that where they were he could not sell it, nor even give it away as a gift, and deciding not to take any prisoners, men or women, along with him, the Cid held parley with the people of Castejón, while sending to Hita and Guadalajara to see how much they might pay for his share. Whatever amount they might agree to, the Cid and his men would come out ahead.

The Moors valued his fifth at three thousand silver marks. The Cid was satisfied with this offer, and three days later the amount was duly paid.

The Cid and all his men reckoned that they could not stay in the castle. It would be defensible, but there would be no water.

"These Moors are peaceful, for they have a treaty with the king.[6] Don Alfonso is after us, with all his forces. I want to leave Castejón—listen up, Minaya and all you men! What I'm about to say to you, you shouldn't take the wrong way. We can't stay in Castejón. King Alfonso is not far off, and he'll be coming after us. But I don't want to demolish the castle. I'm going to free two hundred captives, a hundred men, a hundred women. I don't want them speaking ill of me on account of my capturing the place from them. You've all been taken care of, with no man left unsatisfied. Early tomorrow, let's ride on out of here. I wouldn't want to do battle with my lord king Alfonso."

All were pleased by the Cid's words. They were all now wealthy men as they set out from the castle they had captured, with the Moors, men and women alike, blessing them as they went on their way.

They headed up the Henares, as fast as they could ride, crossing the Alcarria and passing by the Caves of Anguita. Fording the waters of the Tajuña, they came into the plain of Taranz, riding down through that country as fast as they could.

Between Fariza and Cetina the Cid made to set up camp. Great was the loot he captured as he went through that country. The Moors, meanwhile, had no idea of the strategy the Cid and his men had planned.

Next day My Cid, the man of Vivar, [550] moved out, passing by Alhama and following the bend in the stream as he headed downriver. Further on, he passed Bubierca and Ateca.

---

6. In the system of *parias* (tribute payments), Muslim *taifa* kingdoms were obliged to render tribute to Christian kings. Some historians have characterized this practice as a protection racket that involved extortion and intimidation. At the same time, the Christian rulers who were payees under the system guaranteed the protection of their clients from attack by both Muslims and Christians.

On a high, rounded hillock, a readily defensible place over-looking Alcocer, the Cid set up camp. Nearby ran the Jalón, so he could not be cut off from water. My Cid, Don Rodrigo, decided then to take Alcocer.

He deployed his forces very effectively, establishing secure positions on the hill. Some men were stationed on the slopes, others along the river bank. The good Campeador, born in a lucky hour, ordered all his men to dig a trench around the hill, down close to the water, so there could be no sneak attack, day or night, and also so the people of the vicinity would know he was there to stay.

Throughout those lands, the news quickly spread: that the Cid had established a settlement there, that he had left Christendom to come live in Moorish territory. None dared pasture their herds anywhere in his vicinity. The Cid and all his vassals bided their time, as the fortress of Alcocer agreed to pay tribute. The inhabitants of Alcocer willingly rendered tribute to the Cid, as did also those of Ateca and the township of Terrer.

You can be sure all this left the inhabitants of Calatayud very worried indeed.

There the Cid remained for fifteen whole weeks. When he saw that Alcocer was not really about to surrender, he devised a stratagem that he immediately put into effect. Leaving just one tent set up and gathering up the rest, the Cid and his men headed down the Jalón, his standard held up high, each man dressed in armor and with his sword belted on. It was all cleverly done, to lure the enemy out into an ambush.

When they saw all this, Lord, how the people of Alcocer did rejoice!

"The Cid has run out of bread for his men and fodder for his horses! He was barely able to get his tents out of there—look, he had to leave one behind. My Cid left in a hurry, as if he were barely ahead of pursuers. Let's go after him, and we'll win plenty of loot, before those people from Terrer get their hands on it—if we don't, they won't share any of it with us. The tribute he's taken from us so far he'll be paying us back twofold."

In a dreadful hurry, they rushed out from Alcocer. When My Cid saw them outside their town, he fled as if pursued, heading down the Jalón with his men around him.

The people of Alcocer cried: "Our prize is getting away!" Old and young alike rushed forth, heedless of everything but the scent of plunder. They left the gates wide open, with nobody standing guard.

The good Campeador turned his head to look back, saw that the townsfolk had put a good distance between themselves and the castle. As he ordered the standard-bearer to turn around, he and his men wheeled about and then spurred on apace.

"Smite them, my knights, all of you, unflinching! With God's help, the booty is ours!"

The Cid and his men fought hand-to-hand with them, there in the middle of the plain.

Lord, how great was the rejoicing that morning! [600]

My Cid and Álvar Fáñez spurred on ahead. They had excellent horses, you know, yielding to the riders' every command. As they rode into the space between the Moors and the fortress, the Cid's vassals attacked the enemy, giving no quarter—in a little over an hour they slew three hundred of them. As the Moors caught in the trap set up a great outcry, the vanguard of the Cid's forces headed straight for the fortress. Arriving at the gate, they stood there, swords drawn. Then the rest arrived, for the Moors had been routed. My Cid took Alcocer, you see, by means of this ruse.

Pedro Bermúdez arrived, bearing the standard. He placed it atop the highest point of the citadel. My Cid Ruy Díaz spoke, the man born in a lucky hour:

"Thanks be to God in heaven, and all His saints: now we'll all get better lodgings, riders and mounts alike. Listen up, Álvar Fáñez and all you knights! In this fortress we have won great riches. Dead Moors lie everywhere—I see very few survivors. These captives, male or female, we'll be unable to sell, and if we behead them we earn no profit. Let's gather them up instead, here inside the town. Since we're now lords of the place, we'll take up our quarters in their homes, and make them our servants."

My Cid, with all the loot they had won, set up his headquarters there in Alcocer. He ordered his tent to be brought down from where he had left it up on the hill. All this left the people of Ateca very uneasy, and the inhabitants of Terrer and Calatayud were likewise none too pleased. They sent a message to the king of Valencia, concerning a man known as My Cid Ruy Díaz of Vivar:

"Banished by King Alfonso and thrown out of the country, he has taken up a strongly defended position overlooking Alcocer, lured the inhabitants into an ambush, and taken possession of the fortress. If you do not come to our aid, you will lose Ateca and Terrer, and Calatayud as well, which cannot escape, and things will go badly all along the banks of the Jalón, and likewise further on, on the far side of the Jiloca."

When King Tamín heard this, he was sick at heart:

"Three Moorish kings I see before me—do not tarry. Two of you go there now, taking three thousand Moors, all armed for battle, and with the frontier folk, who will gladly help you, capture him alive and bring him before me. He will have to answer to me for having dared to raid my lands."

Three thousand Moors mounted up and set out on their way, reaching Segorbe by nightfall, where they took quarters. Early next morning they rode out, and halted for the night at Cella. They sent news to all the Moors who dwelt on the frontier, and without delay reinforcements came from every direction. Setting out from the place called Cella de Canal, they traveled all day, without rest, and by sundown reached Calatayud, where they halted for the night. [650]

All throughout those lands the heralds went, and an enormous host gathered under the command of the two kings, Fáriz and Galve. They intended to besiege the noble Cid, there in Alcocer.

Setting up their tents, they established their camp. Their forces quickly grew, and their numbers were great. The patrols sent out by the Moors went about fully armed, day and night. There were many such patrols, and their army was truly vast. Soon the Cid and his men saw their water supply cut off.

The Cid's troops were eager to sally forth and do battle. But he who was born in a lucky hour firmly forbade this. They had him surrounded there for three whole weeks.

At the end of the three weeks, at the beginning of the fourth, the Cid again took council with his men:

"They've cut off our water, and we'll soon run out of bread. If we try to get away by night, they won't let us. Their forces are too great for us to take on. Tell me, my knights, what you would like to do."

Minaya spoke up first, a most worthy knight:

"We have set out from fair Castile and come to this place. If we don't engage the Moors in combat, they won't be giving us any bread. There are a full six hundred of us, maybe even a few more. In God's name, let's not have it any other way: tomorrow we attack them, with everything we've got."

The Campeador replied:

"You have spoken just as I would have wished. You do yourself honor, Minaya, and will surely continue to do so."

The Cid commanded that all the Moorish prisoners, men and women alike, be sent out of the town, lest any should learn the secret of his plans. All that day and through the night, the Cid and his men engaged in preparations. Early next day, as the sun came up, the Cid and all his men were armed. My Cid spoke out, as you will now hear:

"Let's all charge forward, let nobody hang back except for two foot soldiers to guard the gate. If we die on the field, the Moors will retake the fortress. If we win the battle, we'll get richer. You, Pedro Bermúdez, take my standard. As you're a stout-hearted fellow, tried and true, I know you'll carry it bravely. But don't charge ahead with it unless I command you to."

Pedro kissed the Cid's hand and took the standard from him. They opened the gates and sallied forth.

When the Moorish sentinels caught sight of them, they hurried back toward their army. What a commotion there was among the Moors, as they scrambled to re-arm themselves! With the din of their battle drums, the earth seemed about to open up. Everywhere one could see Moors donning their armor and hurriedly closing ranks. On their side there were two main banners, and they drew up two formations of mixed infantry — who could ever count them? Then the Moorish battalions started forward, [700] aiming to engage the Cid and his men hand-to-hand.

"Hold steady, men!" cried the Cid. "Right here in this spot. Nobody break ranks until I give the order."

Brave Pedro Bermúdez could not abide this. Holding up the Cid's banner, he urged his mount forward:

"God be with you, Cid, my valiant Campeador! I'm going to plant your standard right in the middle of their lead battalion. All those who have true fealty toward their lord — let's see how you rally to his standard!"

"For God's sake, hold your position!" cried the Campeador.

Pedro Bermúdez replied:

"Now there'll be no holding back!"

He spurred his horse and charged right into the thick of the enemy's lead battalion.

The Moors open ranks, letting him charge in amongst them so they can capture the Cid's standard. They deal him mighty blows, but cannot penetrate his armor.[7]

The Cid cried out:

"Go to his aid, for Heaven's sake!"

Holding their shields close to their chests and lowering their spears adorned with pennons, they leaned forward over their saddle-bows and charged forward, stout-hearted, to smite the enemy.

He who was born in a lucky hour cried out:

"Have at them, my knights, for Heaven's sake! I am Ruy Díaz de Vivar, the Cid Campeador!"

They all charge into the thick of the battle line, there where Pedro Bermúdez is surrounded. Three hundred spears they were, each with a pennon hanging from it. Each of them killed a Moor, each one with a single thrust. As they charged back into the fray, as many more fell dead before them.

There you could see so many spears, lowered and raised back up; so many shields speared right through; so many coats of mail pierced and crumpled; so many white pennons crimsoned with blood; so many fine horses trotting around riderless.

The Moors cry out "Mohammed!" while the Christians cry "Santiago!"[8]

---

7. Throughout the poem, the singer tends to lapse into present tense in the midst of recounting past events. More precisely, he goes back and forth between past and present tense. This is part of his oral epic narrative style. In general, I translate accordingly.

8. The name "Santiago" is the traditional Spanish name for Saint James the Apostle, the patron saint of Christian Spain. In this form, it is the traditional Christian battle cry in wars against the Muslims. Elsewhere in the poem, the saint himself is referred to as Saint James the Apostle.

In no time at all, thirteen hundred Moors had fallen dead.

How well he fought, leaning over his golden saddle-bow, did My Cid Ruy Díaz, the valiant warrior! And Minaya Álvar Fáñez, lord of Zorita; Martín Antolínez, the worthy man of Burgos; Martín Muñoz, lord of Montemayor; Álvar Álvarez and Álvar Salvadórez; Galindo García, the loyal man from Aragon; and Félix Muñoz, the Cid's own nephew. From that moment on, everyone there came to the aid of My Cid, the Campeador, and of his standard-bearer.

They killed Minaya's horse, right out from under him. At once the Christian troops come to his aid. His spear was shattered, so he took his sword in hand. Even though he was now on foot, he dealt out mighty blows. My Cid Ruy Díaz, the Castilian, caught sight of him. Riding up alongside a Moorish viceroy mounted on a fine horse, the Cid struck him such a blow with his right arm [750] that he cut him right through at the waist, hurling half the body on to the field.

The Cid then led the horse over to Minaya Álvar Fáñez, crying out:

"Get on this horse, Minaya! You are my right arm! In this day's doings, our forces will be much stronger thanks to you. The Moors are holding steady, they haven't yet withdrawn from the field."

Minaya rode back into the fray, sword in hand, bravely doing battle, dispatching all who come within his reach. My Cid Ruy Díaz, the one born in a lucky hour, struck at the Moorish king Fáriz three times with his sword, missing twice but hitting him the third time. His cuirass drenched in blood, Fáriz wheeled his horse and fled the battlefield.

With that one stroke the Moorish army was routed.

Meanwhile, Martín Antolínez struck Galve such a blow that the garnets flew from the Moor's helmet as the blade cut through to the flesh. You can be sure Galve didn't wait around for a second blow.

Thus were they defeated, the two kings Fáriz and Galve — a great day for Christendom, as the Moors fled the field with the Cid's men in hot pursuit, cutting down the stragglers as they went! King Fáriz found refuge in Terrer, but Galve was turned away. He fled toward Calatayud as fast as he could, with the Cid right on his heels, pursuing all the way.

Minaya Álvar Fáñez's new horse served him well. He killed thirty-four of those Moors, hacking with his sword, arm covered with blood down to the elbow.

"Now I'm satisfied," he declared. "For good news will travel all the way back to Castile, telling how My Cid Ruy Díaz has won this pitched battle."

Many Moors lay dead on the field, and those few left alive were mostly cut down in the headlong pursuit. Presently the men of the one born in a lucky hour returned. Riding along on his charger, his cap pulled back—Lord, how full was his beard!—the hood of his chain mail draped across his shoulders, his sword in hand, the Cid beheld his men gathering around him.

"Thanks be to God," he declared, "to Him who dwells on high, that we have won such a battle."

The Cid's men instantly set to work pillaging the Moorish camp, making off with shields and weapons and much other plunder. Corralling them together, they counted up five hundred and ten horses left behind by the Moors.

Great was the rejoicing among those Christians; no more than fifteen of their own men were missing. In their possession they had more gold and silver than they could count up. All those Christians were now richer men on account of this plentiful loot. [800] When they moved the Moorish prisoners from Alcocer back into the fortress, the Cid even ordered that they also be given something.

The Cid rejoiced greatly, along with all his vassals, as he divided up all that money and all that abundance of goods. In the fifth that fell to the Cid there were a hundred horses. Lord, how delighted were all his vassals, foot soldiers and cavalrymen alike, by their lord's generosity! He who was born in a lucky hour arranged everything fairly—every man with him was content with his share.

"Hear me, Minaya, you who are my right arm! From these riches that the Creator has given us, take as much as you please, with your own hand. I mean to send you to Castile with news of this battle we've won. To King Alfonso, with whom I am in disgrace, I wish to send thirty horses as a gift, all of them saddled and nicely bridled, and each one with a sword hanging from the saddle-bow."

Minaya Álvar Fáñez replied:

"That I will do, right gladly."

"Behold this boot, brim-full with gold and silver. From it you can have a thousand masses said in Santa María's church, in Burgos. Whatever's left, give to my wife and daughters, so they can pray for me night and day. If I live through this, I'll make them wealthy women."

Minaya Álvar Fáñez gladly accepted this mission, and men were assigned to go with him.

Night was falling and the animals were being fed, as My Cid Ruy Díaz took counsel with his men:

"You are leaving now, Minaya, for fair Castile! You can truly tell our friends that God was on our side when we won that battle. When you return from your mission, you should find us here; if not, catch up with us as soon as you find out where we are. We have to get our livelihood with spear and sword — otherwise we can't survive in this barren land."

Minaya was soon ready, and left next morning, while the Campeador remained there with his men. The land all around was barren, a real wasteland. Day and night, Moors from the borderlands and others, outlanders, spied on the Cid.

When King Fáriz had recovered, the Moors took counsel with him. Together, the people of Ateca, and those of Terrer la Casa, as well as those of Calatayud — the principal town of the three — confirmed the amount and set it down in writing: the Cid would ransom Alcocer back to them for three thousand silver marks.

As My Cid Ruy Díaz ransomed back Alcocer, how happy he made all his vassals! Cavalrymen and foot soldiers alike — he made them rich men: you couldn't find a single needy one among them.

Who serves a generous lord, lives ever a life of ease. [850]

As My Cid was about to leave the fortress, Moorish men and women began to cry out their sorrow:

"You are going away, My Cid! May our blessings go with you! We will always remain grateful for the generosity you have shown us."

As the Cid departed from Alcocer, the Moorish folk, men and women alike, began to weep.

Raising his standard high, the Campeador set forth. He headed down the Jalón, spurring on straight ahead. As they left the Jalón behind them, the bird omens were very good.

The people of Terrer were pleased, and even more so those of Calatayud. But the people of Alcocer grieved, for he had shown them great generosity.

My Cid spurred on, riding straight ahead until he stopped to make camp on a hill overlooking Monreal. The hill was wonderfully big and high; the Cid, you know, felt safe from attack in all directions.

First he subjected Daroca to tribute, then Molina, on the other side, and thirdly Teruel, further on. He also held sway over Cella de Canal. God bless and keep My Cid Ruy Díaz!

Álvar Fáñez Minaya, meanwhile, had reached Castile and presented the king with a gift of thirty horses. Beholding them, the king smiled, delighted:

"Minaya, God be with you—who has given me these animals?"

"My Cid Ruy Díaz, he who girt on sword in a lucky hour. He has vanquished two Moorish kings in battle: great indeed, my lord, is the plunder he has taken. To you, great king, he sends this present. He kisses your feet, and both your hands, begging that you pardon him, so help you God."

The king said:

"It is very early for a banished man, still in disgrace with his lord, to be welcomed back, after only three weeks. But as it was taken from Moors, I accept this gift. I am even glad that My Cid has captured all this loot. In addition to all this, I pardon you, Minaya. All your fiefs and estates are restored to you. From now on, you have my permission to freely come and go. But concerning the Cid Campeador, I say nothing more at this time. However, I want to assure you, Minaya, that I grant my leave, throughout my kingdom, to any and all worthy and valiant men who wish to, to go and help the Cid, exempting their estates from all penalty."

Minaya Álvar Fáñez kissed his hands:

"All my thanks and gratitude to you, my king and natural lord. This much you do for the time being—later on you will do more."

"Make your way through Castile, Minaya; you will be given free passage. Go freely on your way, and join My Cid in the quest for plunder."

Now let me tell you more of the one who was born, and who girt on sword, in a lucky hour.

On that hilltop he set up his camp. [900] Whether in the hands of Moors or Christians, the town will always be officially known, from here on in, as the Hill of the Cid. While camped in that place he pillaged much of the surrounding country, exacting tribute from all the towns along the Martín River.

News of his deeds reached Saragossa. The Moors were not pleased—in fact, they were downright troubled. The Cid remained there for fifteen entire weeks. Seeing that Minaya was delayed in getting back, the intrepid warrior and all his men withdrew from the Hill, marching away by night and leaving nothing behind. Beyond Teruel the Cid Ruy Díaz advanced, establishing his camp in the pine woods of Tévar. All those lands too he plundered, including Saragossa, which he subjected to tribute.

Three weeks after the Cid had accomplished all this, Minaya returned, with two hundred mounted warriors, all armed with swords; the foot soldiers with him, you know, were too numerous to count. As soon as the Cid saw Minaya coming, he galloped out to meet him, embracing him warmly and kissing him on the mouth and eyes.

Minaya told him everything, holding nothing back. The Campeador smiled, delighted:

"Thanks be to God, and all His holy powers! As long as you're alive, Minaya, things will go well for me!"

Lord, how the whole army rejoiced at Minaya's return, as he sent them greetings from cousins and brothers, and from all the companions they had left back home! Lord, how happy was he of the flowing beard, that Álvar Fáñez had paid for the thousand masses, and that he brought back greetings from the Cid's wife and daughters! Lord, how glad the Cid was, and how greatly he rejoiced!

"May your days be many, Álvar Fáñez!"

Wasting no time, he who was born in a lucky hour ravaged the lands of Alcañiz, pillaging the country all around. On the third day after he set out, he returned to his headquarters.

Presently, news of these developments traveled far and wide. The people of Monzón and Huesca were very worried. Those in Saragossa were untroubled, for they already were paying tribute and had no fear of treachery on the Cid's part.

With this plunder the Cid and his men returned to their camp, all of them rejoicing at the plentiful loot they had won for themselves. The Cid was very pleased, and Álvar Fáñez even more so. The intrepid one smiled, beside himself with joy:

"Now then, my knights, I will tell you a true thing: he who stays put may see himself losing ground. Early tomorrow, then, let's get ready to mount up and ride on, leaving this camp behind us." [950]

Next day, the Cid moved to the Gallocanta Pass. From there he raided Huesca and Montalbán. For ten days they carried out those raids, while the news traveled far and wide of how the exile from Castile was causing the people thereabouts such grief. The news reached everywhere.

The news came to the ears of the Count of Barcelona, as to how his whole country was being ravaged by My Cid Ruy Díaz. The count was most displeased, considering this a grave affront.

The count was very foolish and spoke silly words:

"My Cid, the man from Vivar, has wronged me. At my own court he showed me the gravest disrespect: he struck my nephew and has never answered for it.[9] Now he raids my own lands, and those under my protection. Up to now, I have never challenged him, nor retaliated against him. But now that he is really asking for it, I will go and seek him out, demanding that he make amends."

In considerable numbers, reinforcements speedily assembled. Both Moors and Christians made up the numerous host that joined forces with the count. Then they all headed after the Cid, the noble man of Burgos. Three days and two nights they traveled, finally overtaking the Cid at the pine forest of Tévar. The count arrived at the head of so powerful a force that he was sure of taking the Cid prisoner.

Meanwhile, the Cid, in possession of great plunder, descended from a hill and came down into a valley. A message arrived for him from Count Raymond. My Cid, when he heard it, sent back his reply:

---

9. The passage refers to an incident not previously mentioned in the narrative. The confrontation mentioned by the Count of Barcelona is one of many found in chronicles and other works about the Cid and his exploits, and would have been well known to audiences of the time as part of the legend and lore of the Cid.

"Tell the count not to take offense. Nothing of what I take away with me belongs to him; he should let me go in peace."

The count replied:

"That is far from the truth! He will have to answer to me for past and present wrongs — the exile will soon see whom he has dishonored!"

The herald returned as fast as he could. From that moment on, the Cid understood that there was no leaving there without doing battle.

"Now then, my knights, set the loot safely aside. Get ready as quick as you can, and arm yourselves: Count Raymond is going to attack us with everything he's got. His host is enormous and includes both Moors and Christians. There is no way he's going to let us get away without a fight. Since they'll be coming after us, let the battle take place here. Get the horses ready, and let every man don his battle gear. They'll be charging downhill, and they'll all be wearing breeches — no boots. They're using racing saddles, with the cinches loose, while we're using Galician saddles, with boots over our breeches. A hundred of our knights should be enough to defeat their whole army. Before they reach the plain, we'll attack them with our spears. For every one you hit, three more will be thrown from their saddles. Count Raymond will soon see just who he's come after, here among the pines of Tévar, when he tries to strip me of my plunder!"

They all made ready, as My Cid spoke these words. [1000]

Fully armed and mounted on their steeds, they all watched the Frankish forces move down the slope.[10] At the very bottom of the hill, down close to the flat ground, My Cid, he who was born in a lucky hour, commanded his men to strike at the enemy. They all responded eagerly, attacking with a will. Deftly they wielded their pennons and spears, smiting some and unhorsing many others.

Thus did he win this battle, the man born in a lucky hour. Count Raymond, meanwhile, had been taken prisoner by the Cid's men.

---

10. The County of Barcelona was part of the so-called "Spanish March," established around 800 as a buffer zone between the Frankish realm of Charlemagne and the Muslim realms of the Peninsula.

There the Cid won the sword Colada, worth more than a thousand silver marks; there he won that battle by which his beard accrued much honor.[11]

The Cid took Count Raymond to his own quarters, where he ordered his attendants to guard the prisoner. The Cid strode out of the tent, as all his men gathered around. The Cid was very pleased, for they had won vast quantities of loot. They prepared a great banquet for My Cid, Don Rodrigo. Count Raymond looked on with contempt as they brought him food, setting the dishes before him. He refused to eat, disdainfully rejecting everything they offered.

"I won't eat a single morsel, not for all the wealth in Spain. I'd sooner lose body and soul alike, now that I've been defeated in battle by such a bunch of ill-shod louts."

My Cid Ruy Díaz—hear his words:

"Eat, Count: have some bread, drink some wine. If you do as I say, you'll soon be released. If not, as long as you live, you'll never again see Christendom."

Count Raymond replied:

"You eat, Don Rodrigo, and look to your own comfort. I will let myself die, for I refuse to eat."

For three days they could not get him to eat. Meanwhile they went about dividing up those plentiful spoils. During all that time they could not get him to eat so much as a bread crumb.

The Cid said:

"Eat something, Count, for if you don't, you'll never again see Christendom. But if you eat, you'll make me happy. I'll let you and two of your nobles go, releasing you free and clear."

When the count heard this, he cheered up considerably.

"If you do this, Cid, this thing you've promised, as long as I live I'll never get over my admiration."

---

11. In the world of this poem and its audience, a man's beard has a mystical, even superstitious significance. It is a folkloric synecdoche that, like Samson's hair, symbolizes the hero's virility, honor, standing, and warlike prowess. The beard stands for the man. We have already seen that one of the Cid's epithets is "he of the flowing beard." He also solemnly swears by his beard.

"So eat then, Count, and after you've dined, I'll let you and two others go. However, all you've lost and all I've won in the field, know that you'll get nothing back from me, not so much as a farthing. Because I need it all, for these my vassals, who undergo hardship along with me. Taking from you and from others, we'll get by, and lead this life as long as it pleases our Holy Father above, as men in disgrace with their king and forced to live in exile."

Delighted, the count asked them to bring water for his hands, and they quickly did so, setting it down in front of him. [1050] Along with the two knights that the Cid was releasing with him, the count dined — Lord, what a good appetite he had! Beside him, looking on, sat the one born in a lucky hour:

"If you don't eat enough to satisfy me, Count, we'll both stay here, never to part company."

Then the count replied:

"Right gladly will I do as you wish."

Along with his two knights the count ate quickly. The Cid was satisfied, as he remained there watching him, for the count's hands busily moved about the table as he helped himself to the food.

"If you don't mind, My Cid, we are now ready to leave. Order our mounts brought to us, and we will soon be on our way. Never since the day I was made count have I dined so agreeably. I will never forget how much I enjoyed this meal."

They brought them three palfreys, each of them very well saddled, and also handsome garments, fine fur capes and cloaks. Count Raymond placed himself between his two companions, as the Castilian escorted them out to the edge of the encampment.

"Now be off with you, Count, free and clear. I'm most grateful for the spoils you leave behind here with me. If it ever occurs to you to try and get even, just come looking, and you'll surely find me. If not, send someone else after me. Either you'll leave behind some of your goods, or else you'll carry off some of mine."

"You can relax on that score, My Cid: you have nothing to fear from me. I've paid you a whole year's worth of tribute. Coming after you will be the last thing on my mind."

The count gave spur to his horse, intent on getting away quickly. He turned his head, looking back, afraid that the Cid might change his mind—something the intrepid one would never do, not for all the riches in the world. Never in his life did the Cid play false.

When the count had departed, the man from Vivar rejoined his men, and celebrated with them the winning of all that fabulous plunder.

Second Book: The Marriage
(Verses 1087–2277)

The Cid besieges and conquers the Moorish city of Valencia. He sends his trusted friend and vassal Minaya Álvar Fáñez with gifts to the Castilian court, to ask the king for permission to bring Jimena and their daughters to Valencia. The king grants the Cid's request, pardoning him and rescinding all punishments. This excites the envy of the Cid's great enemy, García Ordóñez, and of his allies the Scions of Carrión.[12] The Cid's

---

12. These are the chief villains of the story: Fernando and Diego González. The names are those of historical figures, members of the highest aristocracy. Little or no evidence supports the notion that they were the historical Cid's enemies or that they married his daughters. The poet calls them always "Infantes de Carrión." *Infante*, which has the same origin as the English "infant," can mean "crown prince" or "heir." The latter fits better here, because these characters are not royalty. Some translators call them "The Heirs of Carrión," or simply retain the Spanish word "Infante." I prefer "Scions of Carrión" because the poet uses "Infantes" to mean more than simply "heir." It has a pejorative ring to it, as if to the poet and his audience it meant something like "rake" (i.e., the idle and dissipated son of a prominent family). "Scion" means "offspring," "heir," but retains a hint of its original sense of "sprout," "twig."

García Ordóñez was a Castilian noble and prominent military leader. Shown to be the Cid's archenemy in the story, as well as the ally and collaborator of the Scions of Carrión, he also figures in chronicles and other accounts. These suggest that a real conflict between the two historical men might be the basis of the poet's depiction of this character. For the poet, García Ordóñez, like the Scions of Carrión, personifies the old, effete aristocracy dramatically contrasted with the up-and-coming frontier nobility exemplified by the Cid and his men.

prominence and success induces the Scions of Carrión to seek a marriage with his daughters. The king agrees to support their suit, and the Cid eventually accepts the match, not without misgivings. The marriage takes place and is celebrated by a great feast.

Here begin the real exploits of My Cid, the man of Vivar.

His men were now so rich, they could not count up all their wealth. The Cid had occupied the Olocau Pass, left behind Saragossa and the lands thereabouts, and moved on from Huesca and the lands of Montalbán. Along the salty sea he began his campaign, heading toward where the sun rises in the east. The Cid took Jérica and Onda and Almenara, and conquered all the country around Burriana.

The Creator helped him, the Lord who dwells in Heaven. Along with all those other lands, he took Murviedro. Now My Cid saw that God was truly with him.

Within Valencia, they were quite alarmed.

The Valencians were downright restless, you can be sure — they were not at all pleased. Taking counsel amongst themselves, they resolved to surround the Cid and his forces. Traveling by night, at dawn of the next day [1100] they set up their tents near Murviedro.

Beholding all this, My Cid exulted:

"Thanks be to thee, oh Spiritual Father! We are in their lands, doing them all manner of harm. We drink their wine and eat their bread: if they come to besiege us, they have every right to do so. Short of a fight, this business will never be settled. Let messengers go forth, and send word to all those bound to come to our aid: some to Jérica, others to Olocau and from there to Onda, still others to Almenara, and to those in Burriana, also — tell them all to get here right away. We shall start this battle, and I trust in God that these reinforcements will increase our advantage."

On the third day, they had all gathered together. The man born in a lucky hour began to address them:

"Hear me, all my battalions, the Creator bless and keep you! Since we departed from Blessed Christendom — a thing we did against our will, we had no any other choice — things have gone well for us, thanks be to God. Now the Valencians have us surrounded. If we want to stay in these lands, they must be taught a harsh lesson. Let night fall and morning come. Then get ready, mounted up and fully armed, and we'll go take a look at that horde of theirs, like the exiles we are, cast out from a distant land. Now we'll see who's ready to earn his keep."

Now hear what Minaya Álvar Fáñez said:

"Campeador, your wish is our command. Give me a hundred knights, that's all I ask of you. You and the others strike them head on. Hit them hard, no holding back, while I with my hundred men will come at them from the other side. With God's help, on which I firmly rely, the field will be ours."

The Cid was much pleased at Minaya's words.

Then it was the next morning, and they were all getting ready to don their armor. Each and every one of them knew exactly what he was supposed to do. At daybreak My Cid launched the attack.

"In the name of the Creator and of Saint James the Apostle, have at them, my knights, with heart, and zeal, and force of will! For I am Ruy Díaz, the Cid, the man from Vivar!"

There you would have seen so many tent cords snapped, and everywhere stakes yanked up and tent poles knocked down. The Moors were many, and quickly moved to regroup. But there was Álvar Fáñez, attacking them from the other side. Much as it distressed them, they had no choice but to surrender or flee. Those who could fled on horseback.

Great was the rejoicing all over that battlefield! Two kings of Moors were killed in the pursuit, as the Cid's men chased the routed army all the way to Valencia.

Great was the plunder taken by the Cid, as his men pillaged the field and then headed back. Along the way they took Cebolla and everything before it, [1150] before arriving at Murviedro with that immense haul of loot.

News of My Cid's exploits, you can be sure, resounded far and wide.

The Valencians were afraid, uncertain of what to do; meanwhile, news of the Cid reached even beyond the sea.

The Cid and all his men rejoiced, glad that with God's help they had won this great victory. Their raiding parties were sent out. Moving by night, they reached Cullera, then Játiva, and even, a bit further south, the town of Denia. All along the coast, the Cid relentlessly plundered Moorish country. He captured Benicadell, and all roads in and out.

When the Cid Campeador took possession of Benicadell, the people of Játiva and Cullera were troubled indeed, while the dread that overcame Valencia was indescribable.

There in Moorish country, capturing and setting up garrisons as he went, sleeping days and marching by night, the Cid spent three years conquering all those towns. The Valencians had been taught a harsh lesson; they dared not come out to take him on. Meanwhile, he cut down their farmlands, doing them great harm. In each of those years he took away their bread.

Bitterly the Valencians bemoaned their plight, at their wits' end as to what they could do. Bread was nowhere to be found; fathers could not help their sons, nor sons their fathers, nor could friends comfort one another.

A grievous plight it is, my lords, to suffer dearth of bread, to watch one's wife and children starve to death.

They saw the misery at hand, saw how helpless they were, and resolved to send for the king of Morocco. But he was waging a great war against the king of the Atlas Mountains, and could give them neither aid nor comfort.

Learning of this, the Cid was heartily pleased. Leaving Murviedro, he marched all night and reached Monreal by daybreak. Throughout Aragon and Navarre he ordered to be proclaimed, and to Castilian lands he sent his heralds to announce:

Whoever sought to leave poverty behind and obtain riches instead, should come and join up with the Cid, who was planning to go on an expedition, intending to lay siege to Valencia and hand it over to the Christians.

"Whoever wants to come with me, and lay siege to Valencia: let every man come of his own free will, no one is being coerced. I'll wait for three days in Cella de Canal."

Thus spoke My Cid, the man born in a lucky hour. Then he turned back toward Murviedro, for he had conquered it, right and proper, for himself.

The proclamations, you know, went out far and wide. Enticed by the smell of loot, they did not tarry: from everywhere came great numbers of Christians, to join up with the Cid. My Cid, the man of Vivar, saw himself growing ever richer. [1200] Delighted, he beheld the host assembled before him. Wasting no time, Don Rodrigo headed straight for Valencia and immediately began to lay siege to it. He surrounded it completely, leaving no way to escape: he blocked off every way out, and every way in.

News of all the Cid's operations soon spread far and wide. The ones joining up with the Cid, you can be sure, outnumbered those leaving his service.

He held the city to a time limit, to see if anybody might come to their aid. Nine whole months he laid siege to the town, you know, and when the tenth month came around, they had no choice but to surrender.

Great was the rejoicing all around, when the Cid took Valencia and entered into the town! All those who had fought on foot instantly became knights, while the gold and the silver— whoever could count it all up? They were all rich men now, all those there with him.

My Cid Don Rodrigo ordered the fifth part of the loot to be set aside. Thirty thousand marks in coined money fell to his share, and as for the other goods, they were beyond all tally. Meanwhile, the Cid and all his men rejoiced to see his standard placed at the topmost point of the citadel.

Now, as the Cid took his rest, his companies all around him, reports reached the ears of the king of Seville, to the effect that Valencia had been conquered, for no one had come to their aid. He came to confront the Cid with thirty thousand men-at-arms. Amid the fertile plain they joined battle, and the Cid, the long-bearded one, routed them utterly. All the way into Játiva his men pursued them. The skirmish at the crossing of the Júcar was a real sight to see, as the Moors floundered about and gulped down river water, like it or not.

The king of Morocco escaped with just three wounds, as the Cid made off with all that loot. The spoils were great from conquering the town of Valencia, but this raid, you know, was even more profitable. Even the lowliest soldier received a hundred silver marks. Now indeed did the Cid's fame spread far and wide.

Great was the rejoicing among all those Christians there with My Cid Ruy Díaz, the man born in a lucky hour. Now his beard was really growing, getting longer and longer. From his own mouth, My Cid had sworn this oath:

"For love of King Alfonso, he who cast me out from his kingdom, no scissors will cut as much as a single hair from it, and let this be talked about among Moors and Christians alike."
My Cid, Don Rodrigo, rested there in Valencia. With him was Minaya Álvar Fáñez, who never left his side. Riches were lavishly bestowed on all those who had left their homeland to join him; he granted them all houses and estates, which made them very happy. Now they all really felt the Cid's love for them, both those who set out with him at the beginning and those who came afterward—they were all very content.

My Cid saw that with the riches they had acquired many were ready to leave as soon as they could. [1250] My Cid issued the following order, after consulting with Minaya:

Any man of his who departed without taking proper leave and kissing his lord's hand, would, if arrested or captured, be stripped of his possessions and hanged on the gallows.

All these measures were duly carried out. The Cid then took counsel with Minaya Álvar Fáñez:

"If you approve, Minaya, I want to verify the names of all those here who have won riches. I want to record their names in writing, and let all of them be counted, so that if anybody sneaks away or is unaccounted for, his goods will be handed over to these vassals of mine, who watch over Valencia and are constantly on patrol."

"That is a good idea," agreed Minaya.

The Cid ordered them all to come to court and be assembled before him. Once he had them there, he ordered them all counted up by name. My Cid, the man of Vivar, had three thousand, six hundred men. Gladness filled his heart, and he smiled:

"Thanks be to God, Minaya, and to Holy Mother Mary! There were far fewer with us when we left the town of Vivar; now we have riches, and will soon have more. If you agree, Minaya, and if it isn't too much trouble, I'd like to send you to Castile, where we hold lands, to see my liege-lord, King Alfonso. From this plunder that we've won here, I want you to go and give him one hundred horses. Then kiss his hand on my behalf, and earnestly entreat him—if it please his majesty—to let me take my wife and daughters out of Castile and bring them here. I'll send for them; you, meanwhile, learn this message by heart: 'A company will be sent to escort My Cid's wife and two young daughters, so that they will be brought here in most honorable fashion, to these foreign lands that we have managed to conquer.'"

Minaya then replied:

"Gladly."

After they had discussed this, they looked to the preparations. My Cid gave Álvar Fáñez a hundred men, to serve him on the way, and ordered them to take with them a thousand silver marks to the monastery of San Pedro, to give to the abbot Don Sancho.

As everyone rejoiced at these developments, a tonsured man arrived from the east, Bishop Jerome by name.[13] A learned man, and very wise, he was also a good fighter, whether on foot or on horseback. He had been going about informing himself as to the exploits of My Cid. Now the good bishop sighed with longing at the prospect of taking on the Moors in battle. If he could only fight to his heart's content, smiting the enemy with his own hands, he would never be mourned by his fellow Christians, not in all the days of the world.

When My Cid heard about this, he was very happy.

"Listen, Minaya Álvar Fáñez, by the Lord who dwells on high! If God wants to send us help, let's give Him many thanks. I intend to establish a diocese here in Valencia, and mean to give it to this good Christian. [1300] You, when you return to Castile, will bear glad tidings."

Álvar Fáñez was pleased with Don Rodrigo's words. Soon afterward, Don Jerome was named bishop of the see of Valencia, a post that would surely make him a rich man. Lord, how all Christendom rejoiced to see the land of Valencia provided with its own lord bishop!

Minaya rejoiced as he took his leave and went on his way.

With the Valencian lands now at peace, Minaya Álvar Fáñez made his way toward Castile. I will pass over all the places where he stopped to rest, having no desire to give a full account of them. He asked for Alfonso, wondering where he might find him. The king had gone to Sahagún a short time

---

13. The tonsure was a ritual shaving of the head: leaving a circular patch on the crown, it marked one's membership in a religious order.

before, then had returned to Carrión; that was where Minaya would find him. Glad to hear this, Minaya Álvar Fáñez headed for that place, bearing the gifts the Cid had sent with him.

King Alfonso had just come out from mass, when Minaya Álvar Fáñez appeared at just the right moment and fell to his knees in front of all the people. Right at King Alfonso's feet he fell, expressing grievous sorrow. Kissing the king's hands, he spoke these timely words:

"A favor, Lord Alfonso, I beg of you, for the love of God! My Cid the Campeador kisses your hands, kisses your hands and feet, as befits so fine a lord. He begs you grant him this favor, so help you God. You cast him out from the land, and he remains in disgrace with you. Although in a strange country, he does the best he can: he has conquered Jérica, and the place called Onda; he has also taken Almenara and Murviedro, an even bigger place, and likewise Cebolla, and Castejón, further on, and Benicadell, an impregnable height. Along with all these places, he is also now lord of Valencia. My lord Campeador has appointed a bishop and has fought five pitched battles, winning them all. Great are the spoils that the Creator has granted him, and behold, here before you, the proof of it, I tell you verily: one hundred horses, stout and swift, all fully harnessed with saddles and bridles—kissing your hands, he bids you accept them as a gift. He still considers himself your vassal, and holds you to be his lord."

Raising his right hand, the king crossed himself:

"Concerning these great spoils the Campeador has won— Saint Isidore preserve me!—I rejoice in my heart, and rejoice as well at the Campeador's exploits. I hereby accept these horses he sends me as a gift."

Although the king was pleased, Garcia Ordóñez was much aggrieved:

"It seems like there's barely a man left alive in Moorish country, seeing how the Cid Campeador can do anything he pleases."

The king said to the count:

"That's enough of that. In any event, he serves me better than you do."

Then Minaya spoke out boldly: [1350]

"The Cid begs a favor of you, if it please your majesty, on behalf of his wife, Doña Jimena, and of his two daughters. He begs that they might leave the monastery where he left them, and go join the good Campeador in Valencia."

Immediately the king answered:

"Granted, with all my heart. I will have them supplied with provisions as long as they are within my lands, and will see to it that they are protected from all shame, harm, or dishonor. After the noble ladies cross the border of my kingdom, look to serve them as best you can, you and the Campeador.

Now hear me, all my vassals and all members of my court! I do not want the Campeador to suffer the slightest loss. And to all the men-at-arms who call him lord, I hereby restore to them whatever property of theirs I have confiscated. Let them have the use of their lands, wherever the Campeador may be. I guarantee the safety of their persons from all harm and violence; this I do so they may better serve their lord."

Minaya Álvar Fáñez kissed his hands.

The king smiled, and spoke most generously:

"All those who wish to go and serve the Campeador: let them be free and clear of all obligation to me, and God speed them on their way. We shall benefit more from this than from meting out further punishment."

At that moment, the Scions of Carrión began to talk things over.

"The fortunes of My Cid, the Campeador, keep growing and growing. We would do very well to marry his daughters: that would be really profitable for us. But we don't dare propose the match ourselves. My Cid is from Vivar, and we belong to the clan of the Counts of Carrión."

They spoke to no one, and nothing came of the matter for the time being.

Meanwhile, Minaya Álvar Fáñez took his leave of the good king.

"So then, you are leaving us, Minaya. Go, and God's grace be with you! Take one of my royal couriers with you, I think he'll be of use to you. If you're taking the ladies with you, let them be waited upon just as they please. As far as Medinaceli, let them be given everything they have need of, from that point on, let the Campeador look to their well-being."

Minaya took his leave and departed from the court.

The Scions of Carrión accompanied Minaya Álvar Fáñez.

"You are always so obliging about everything. Do likewise regarding this: send greetings to My Cid from us. We are at his service, as much as is in our power. If the Cid should be well disposed toward us, he will lose nothing thereby."

Minaya replied:

"I see nothing wrong with conveying your message."

Minaya continued on his journey, and the Scions of Carrión headed back.

Minaya made his way to San Pedro, where the ladies were staying. Great indeed was the rejoicing as they saw him arrive! Minaya got down from his horse and went to pray to Saint Peter. After he had finished his prayer, he turned to the ladies:

"My deepest respects, my lady Jimena. God keep you from all harm, and likewise both your daughters. My Cid sends you greetings, from the place where he now lives. I left him in good health, and in possession of great riches. The king has graciously deigned to release you to me, [1400] so that I may conduct you to Valencia, of which we are now the rightful lords. If the Cid could only see you again, safe and sound, he would be overjoyed, and his sorrows would be over."

Doña Jimena replied:

"The Creator will it so!"

Minaya assigned three knights to go to where My Cid resided in Valencia:

"Tell the Campeador, God keep him from all harm, that the king has released his wife and daughters to me, and that he ordered us to be given provisions as long as we are in his territory. Two weeks from now, if God keeps us from harm, his wife and I, and his two daughters, will all be there, along with all the excellent ladies in their company."

The knights set forth, very mindful of their task, while Minaya Álvar Fáñez remained in San Pedro. You could see knights arriving from everywhere, wanting to go to Valencia to join up with My Cid, the man of Vivar.

They asked Minaya to support them in this, and he replied: "This I will gladly do."

Sixty-five knights came to join Minaya, increasing his forces by that many. He was thus able to take a hundred men along with him, a goodly number to accompany the ladies. Meanwhile Minaya gave five hundred marks to the abbot. I will tell you what Minaya did with the other five hundred. The good Minaya made sure to provide Doña Jimena, and her daughters with her, and the ladies that kept them company, with the finest garments to be found in Burgos, along with palfreys and mules, so they could make the best impression. When he had provided them with all they needed, the good Minaya made ready to set out.

But then, all at once, Raquel and Vidas showed up, falling to their knees before him:

"A favor, Minaya, most worthy knight! The Cid has ruined us, if he does not come to our aid. We would gladly forgo the interest, if he would only give us back the principal."

"I will talk to the Cid about this matter, if, with God's help, I manage to get back to him. For the service you have rendered, there will be suitable compensation."

Raquel and Vidas replied:

"May God will it so! If not, we will leave Burgos and come looking for the Cid."

Minaya Álvar Fáñez went back into the monastery. There, many more men joined up with him, as he made ready to ride forth.

At the moment of departure, the abbot was sad at heart:

"God keep you, Minaya Álvar Fáñez! Kiss the Campeador's hands on my behalf, and bid him not forget this monastery. For in continuing to look out for us, the Cid's fortunes will never cease to improve, as long as he lives."

Minaya replied:

"I will do so gladly."

Then they took their leave and rode forth, and with them the king's courier, who was assigned to watch over them. Making their way through Alfonso's kingdom, they were amply provisioned along the way. [1450] From San Pedro they reach Medinaceli in five days.

And now, as we behold them in Medinaceli, the ladies and Álvar Fáñez, I will tell of the knights who carried the message to Valencia.

On hearing the news, My Cid rejoiced, his heart filled with gladness, and he spoke these words:

"He who sends a good messenger should expect nothing less. You, Muño Gustioz, and you, Pedro Bermúdez, come here!

And Martín Antolínez, a loyal man of Burgos, and Bishop Jerome, you worthy tonsured man: ride forth, all of you, with one hundred of my knights, all armed for battle. Go by way of Albarracín, and then to Molina, further on. That place is held by Abengalbón, my friend and ally. From there he will surely accompany you with another hundred knights. Go now, head toward Medinaceli as fast as you can ride. There, as I've been told, you will find my wife and daughters, along with Minaya Álvar Fáñez. Bring them here to me, honoring them in every way you can. Meanwhile I will remain here in Valencia, a conquest dearly bought. It would be folly to leave it undefended. So I will stay here in Valencia, since I now hold it as my own domain."

These words spoken, his men set out, riding for as long as they could without stopping. They passed through Albarracín, then stopped to spend the night in Bronchales. Next day they halted in Molina. As soon as he heard the news of their arrival, the Moor Abengalbón, rejoicing greatly, went out to welcome them.

"Come, vassals of my dear friend! No bother at all, believe me—I am delighted indeed to see you!"

Then Muño Gustioz spoke up, not waiting for anybody else:

"Greetings to you from My Cid, who asked me to bid you help him by preparing to ride forth immediately with one hundred knights. His wife and daughters are waiting in Medinaceli. He wishes you to go and escort them back here, and then to accompany them, not leaving their side until they get to Valencia."

Abengalbón replied:

"That I will gladly do."

That night he feasted them handsomely. The following morning, they all rode out. Only a hundred knights had been requested; Abengalbón brought two hundred with him.

They went through forests, vast and wild, then, undaunted, crossed through the Thickets of Taranz. From there they descended through the valley of the Arbujuelo.

Meanwhile, in Medinaceli, Minaya Álvar Fáñez, taking all precautions, sent two knights to find out who was coming. Without delay, they eagerly set out. One ended up staying with the new arrivals, while the other returned to report back to Álvar Fáñez:

"A company of the Cid's men is coming to meet up with us. Pedro Bermúdez is with them, and Muño Gustioz—your faithful friends, both of them—and Martín Antolínez, the man from Burgos, [1500] and Bishop Jerome, a loyal tonsured man, and the Moorish governor Abengalbón, who leads a detachment of his own men. To please My Cid, and honor him as best they can, they are all traveling together, and will be here soon."

To this Minaya replied:

"Let us ride out to meet them."

They rode swiftly, eager to get there as quickly as they could. At least a hundred set out, a sight to behold, with trappings of brocade, bells on their steeds' harness, bucklers slung from their shoulders, and each man carrying a lance from which a pennon flew. All this was so the newcomers could see how thoughtfully Minaya had provided for them, as he went forth from Castile with those ladies he escorted.

The advance guard, scouting out the land, immediately began to brandish their weapons playfully, and there was loud rejoicing along the banks of the Jalón. As the newcomers arrived, they all went to pay their respects to Minaya Álvar Fáñez. When Abengalbón arrived, as soon as he caught sight of Minaya he hurried, smiling broadly, to embrace him and kiss him on the shoulder, for such was the Moorish custom.

"A very fine day to you, Minaya Álvar Fáñez. The presence of these ladies you bring with you, the Cid's legitimate wife and daughters, magnifies the honor of us all. We all must do you honor, for such is the Cid's destiny. Even if we wished him harm, we could not prevail against him—whether in peace or war, we will always render him tribute. I regard as dull-witted any man who does not understand this."

Minaya Álvar Fáñez said, a smile on his lips:

"Abengalbón, you are indeed the Cid's faithful friend! If God conducts me again into the Cid's presence, and I behold him alive, you will lose nothing for having done all this for the Cid. Now let us take up our lodgings, for the dinner is all prepared."

Abengalbón replied:

"I am pleased to accept your invitation, and before three days are out I will repay it twofold."

They entered in to Medinaceli, with Minaya seeing to their every need. They were all very happy with the kind treatment they received. The king's courier ordered that the expenses be charged to the royal account. The Cid, even though residing in Valencia, was thus honored by the ample provisions furnished for his people, there in Medinaceli. The king paid for everything, and Minaya departed owing nothing.

The night came and went, and morning dawned. Mass was heard, and then they all rode out, leaving behind Medinaceli and crossing the Jalón. They spurred on their horses, hurrying up the Arbujuelo and speedily traversing the fields of Taranz, after which they came to Molina, where Abengalbón was governor.

Bishop Jerome, a good Christian, tried and true, watched over the ladies day and night, with his warhorse led along to his right, and weapons and armor transported behind him. The ladies all rode together between him and Álvar Fáñez.

They entered into Molina, a fine and prosperous town, [1550] where the Moor Abengalbón treated them very well indeed. Anything they wanted, he provided—they lacked for nothing. He even ordered the horses of Minaya and the ladies to be reshod—Lord, what honor he showed them!

Early next morning they rode forth without delay. The Moor attended them unstintingly, all the way to Valencia, spending freely of his own wealth and accepting nothing at all from them.

Amid great rejoicing and glorious tidings they approached to within three leagues of Valencia.

The message came to Valencia, to My Cid, the man born in a lucky hour. Never in all his life had he known such joy. For now he had news of those he loved most in all the world. He ordered two hundred knights to ride forth at top speed, to welcome Minaya and the noble ladies with him. The Cid, meanwhile, remained in Valencia, watchful as ever and on the alert, confident that Álvar Fáñez had things well in hand.

And now behold those knights, welcoming Minaya, the ladies, the girls, and all their companions. My Cid ordered all the men in his household to keep watch over the citadel, the town's lofty towers, all its gates, and all roads in and out. He then sent for his horse Babieca, which he had newly won in battle. My Cid, he who girt on sword in a lucky hour, wanted to know how fast the horse was, and how well it would respond to the bit. In front of the main gate of Valencia, where he would be safe from attack, he was determined to perform a display of arms for his wife and daughters.

As the ladies were being welcomed with all due honor, Bishop Jerome made his way into the town. Dismounting from his horse, he headed for the chapel. All the clerics Jerome could gather together, of those who could arrange to interrupt their recitation of canonical hours, went out with him, clad in surplices and bearing silver crosses, to welcome the noble ladies and the good Minaya.

Wasting no time, the man born in a lucky hour put on his tunic, his beard flowing superbly. When they had saddled and caparisoned Babieca, My Cid rode out, taking wooden jousting weapons with him. Mounted on the horse called Babieca, the Cid galloped over a stretch of ground, with such marvelous speed that from that day on Babieca's worth was known throughout the length and breadth of Spain.

At the end of his ride, the Cid got down from his horse, and went over to his wife and two daughters. When Doña Jimena saw him, she fell to her knees in front of him:

"Thank you, Campeador, you who girt on sword in a lucky hour! You have saved me from many shameful indignities. Now, behold me here, along with both your daughters—thanks to you and to God they are good girls, well brought up."

The Cid hugged his wife and daughters tight, as they all wept tears of joy. [1600] Likewise delighted, all his spirited companies made a sportive show of brandishing their weapons and tilting at wooden castles.

Hear now what he said, the man born in a lucky hour:

"You, my dear and honored wife, and both my daughters, my very heart and soul: come with me into this city of Valencia, this heritage I have won for you."

Mother and daughters kissed his hands, and entered with him into Valencia, amid general rejoicing and acclaim.

My Cid took them with him into the citadel. There he took them up to the very top of the highest tower. From that vantage point, shining eyes looked all around. They saw how Valencia lay around them on one side, and beheld on the other the blue expanse of the sea. They saw the broad, luxuriant croplands of the Huerta, and lifted up their hands in prayer, thanking God for a prize so rich and great.[14]

My Cid and all his companies were very pleased. Winter was coming to an end, and the beginning of March was upon them.

Now I wish to tell you of events beyond the sea, and of that King Yusuf who dwelt in Morocco.

The king of Morocco was stirred to wrath by My Cid, Don Rodrigo:

"For he has wrongfully entered into my domains, and he gives thanks for this to none other than Jesus Christ."

The king of Morocco summoned all his forces together. With fifty thousand men-at-arms, all told, they embarked in ships and set out to sea and headed toward Valencia, intent on attacking My Cid, Don Rodrigo.

Their ships reached land, and their troops swarmed ashore. They had arrived in Valencia, that My Cid had conquered. There the infidel hordes set up their tents and established their camp.

News of these developments soon reached My Cid.

"Thanks be to the Creator and to our Holy Father! All the wealth that I have won, I see before my eyes. I have won Valencia with the sweat of my brow, and now hold it by right of possession. Nothing short of death will make me give it up. Thanks to the Creator and to our Holy Mother Mary, I now have my wife and daughters here with me. A piece of good luck now comes my way, from the lands beyond the sea. I must now take up arms, I have no choice. Now my wife and daughters will see me fight, and see how we win a place for ourselves here in these foreign lands, and see for themselves, with their own eyes, how our bread is won."

He took his wife and daughters up into the citadel. Lifting up their eyes, they saw all the tents set up.

"What is all this, Cid, the Creator be with you?"

"There, there, my beloved wife! Don't worry! All this means more wealth for us, a marvelous fortune—no sooner do

---

14. The Huerta was, and still is, an extensive tract of irrigated land given over to the cultivation of vegetable crops and fruit trees.

you arrive, then these infidels show up to give you a present! Your daughters are now of marrying age—now, here come these fellows, providing us the dowry!" [1650]

"Thanks be to thee, oh God, our Heavenly Father!"

"Now then, my wife, stay in this palace, or even up here in the citadel if you like. Don't be afraid at seeing me in combat. By God's favor, and that of Holy Mary, our mother, my heart now soars because you are here with me. With God's help I am bound to win this fight."

The tents were all set up, and day was dawning. Eagerly the infidels beat their war drums.

My Cid rejoiced and said:

"Oh, what a fine day this is!"

His wife was afraid, her heart was about to break. Her waiting ladies and both her daughters felt the same—never since the day they were born had they heard such a thunderous beating of drums.

The noble Cid Campeador grasped his beard:

"Don't be afraid, for all this will be turned to your advantage. Before fifteen days are out, if it please the Creator, those drums will be brought before you, and you'll see that's all they are: drums. From then on, they'll belong to Bishop Jerome. They'll be hung up in Santa María church, for all to see."

As the Cid Campeador made this vow, the ladies took heart and lost all fear.

Meanwhile the Moors from Morocco, riding in full force, entered boldly into the surrounding farmlands. Catching sight of them, the lookout rang the alarm bell. Quickly the Christian companies made ready, and bravely sallied forth from the town. Wherever they encountered the Moors, they attacked them instantly. Soon, they chased them out of the surrounding farm country, smiting them without mercy and killing a full five hundred by day's end.

All the way to the enemies' tents the pursuit lasted, and many great feats of arms were performed by the time they turned back. Álvar Salvadórez was taken prisoner in the encounter. Back to the Cid sped those who received their daily bread from him, to give him an account of what he had already seen with his own eyes. My Cid rejoiced at all that his men had accomplished.

"Hear me, oh knights! There can be no holding back. Today was a good day, and tomorrow will be even better. Tomorrow before dawn, all of you be up and fully armed. Bishop Jerome will say mass, and then you get ready and ride into battle. The good bishop will give us absolution and we'll have at them, in the name of the Creator, and of Saint James the Apostle. Better for us to conquer them outright than for them to deprive us of our bread."

Instantly, they all replied as one:

"Gladly, and with all our hearts!"

Minaya then spoke up, determined to waste no time:

"Since that is your wish, Cid, assign me another task. Give me a hundred and thirty knights to fight wherever they might be needed. When you have started your attack, I will come in from the other side. From one side or from both, either way, God will be with us."

Right away the Cid replied:

"Right gladly!"

That day was done, and night had fallen. The Christian forces lost no time in making their preparations. [1700] At the second cock-crow, before the dawn, Bishop Jerome sang the mass for them. When the mass was said, he gave them a general absolution:

"I take away the sins of whomever should die in battle, fighting face to face with the enemy, and God will have his soul. For you, Cid Don Rodrigo, you who girt on sword in a lucky hour, I have sung this morning's mass. I beg of you this boon, and let it be granted me: I wish to be allowed to strike the first blows."

The Campeador replied:

"From this very moment, let it be so ordered."

They all sallied forth fully armed past the towers of Valencia. My Cid instructed his vassals very well, and posted very reliable men to guard the gates.

My Cid charged forth, fully armed and equipped, on his horse Babieca. Bearing their battle standard high, they sallied out from Valencia. Four thousand men less thirty went forth at the Cid's side, eagerly attacking the fifty thousand Moors, while Álvar Álvarez and Álvar Salvadórez and Minaya Álvar Fáñez fell upon them from the other side.

They routed the enemy—such was the Creator's will. Wielding his spear with one hand and his sword with the other, blood dripping down to his elbows, My Cid killed so many Moors you could not even count them. He dealt three blows to King Yusuf, who ducked out from under the Cid's sword—for the Moor's steed was very swift—and fled to take refuge in the towering castle of Cullera. My Cid, the man from Vivar, led the pursuit all the way there, accompanied by a number of his stout-hearted vassals. From there the man born in a lucky hour turned back, delighted with the spoils they had taken. On that occasion he saw Babieca's true worth, from head to tail.

All this plunder remained in his hands. Fifty thousand prisoners were counted, for no more than a hundred and four had gotten away. My Cid's companies had plundered the field, and the captured gold and silver amounted to three thousand marks. As for the rest of the loot, there was too much to count.

My Cid was happy indeed, and all his vassals with him, that with God's favor they had won the field. With the king of Morocco thus defeated, the Cid left Álvar Fáñez in charge of everything and went back into Valencia with a hundred of his knights. His face was wrinkled from wearing the helmet he had taken off, as he rode in on Babieca, sword in hand. The ladies welcomed him back, for they had been eagerly awaiting his return.

My Cid halted in front of them, reining in his horse.

"Most humbly I salute you, ladies. I have won you a great prize, for while you held Valencia, I have prevailed in the field. [1750] This has been God's will, and that of all His saints: that to celebrate your arrival so great a prize has been granted us. Do you see the sword, all bloody, and my horse, all covered with sweat? This is how Moors are vanquished in the field. Praying to the Creator to let me live on yet another year or two, you will surely gain in honor, and men will kiss your hands."

This My Cid said as he got down from his horse. When they beheld him, dismounted and standing there before them, the ladies-in-waiting, his two daughters, and his noble wife, all fell to their knees in front of the Campeador.

"We are in your hands, and may you live many more years!"

Turning with him, they went back into the palace and sat down with him on couches of the finest workmanship.

"Now then, beloved wife, my lady Jimena — did you expect anything less of me? — these ladies who accompany you, who have served you so faithfully, I wish to marry to these vassals of mine. Furthermore, to each of them I give two hundred silver marks. Let it be known throughout Castile, just whom they have served so well. As for your daughters' settlement, we will talk of that later on."

They all arose and kissed his hands, and there was great rejoicing in the palace: the matter was concluded just as the Cid had promised.

Meanwhile, Minaya Álvar Fáñez was still out in the field with all his men, counting up and keeping track of all the loot. They found such a treasure of tents, weapons, and costly garments that it was beyond all tally. And I want to tell you something even more amazing: they could not even count the number of saddled horses running around loose with nobody to take them in hand. The Moors of those parts managed to capture a number of them. But even with the loss of these strays, the renowned Campeador still received as his share the pick of the whole herd, fifteen hundred fine horses in all.

As My Cid took possession of all these animals, the rest of his men considered themselves well satisfied. So many costly tents, so many finely wrought tent poles won in battle, by My Cid and all his men!

The king of Morocco's tent, the finest of them all, was held up by two poles inlaid with gold. My Cid ordered that this tent be left standing, and that no Christian remove it from where it stood.

"A tent like this, brought over from Morocco, I want to send word to Alfonso the Castilian." This the Cid intended to do so that Alfonso could more readily believe the news of how much wealth My Cid now possessed.

With all these riches they entered into Valencia. By the time that excellent tonsured man, Bishop Jerome, had enough of fighting with both hands, there was no counting the Moors he had killed. What fell to him as his share was considerable indeed: My Cid, Don Rodrigo, the man born in a lucky hour, ordered the tenth part, out of his own fifth, to be handed over to the bishop.

The Christian folk rejoiced throughout Valencia, so great was their plunder in goods, horses, and weapons. [1800] Doña

Jimena and her daughters were very happy, as were all the other ladies, who considered themselves as good as married.

Soon after that, the noble Cid said:

"Where are you, Minaya, you stout fellow? Come here. For the share that's fallen to you, no need to thank me. From this fifth share of mine, I tell you true: take as much as you like, and leave the rest. And tomorrow morning, bright and early, make no mistake, you'll be heading out with horses taken from my share of the loot, all of them saddled and harnessed, and each with a sword hanging from the saddle. For love of my wife and both my daughters, because the king sent them to be happy here with me, these two hundred horses are being sent as a present, so King Alfonso will have no cause to speak ill of the man who rules in Valencia."

He commanded Pedro Bermúdez to accompany Minaya. Early the next day they rode forth without delay, taking with them a company of two hundred men and bearing the Cid's greetings for the king. These were to the effect that the Cid kissed the king's hands in fealty; that from this battle he had won the Cid sent as a present two hundred horses; and that he would serve King Alfonso as long as breath was in his body.

They left Valencia and set out riding, bearing with them such a quantity of plunder that it had to be carefully guarded. Traveling day and night, they passed through the mountains that separated the two lands, and began to make inquiry as to the whereabouts of King Alfonso.

They continued their journey, crossing over mountains, traversing forests, and fording rivers, coming at last to Valladolid, where the king was in residence. Pedro Bermúdez and Minaya sent the king a message, asking that he give permission for the Cid's embassy to be received, and informing him that My Cid of Valencia was sending him a present.

Beside himself with happiness at hearing this news, the king ordered all the members of his entourage to ride out instantly. The king himself rode out at the head of this company, eager to see these messengers sent by the man born in a lucky hour.

Know then that the Scions of Carrión also happened to be there, along with Count García, the Cid's archenemy.

Some among that company were very pleased, but others were downright annoyed.

Catching sight of the vassals of the man born in a lucky hour, Alfonso and his men thought it was a Moorish army coming toward them, for no herald had been sent ahead. King Alfonso crossed himself as he came to a halt. Minaya and Pedro Bermúdez came riding up and jumped down from their horses. Kneeling down before the king, kissing the ground and both his feet, they said:

"A favor, oh mighty King Alfonso! On behalf of My Cid Campeador we kiss your hands, and declare that he still regards you as his lord, and holds himself to be your vassal. The Cid values most highly all the honor you have done him. Only a few days ago, lord king, the Cid won a great battle against that king of Morocco, Yusuf by name, [1850] who, with all his fifty thousand men, was vanquished in the field. The plunder taken was great beyond the telling. All the Cid's vassals have become rich men. Now he sends you these two hundred horses, and kisses your hand."

King Alfonso replied:

"I accept them gladly, and thank the Cid for sending me so fine a gift. May the hour soon come when I may return the favor."

Many were pleased to see this, and kissed Minaya's hands. But it greatly troubled Count García, who was thoroughly vexed. He went aside to confer with ten of his kinsmen:

"Isn't it amazing to see how the Cid's honor just keeps growing and growing! The more his glory increases, the more we are put to shame. By winning some absurd victory over a few kings on the battlefield, and leading a bunch of horses back here, as if he found their riders all lying around dead! All these so-called deeds of his spell trouble for us."

King Alfonso spoke and made this declaration:

"Thanks be to the Creator, and to Saint Isidore of León, for these two hundred horses sent to me by My Cid. From now on he will be able to serve my kingdom with even greater distinction. Regarding you, Minaya Álvar Fáñez and you, Pedro Bermúdez, I hereby command that both be most honorably attended to and clothed, and outfitted, furthermore, with any weapons and equipment you require. All this so you may look your best before Ruy Díaz, My Cid. I also give each of you three horses—choose from among these right here. As it seems to me, and as my heart tells me, some good will come of this whole new turn of events."

They kissed his hands, then went to take their rest. The king, meanwhile, ordered them to be provided with anything they needed.

Now I want to tell you of the Scions of Carrión, conferring in secret about their plans:

"The Cid's fortunes are on the rise. Let's ask for his daughters in marriage. That way, our own honor will increase and we will come up in the world."

They came to King Alfonso with this secret proposal:

"A favor we ask of you, as of our king and natural lord! With your help, we want this to be done—that you ask on our behalf for the hand of the Cid's two daughters. We want to marry them, to their honor and our advantage."

The king pondered and thought:

"I sent the good Campeador into exile. I did him great harm, while he has never done anything but right by me. I don't know if he will approve of this match. But since you request it, let us take the matter under consideration."

Then King Alfonso summoned Minaya Álvar Fáñez and Pedro Bermúdez, and led them aside into a room.

"Hear me, Minaya, and you, Pedro Bermúdez. My Cid the Campeador serves me loyally. He will have the pardon he so richly deserves—let him come to me when I convene my assembly, if such be his wish. There are also messages for the Cid from others in my court. [1900] Diego and Fernando, the Scions of Carrión, have it in mind to marry both the Cid's daughters. Be good messengers, I beseech you, and mention this matter to the good Campeador. There will be honor in it for him, and his estates will grow thereby, if he becomes father-in-law to the Scions of Carrión."

Minaya replied, and Pedro Bermúdez agreed:

"We will ask him to do as you say. From then on, let the Cid do as he sees fit."

"Tell Ruy Díaz, he who was born in a lucky hour, that I will convene the assembly wherever is most convenient to him— wherever he decides, let that be the designated meeting place. In any event, I wish to act in My Cid's best interests, in every way I can."

Taking leave of the king, they returned with this message, heading back toward Valencia with all their men.

When the Campeador heard they were coming, he rode out as fast as he could to welcome them.

Smiling, My Cid hugged them both tight:

"Welcome, Minaya, and you too, Pedro Bermúdez! In any country, it would be hard to find two such men as you. What does my lord Alfonso send me by way of greeting? Did he accept the gift? Was he happy with it?"

Minaya said:

"He is pleased, heart and soul, and sends you his love."

My Cid replied:

"Thanks be to the Creator!"

When the Cid had spoken, they told him the message: how Alfonso of León was asking the Cid to give his daughters to the Scions of Carrión; how the king felt that the Cid would thereby gain in honor and see his fiefdom grow; and how the king proposed this with all his heart and soul.

When My Cid the Campeador heard this, he thought about the matter for a good hour, looking at it from all angles:

"I give thanks to Christ my Lord for this. I was banished, and my lands taken from me. What I now have, I have earned by toil and travail. I thank God that I am again in the king's good graces, and that I am now being asked for my daughters to be married to the Scions of Carrión. They are very proud young men, and members of the king's court. This is not a match I would have found to my liking—but since he who recommends it is one more worthy than ourselves, let us talk about it, undertake the negotiation—and may God guide us in making the right decision!"

"Besides all this, Alfonso said to tell you that he would convene open assembly wherever you like. He would like to see you and personally give you his love; afterward, you and he can come to an agreement as to what is best."

To this the Cid replied:

"Agreed, with all my heart."

"It is up to you to decide," said Minaya, "where you want to have this audience."

"It would not be too much to ask, if it were all right with Alfonso, [1950] for us to go in search of him wherever he might be, showing him all due honor, as befits the king of the land. But whatever he prefers, let that be our wish as well. On the banks of the Tagus, which is a mighty river—let the audience take place there, if this be my lord's wish."

Letters were written then, and carefully sealed. Two knights were immediately dispatched to convey the message to the king:

"Whatever the king wished, the Campeador would do."

The letters were shown to the noble king. When he saw them, he was glad in his heart:

"Greetings to the Cid, in my name, to him who in a lucky hour girt on sword. Let the audience take place three weeks from now. Assuming I still live, I will be there without fail."

Without delay they returned to My Cid. On both sides, they prepared for the assembly. Whoever saw, in the land of Castile, so many fine mules, so many high-stepping palfreys? So many horses, deep-chested and swift; so many handsome pennons attached to sturdy lance shafts, or shields with gold and silver bosses; cloaks, and furs, and glossy silks of Andros?

The king ordered plentiful provisions to be conveyed to the waters of the Tagus, where things were being made ready for the assembly. The king was accompanied by a numerous retinue of nobles. The Scions of Carrión traveled in high spirits, getting some things on credit and paying cash for the rest, thinking, as they did, that riches would soon be theirs, and considering themselves already in possession of all the wealth in gold or silver they could ever wish for.

King Alfonso rode forth without delay, accompanied by counts and dukes and a great force of vassals. The Scions of Carrión brought with them a great company of their own. Accompanying the king were Leonese vassals as well as Galician companies—as for the Castilians, they were beyond counting. They all loosened their horses' reins, heading at top speed for the place where the assembly was to be held.

Back in Valencia, My Cid the Campeador, wasting no time, made ready for the assembly. There were so many sturdy mules and brisk-trotting palfreys, so many shining weapons and stout, swift horses; so many fine capes and cloaks and furs. Everyone, the high and the low, were dressed in bright-colored clothes: Minaya Álvar Fáñez, the famous Pedro Bermúdez, Martín Muñoz, and Martín Antolínez, the worthy man of Burgos; Bishop Jerome, that most excellent tonsured man; Álvar Álvarez and Álvar Salvadórez, and Muño Gustioz, that worthy knight; Galindo García, the man from Aragon—all these made ready to accompany the Campeador, as did all the others there with them.

Álvar Álvarez and Galindo García of Aragon were ordered by the Campeador [2000] to remain behind and devote themselves heart and soul to keeping watch over Valencia, and over all those subject to their authority. The gates of the citadel were to remain closed day and night, for inside were the Cid's wife and his two daughters, his very heart and soul, and the other ladies with them, their faithful servants. The Cid left orders, like the worthy baron he was, that not one of the ladies was to leave the citadel until the man born in a lucky hour had returned.

They rode out from Valencia, pricking with both spurs and urging on their mounts. All these swift, deep-chested warhorses had been won by My Cid in battle—nobody had given them to him as a gift. Now the Cid headed toward the place where he had arranged to have an audience with King Alfonso.

King Alfonso arrived a day before the Cid. When they saw that the Campeador was on his way, they went out to welcome him with all due honors. As soon as the man born in a lucky hour caught sight of the king, he ordered all his men to come to a halt—all save those knights closest to his heart.

With some fifteen of his most trusted henchmen he jumped down from his horse.

Just as the man born in a lucky hour had planned, he fell to the ground, on hands and knees, and took up the grass of the field between his teeth. Weeping, the tears streaming from his eyes, such was the depth of his joy—thus did the Cid perform this act of submission before his lord King Alfonso.

In this way, My Cid prostrated himself at the feet of his lord. The king was much distressed at this:

"Arise, on your feet, this instant, Cid Campeador! Kiss my hands, but not my feet. You will not win back my love unless you do as I say."

Remaining on his knees, the Campeador insisted:

"A favor I beg of you, my natural lord: that here and now you grant me your love, so that all these here may bear witness."

The king replied:

"This will I do, right gladly and with all my heart! I hereby pardon you, and give you my love, and grant you the freedom to come and go throughout my realm."

My Cid spoke in reply:

"My thanks! I accept this, my lord Alfonso, and give thanks to God in heaven, and then to you, and then to all these companies of vassals gathered round."

Still on his knees, the Cid kissed his lord's hand, and then, getting to his feet, kissed him on the mouth.

Everyone was delighted to see this, all save Álvar Díaz and García Ordóñez, who were most displeased.

My Cid spoke out, saying these words:

"For this I give thanks to the Creator. Now that I am again in the good graces of my lord, Don Alfonso, I know that God will henceforth be with me, day and night. I would like for you to be my guest, if it please you, my lord."

The king replied:

"That would not be seemly today, seeing that you have just arrived, and we got here last night. You shall be my guest, Cid Campeador, and tomorrow we will do as you please." [2050]

Kissing his lord's hand, the Cid accepted.

Just then, the Scions of Carrión came to bow down before the Cid:

"We are at your feet, Cid, you who were born in a lucky hour! In every way we can, we will act in your best interests."

My Cid replied:

"The Creator grant it so!"

My Cid Ruy Díaz, he who was born in a lucky hour, was the king's guest that day. So heartfelt was the love he bore him, the king could not get enough of the Cid's company. Nor could he take his eyes off the Cid's beard, which had grown out so quickly. Everyone there marveled to behold My Cid.

Day was done, and night had fallen. On the morning of the next day, the sun rose, shining brightly.

My Cid ordered his men to prepare a meal for everybody there. Afterward, the Campeador's hospitality left them all so heartily satisfied that everybody cheerfully agreed: nobody had eaten better in three years' time or more.

On the morning of the third day, as soon as the sun came up, Bishop Jerome said mass. After mass, they all assembled. Losing no time, the king immediately spoke of the matter at hand:

"Hear me, all you vassals of my court, counts and barons! I wish to make a request of My Cid, the Campeador. Christ grant that it redound to his benefit. I ask that you give your daughters, Doña Elvira and Doña Sol, to be the wives of the Scions of Carrión. The marriage seems to me both honorable and advantageous. The two young men ask you for their hands, and I bid you accept. All those here present, on both sides, your men and mine: let us all be your petitioners: give them to us, My Cid, so help you God!"

"I wouldn't think my daughters marriageable," replied the Campeador, "for they are not yet fully grown, and are still quite young in years. The Scions of Carrión are young men of a renowned family. They are a good match for my daughters, and even for girls of much higher station. I fathered both my daughters, and you raised them. All three of us are in your debt. Here then, I give them into your hands, Doña Elvira and Doña Sol, to give to whomever you wish, for I am content to do your will."[15]

"All my thanks," said the king, "to you, and to all this court."

Then the Scions of Carrión got up and went to kiss the hands of the one born in a lucky hour, and the two parties exchanged swords before King Alfonso.

King Alfonso spoke again, like the great lord he was:

"My most grateful thanks to you, Cid, worthy man that you are, and most of all to the Creator, for giving your daughters to me on behalf of the Scions of Carrión. At this time I take by the hand Doña Elvira and Doña Sol, and give them in betrothal to the Scions of Carrión. I marry these your daughters to these young men, with your willing consent. The Creator

---

15. Fosterage of the kind alluded to by the Cid was very common in royal and noble households of the Middle Ages. This relationship between the two men and their families is clearly very close. Amounting to a kind of artificial kinship, the roles of foster parent and foster child are similar to those established by godfatherhood in traditional European societies. The intimacies of fosterage illuminate the way the poem and its audience understand kinship and its analogues in general. Relationships between in-laws, for example, will be an important theme from now on in the poem.

grant that this match bring you happiness. [2100] Now I hand over to your safekeeping the Scions of Carrión. Let them go with you, for I am about to head back. I give them three hundred silver marks to help with the wedding expenses, or to spend on whatever you see fit. From the time they are under your authority, in Valencia of the Many Gates,[16] sons-in-law and daughters alike are all your children—do with them what you think best, Campeador."

My Cid took them into his keeping, then kissed his lord's hands:

"My most heartfelt thanks I give you, as to my king and rightful lord. It is you who join my daughters in wedlock, for it is not I who gives them away."[17]

When the wedding vows had been exchanged, they all agreed that everybody would return home at sunup on the morning of the following day.

Then My Cid, the Campeador, really gave people something to talk about, as he began to give away so many sturdy mules and sleek palfreys, so many costly garments, finely made, to anyone who wanted to accept his generosity—no one was turned away unsatisfied.

My Cid gave away sixty horses of those he had won in battle. All those present were very happy indeed with the outcome of that audience.

And now night was falling, and everyone was eager to be off.

The king took the Scions of Carrión by the hand, and placed them in the Cid's safekeeping:

---

16. This famous city on the Mediterranean coast is generally referred to in the poem as "la Mayor" or "la Grande"—literally "the Greater" or "the Great." In English, "the Great" used as a toponymic epithet is too vague to convey the delectable magnitude of the city. A more concrete attribute, such as the number of gates—indicative of a town's size and importance—better expresses the covetous intensity with which medieval besiegers of cities, like the Cid and his men, would have regarded such places.

17. The Cid very shrewdly makes the king responsible for the daughters' weddings. If anything goes wrong with the marriages, the king, his own honor compromised, will be obliged to seek redress from the Scions of Carrión.

"Behold your children, seeing that that they are now your sons-in-law. From this day forward, Campeador, be sure and take good care of them."

"I thank you for this, your majesty, and accept your gift. God in heaven grant that it turn out to be truly worthwhile for me."

The Cid then leapt astride his horse, Babieca.

"Here I declare, in the presence of my lord King Alfonso: whoever wishes to go with me now to the wedding or receive a gift from me, let him accompany me now; I think there will be something in it for him.

"And of you I ask this favor, of you, my rightful king: since you give away my daughters in marriage, as you see fit, assign a representative to whom I may give them, since you are taking them from me. I will not give the girls to Scions of Carrión — they will not have that satisfaction."

The king answered:

"Here, Álvar Fáñez: you take the girls into your hands, and you give them away to the Scions of Carrión, in as much as I have here assumed the guardianship of them. Be their sponsor for me throughout the wedding ceremony, as if I were there myself. When next we see each other, give me a full account of the matter."

Álvar Fáñez replied:

"Indeed, my lord, I am most pleased to do so."

All this was arranged, you can be sure, with all due care.

"Now then, my lord king Don Alfonso, my most honored lord, from this audience that we have held here, you must take with you something of mine. I bring you twenty palfreys, all richly equipped, and thirty swift horses, all handsomely saddled. Accept this gift, as I kiss your hands."

The lord King Alfonso replied:

"You quite overwhelm me. But I accept this gift that you offer me. May it please the Creator and all his saints that this favor you do me here be properly rewarded. [2150] My Cid Ruy Díaz, you have shown me great honor. I am well served by you, and hold myself well satisfied. I hope that in my lifetime you receive from me some worthy recompense. Meanwhile, I commend you to God, and hereby depart from this audience. God in heaven grant that this matter turn out for the best."

And now My Cid took leave of his lord, Alfonso. Having no wish to be escorted out of camp by the king, he departed thence without delay. And then, how many illustrious knights could be seen, going to kiss the king's hand in taking formal leave of him:

"May it please your majesty to give us permission, so we may go under My Cid's protection to Valencia of the Many Gates, there to attend the wedding of the Scions of Carrión and of My Cid's two daughters, Doña Elvira and Doña Sol."

The king was pleased to grant their request, and gave them all leave to go. In this way the Cid's following increased, and that of the king diminished, as a great company rode with the Campeador straight on toward Valencia, that he had taken in a lucky hour.

And the Cid ordered Pedro Bermúdez and Muño Gustioz — in all the Cid's household, there were no two better men — to keep an eye on Fernando and Don Diego, so they could get to know the ways of the Scions of Carrión. Along with Fernando and Diego went Ansur González, a loud-mouth, long in the tongue, but not much use for anything else.

The Scions of Carrión were treated with all due respect.

Soon they were back in Valencia, which My Cid had conquered, and there was great rejoicing when they got there.

My Cid said to Don Pedro and to Muño Gustioz:

"Find lodging for the Scions of Carrión and stay with them — those are my orders. When morning comes, and the sun is up, they will see their brides, Doña Elvira and Doña Sol."

That night, everyone went to their quarters. My Cid, the Campeador, went in to the citadel, where he was welcomed by Doña Jimena and both his daughters:

"Welcome, Campeador, you who girt on the sword in a lucky hour! May we behold you with our own eyes for many days to come!"

"Thanks be to the Creator, I am back at last, my noble wife! And I bring you sons-in-law, which will bring us much honor. Thank me, my daughters, for arranging such fine marriages for you both!"

His wife and both his daughters kissed his hands, along with all their ladies-in-waiting.

"Thanks be to the Creator, and to you, Cid, you of the flowing beard! Everything you do turns out well. In all your days, our daughters will never know want."

"Now that you have arranged our marriages, we will surely be rich women."

"My wife, Doña Jimena, thanks be to the Creator! And to you, my daughters, Doña Elvira and Doña Sol: by this marriage of yours we will all gain in honor. But know this truly: it was not I who arranged the matter. It was the king, Lord Alfonso, who asked for your hands, [2200] entreating me so urgently and in such heartfelt terms, that I could not by any means deny him. I placed you in his hands, both of you—believe me, it is he who gives you away in marriage, not I."

Now they began to decorate the palace, carpeting the floors and covering the walls with so many silks and satins and other precious fabrics—you would have gladly stayed for dinner in that palace!

All the Cid's knights quickly assembled, while the Scions of Carrión were sent for. The Scions rode directly to the palace, elegantly dressed and splendidly accoutred. Lord, what an impressive entrance they made—how calmly they strode into the palace!

My Cid and all his vassals welcomed them, after which the Scions of Carrión bowed deeply before the Cid and his wife, and then went to sit down on a couch of finest workmanship.

All the Cid's men were of one mind, listening attentively to the man born in a lucky hour.

The Campeador got to his feet:

"Since do this we must, why tarry any longer? Come here, Álvar Fáñez, my dearly beloved vassal. Behold my two daughters: I hand them over to you. Know then that I have promised this to the king, and will not fail in any way to carry out what the king has arranged. Give my daughters with your own hand to the Scions of Carrión, let them receive the nuptial blessing, and let us bring this matter to a conclusion."

Then Minaya replied:

"This I will do gladly."

The girls stood up, and Minaya handed them over to the Scions of Carrión, to whom Minaya then addressed these words:

"Here, in the presence of Minaya, you two brothers, by the hand of King Alfonso, who entrusted this task to me: I give you these ladies, both of noble birth, for you to have and to hold as your lawfully wedded wives."

The two young men accepted the girls, willingly and with open affection. They then went to kiss the hands of the Cid and his wife. When they had done this, everyone went out from the palace, hurrying toward the cathedral of Santa María.

Bishop Jerome, meanwhile, had hastily donned his vestments and was waiting for them at the church door. He gave them the nuptial blessing and sang the mass.

On leaving the church, the men all mounted up and rode speedily out to the sandy beach of Valencia. Lord, how well they jousted, the Cid and all his vassals! The Cid himself, the man born in a lucky hour, changed mounts three times. He was very pleased with what he saw, as the Scions of Carrión rode well in the tournament.

Then they all went back in to Valencia, accompanying the ladies. The wedding feast was splendid, there in the famous citadel. The next day, the Cid had seven wooden castles set up, and all seven were knocked down by dinner time.[18] [2250]

For two whole weeks the wedding feast lasted, and on the fifteenth day, all the noble guests made ready for their departure. What with palfreys and mules and fleet warhorses, My Cid Ruy Díaz, the man born in a lucky hour, gave away over a hundred riding animals, not counting anything else. As if that were not enough, there were cloaks and furs and many other garments. As for coined money, that was beyond counting. Talking among themselves, the Cid's vassals all agreed to give presents of their own. Each and every person willing to accept such gifts was well supplied: all those attending the wedding returned as wealthy men to Castile.

Now the guests were all departing, taking their leave of Ruy Díaz, the man born in a lucky hour, and of all the ladies

---

18. The mock warfare of medieval tournaments commonly involved elaborate sets, such as the wooden castles mentioned here. Although such contests were intended as practice, and as a sportive way to exhibit martial prowess, they were quite violent, often resulting in injury, and occasionally death, for the participants.

and noblemen. All the guests were much pleased with My Cid and his vassals, and spoke highly of them, as was only fitting.

And Diego and Fernando, the sons of Count Gonzalo, were also very happy. All these guests returned to Castile, while the Cid and his sons-in-law remained in Valencia.

The Scions of Carrión remained there nearly two years, and were well treated in every way. And the Cid himself was happy, along with all his vassals.

May it please our Father in heaven, and Holy Mother Mary, that this marriage bring contentment to the Cid and any man who holds him dear!

And now the verses of this book are coming to an end.

May the Creator and all his saints bless and keep you!

Third Book: The Outrage
(Verses 2278–3730)

The Scions of Carrión show themselves arrant cowards, fleeing in terror from an escaped lion at court, and panicking in the face of the enemy in battle. The object of raucous contempt at the Cid's court, they resolve to exact vengeance for their humiliation. On the way back to Carrión with their brides, they stop in the Oakgrove of Corpes, a wild and isolated place. There they savagely beat the girls and leave them for dead. Hearing of this atrocity and grievously offended, the Cid demands justice from the king. At a special assembly convened by the king, the Cid is awarded restitution of various wedding gifts. A final claim, that the Scions of Carrión have committed treachery against the Cid's daughters, is settled by judicial combat,[19] in which the Scions

---

19. Judicial combat was a procedure in Germanic law for resolving disputes that could not be settled by the confession of a defendant or by the testimony of witnesses. Its depiction in this epic reflects the lingering influence of Visigothic law and custom in Christian Spain (see Visigoths in the Compendium of Proper Names). Also known as trial by combat and judicial duel and practiced in the European Middle Ages until the fifteenth century, it determined that the winner of the duel was in the right and the loser in the wrong.

of Carrión and their brother Ansur are defeated and humiliated by the Cid's three champions. After this triumph, the Cid's daughters marry the crown princes of Navarre and Aragon. The Cid dies a happy man.

My Cid was in Valencia, along with all his vassals, and with him were his sons-in-law, the Scions of Carrión. The Campeador lay sleeping on a couch, when all at once a shocking incident took them by surprise: a lion got loose and escaped from its cage. Amid the general panic in the hall, the Campeador's men wrapped their cloaks around their arms and stood around his couch, standing guard over their lord.

Fernando González saw nowhere to hide—not an open chamber, not a tower in sight—so he crouched down under the Cid's couch.

His brother Diego González, meanwhile, ran right out the door, yelling: "I'll never see Carrión again!" Terrified, he crawled under the beam of a winepress. Later he would emerge with his cloak and tunic all begrimed with filth.

At this point the man born in a lucky hour awoke, and saw his couch surrounded by his worthy barons.

"What's all this, my vassals? What's the matter?"

"Most worthy lord! The lion suddenly attacked us."

Leaning on his elbow, the Cid got to his feet. His cloak draped over his shoulder, he headed straight for the lion.

As it caught sight of him, the lion was so cowed that it lowered its head before My Cid and pressed its face against the floor.

My Cid Don Rodrigo took it by the scruff of the neck, [2300] led it back to its cage, and put it inside.

Everyone present, there in the hall, watched all this in amazement. Meanwhile, the others came back into the hall from where they had taken refuge in the palace.

My Cid asked for his sons-in-law, and they were nowhere to be found. Even though people were calling for them by name, there was no reply. When they finally found them, they came in all pale-faced. You should have heard the derisive laughter echoing throughout the palace!

My Cid the Campeador put a stop to it. But the Scions of Carrión considered themselves grievously offended. They felt deeply humiliated by what they had undergone.

While they were thus nursing their grievance about what had happened, an army arrived from Morocco to lay Valencia under siege. Fifty thousand of the biggest tents were pitched there. The leader was King Búcar — I think you've heard tell of him.

The Cid and all his men were overjoyed to see this chance for more plunder that the Creator was sending their way.

But the Scions of Carrión were sick at heart, you can be sure, dismayed at the sight of all those Moorish tents. The two brothers went off to one side to confer:

"We've been looking at what we stood to gain, not what we stand to lose. Now there's no way we can avoid fighting in this battle. It's as if made to order for us never to see Carrión again — the Cid's daughters are going to be left widows!"

Muño Gustioz overheard their conversation and went to tell My Cid Ruy Díaz, the Campeador:

"Look how scared those daring sons-in-law of yours are! Now that they're about to go into battle, they get homesick for Carrión. Go and comfort them, God keep you, so they can stay safely behind and take no part in this. With you as our leader and the Creator on our side, we'll win this battle."

My Cid Don Rodrigo went out to them, a smile on his face:

"God keep you, my sons-in-law, you Scions of Carrión. You are newly wedded to my daughters, bright as the sun. I yearn for battle, and you for your home in Carrión. Take things easy, here in Valencia, just as you please, for I know how to deal with these Moors. I will venture forth to defeat them, by the grace of God."

* * * Gap in manuscript of about one page * * * [20]

". . . may the time soon come when I can repay you twofold."

---

20. A comparison with the late thirteenth-century *The Chronicle of Twenty Kings* (see Related Texts E), that narrates the life and exploits of the Cid, suggests that the missing folio probably tells how Fernando rode to meet a Moorish warrior in battle, then panicked and fled in terror. Pedro Bermúdez fights and kills the Moor, then generously gives the slain enemy's horse to Fernando, assuring him that he will support Fernando's claim to have slain the Moor himself.

They both rode back together, with Don Pedro confirming Fernando's boastful account.

My Cid and all his vassals were very pleased:

"If it be the will of God, our Father who dwells on high, both my sons-in-law will prove themselves in battle."

As they were saying this, the troops gathered together. While the drums sounded amid the Moorish host, many of the Christians were really taken aback—being newly arrived, they had never seen such a thing before.

Diego and Fernando were even more taken aback than the others. If they had their way, they would never have come to Valencia in the first place.

Listen now to the words of the man born in a lucky hour: [2350]

"You there, Pedro Bermúdez! My dear nephew! Look after Don Diego for me, and for Don Fernando, too. They're both my sons-in-law—I hold them dear. For with God's help, the Moors will be driven from the field."

"For pity's sake I tell you, Cid: today the Scions of Carrión won't have me to babysit them. Let somebody else look out for them, they couldn't matter less to me. I want to strike from the front, with my men. You and yours hold steady, guarding the rear. If there's any trouble, you can quickly come to my aid."

At that moment Minaya Álvar Fáñez came up:

"Hear me, loyal Cid, Campeador! The Creator himself will fight this battle, along with you, so worthy to be at His side. Have us attack them, from whatever side you think best: each man is bound to do his duty as your vassal. That's the way things will turn out: with God's help and your good fortune."

My Cid replied:

"Let's take our time; no hurry."

Just then Bishop Jerome came up, fully armed for battle, and halted before the Cid, the man whose luck never ran out:

"Today I said the mass of the Holy Trinity for you. This is why I left my country and came to seek you out: to satisfy the longing I had to kill a few Moors. I would like to honor both my order and my own hands, and lead our men into the fray. I carry a banner and a shield with the roe deer emblazoned on both. If it please God, I'd like to try them out, to gladden my heart and to make you better content with me. If you fail to grant me this favor, I intend to take my leave of you."

Then My Cid replied:

"Your wish pleases me. Here come the Moors: have at them. We'll watch from here to see how the abbot handles himself in battle."

Bishop Jerome spurred his horse and went to attack the enemy on the edge of their camp. Thanks to his own good luck and to God who loved him, he killed two Moors at the outset, with his lance. When he had broken the shaft, he drew his sword.

He gave it all he had, the bishop did — Lord, how well he fought! He killed two with the lance, and five more with his sword. The Moors were many, and came at him from all sides. They dealt him mighty blows but could not dent his armor.

The man born in a lucky hour was watching him intently. Embracing his shield and lowering his lance, he gave spur to Babieca, his swift-running horse, and went to smite the enemy with all his heart and soul.

Charging into their front ranks, the Campeador knocked seven to the ground and killed four others outright. As was God's will, this was the beginning of the rout. The Cid and his men launched into the pursuit. You should have seen all those snapping tent-ropes, all those stakes ripped up, [2400] and all those tent-poles, finely wrought, crashing to the ground.

The Cid's men chased Búcar's followers from their tents.

They chased them out of their tents and were right on their heels in pursuit — you should have seen all the arms lopped off, still in their armored sleeves, and so many severed heads, the helmets still on, being tossed here and there. Seven whole miles the pursuit lasted.[21]

Meanwhile, My Cid went after King Búcar:

---

21. In the original Old Spanish (l. 2407), the term used is *migeros* ("miles"). The English word "mile," like the modern Spanish *milla*, comes from the Latin *mille passus*, "a thousand paces." In the context of medieval Spanish works translated into English, "miles" seems a reasonable choice. "Kilometer" would be anachronistic in the medieval context, since the metric system dates back only to the late eighteenth century. In this translation, metric terms will be used in explanatory contexts, such as footnotes and compendium entries.

"Come back here, Búcar! You came from across the sea. Now you have to deal with the Cid, the man with the flowing beard. Let's exchange greetings, and strike up a friendship!"

Búcar replied to the Cid:

"God forbid any such friendship! I see you holding your naked sword, spurring your horse on. It looks like you want to try your blade out on me. But unless my horse stumbles and throws me to the ground, you'll not catch me before I reach the sea."

To this My Cid replied:

"That is not going to happen!"

Búcar had a fine horse, and it galloped at breakneck speed, but Babieca, the Cid's horse, gradually overtook him. The Cid caught up with Búcar three yards from the sea. Raising up Colada, he smote the Moor a mighty blow, jarring the rubies of his helmet loose and cutting right through, helmet and all—right down to the waist the sword's blade slashed.

Thus did My Cid slay Búcar, the king from beyond the sea, and win the sword Tizón, worth a thousand golden marks. The Cid won this great and marvelous battle, winning honor for himself and for all the men there with him.

With their plunder they headed back—you can be sure they all took part in stripping the field completely—and returned to the tents, where they found the man born in a lucky hour.

My Cid Ruy Díaz, the famous Campeador, with those two swords he valued so highly, rode at top speed through that scene of butchery, his face all creased, his hood of chain mail pulled up, the cap a little wrinkled against his hair. My Cid saw something that made him glad: he raised his eyes, looking straight ahead, and saw coming toward him Diego and Fernando, both the sons of the count, Don Gonzalo.

My Cid rejoiced, smiling happily:

"Here you come, my sons-in-law, you are indeed my sons! I can tell that you take pleasure in doing battle. There will be good things said about you, when the news reaches Carrión, about how we have defeated King Búcar. As I trust in God and all his saints, we'll have good reason to be happy with this victory."

From all around his vassals came, among them Minaya Álvar Fáñez, who was just arriving. Hanging by its strap from his neck, his shield was all dented with sword blows, [2450] and the strokes of countless lances. Of the men who had dealt those blows, none had touched him. The blood dripped down from the elbow, from the twenty Moors he had killed in battle.

"Thanks be to God, to our Father on high, and to you, Cid, you who were born in a lucky hour. You killed Búcar, and we have taken the field. All these goods belong to you, and to your vassals, and to these your sons-in-law, who have acquitted themselves well this day, getting their fill of fighting with Moors on the battlefield."

My Cid replied:

"I am very pleased about that. Seeing how they've acquitted themselves well on this occasion, their reputation will only improve later on."

The Cid's words were well meant, but the Scions of Carrión took them the wrong way.

All the plunder was carried back to Valencia, as the Cid and all his companies rejoiced, for each man's share came to six hundred silver marks. The Cid's sons-in-law, when they received their share of the loot from this victory, and had it in their possession, thought they would never again know want in all their days.

Everybody arrived back in Valencia magnificently arrayed, eating very well, and with furs and cloaks of the finest. My Cid and all his vassals were happy indeed.

It was a great day in the Campeador's palace, now that they had all won this battle and the Cid had killed Búcar. The Cid held up his hand and grasped his beard:

"Thanks be to Jesus Christ, the lord of all the world, now that I have seen what I so longed to see: both my sons-in-law fighting by my side on the battlefield. Good things will be said of them when the news gets back to Carrión: how they've done right by themselves, and are going to prove useful to all of you from now on. Part of this mighty plunder we have all won together is ours; the rest remains in the hands of the Scions of Carrión."

My Cid, the man born in a lucky hour, saw to it that all of them received their fair share of the spoils from the battle, and that his fifth part should not be forgotten. Everyone did as he commanded, for they were all in agreement: to the Cid, as part of his fifth, there fell six hundred horses, as well as many pack animals and numerous camels — there was no counting them, there were so many.

All this loot was won by the Campeador:

"Thanks be to God, the Lord of all the world! Before this I was poor, and now I'm rich, for I have wealth and land and gold and estates, and the Scions of Carrión are my sons-in-law. I win battles at the Creator's pleasure, and Moors and Christians live in fear of me. Over there, in Morocco, the land of mosques, they worry that maybe I might attack them some night. [2500] But I have no such intention. I won't be going to look for them: I'll be staying here in Valencia, while, with God's help, they render tribute to me, or to whomever I say."

Great was the rejoicing throughout Valencia, among the Cid and all his companies and vassals. Great was the rejoicing of the two Scions of Carrión, for from the battle in which they had fought so bravely they both won five thousand marks' worth. The Scions of Carrión considered themselves very rich men, as they went with all the others to the Cid's palace.

There with the Cid was Bishop Jerome, and the worthy Álvar Fáñez, a valiant knight, and many others the Cid had brought up in his household. When the Scions of Carrión came in, Minaya welcomed them on the Cid's behalf:

"Come in, kinsmen. Your valor increases the honor of us all."

As they came in, the Campeador was much pleased:

"Behold, my sons-in-law, my noble wife and both my daughters, Doña Elvira and Doña Sol. May they embrace you warmly and serve you with all their hearts. We have vanquished the Moors in the field and killed King Búcar, that proven traitor. Thanks be to Holy Mary, Mother of Our Lord: from these marriages you will obtain estates, and good tidings will reach the lands of Carrión."

To these words Fernando González replied:

"Thanks to the Creator, and to you, noble Cid, we already have so much wealth it is beyond reckoning. On your behalf we have garnered glory, and we have done battle. Take care of the rest of the loot, for we have our own share well in hand."

All the Cid's vassals smiled at one another, asking who had fought hardest or who had taken part in the pursuit, and no one remembered seeing Diego or Fernando anywhere in the fray.

Mortified by this constant banter, that vexed them day and night, the two Scions of Carrión came up with a nasty plan. Going off to one side, away from the others — they're brothers, two peas in a pod — they started up their scheming.

God forbid any of us should ever have anything to do with such dealings!

"Let's head back to Carrion," they said. "We've lingered here long enough. We have wealth aplenty, heaps of it, more than we could ever spend. Let's ask the Cid if we can take his daughters back home with us to the lands of Carrión, so we can show them our estates. Let's get them out of Valencia and away from where he can get at us. Afterward, out on the road, we'll have our way with them, with nobody there to taunt us any more about the lion episode.

"After all, we're blood kin to the Counts of Carrión. We're taking back with us plenty of goods, all very valuable. [2550] Now we'll teach the Campeador's daughters a good lesson. With all this wealth, we'll be proper grandees from here on in. Why, we could marry the daughters of kings and even emperors! After all, we're kin to the Counts of Carrión! We'll teach the Campeador's daughters a lesson, sure enough. And nobody will be making fun anymore about what happened with the lion."

With this plan in mind, they rejoined the group.

Fernando González spoke, and the whole court fell silent:

"God preserve you, Cid Campeador! May it please the lady Jimena, and most of all you, and also Minaya Álvar Fáñez, and all those here present:

"Let us have our lawfully wedded wives, so we can take them and show them our lands in Carrión. There they'll be set up in the estates we're giving them as their portion and rightful property. Your daughters will behold all our lands, and what the children we have with them will someday share in."

With no inkling of the disgrace that lay in store, the Cid Campeador said:

"I'll not only give you my daughters, but something of my own property to boot. You have given them as portion estates in the lands of Carrión. I will give them as their dowry three thousand silver marks. To you yourselves I will give mules and palfreys, sleek and sturdy, and riding horses, strong and swift, and many robes of the finest cloth.

"I will give you lads my two swords, Colada and Tizón, that I won, as you well know, in honorable battle.

"You are now my sons, for I give my daughters to you. With them you take away my very heart's blood. Let it be known throughout Galicia, Castile, and León, with what riches I send forth my two sons-in-law. Take care of my daughters, for they are now your wives. Take good care of them, and I will be eternally grateful."

And so they promised, the Scions of Carrión, and there and then took into their keeping the Cid's two daughters, to have and to hold, even as they took possession of what the Cid had pledged by way of wedding gifts. When they were well satisfied, the Scions ordered the pack animals to be loaded up.

Great was the applause throughout all Valencia, as all the Cid's men rode forth fully armed to see the Campeador's daughters off, as they set out for the lands of Carrión.

Soon they were heading out, about to take their leave. Both sisters, Doña Elvira and Doña Sol, knelt down before the Cid Campeador:

"A boon we ask of you, father, the Creator bless and keep you! You begat us, and our mother bore us. Here we kneel before you, our lord and lady. You are sending us off to the lands of Carrión. It is our duty to do whatever you tell us to. But we both ask of you this boon: that while we are there in the lands of Carrión, [2600] you keep ever on the alert for news of us."

My Cid hugged them both and bade them farewell.

When he had done so, their mother did as much and more:

"Be on your way, my daughters, and the Creator be with you. You have your father's heartfelt leave, and my own. Go to Carrión, where you are now women of property. For surely, it seems to me, I have found you both good matches."

The girls kissed the hands of their mother and father. Both parents blessed them and gave them their leave.

Now My Cid and the others set out riding, fully armed and superbly mounted. The Scions set out too, from far-famed Valencia, taking their leave of all the ladies and their companions. Through Valencia's fertile fields they all rode merrily out, flourishing their weapons, My Cid and all his companies.

He saw in the omens, he who girt the sword in a lucky hour, that these marriages would not be trouble-free. But it was too late for second thoughts, for he had seen them properly married.

"Where are you, nephew mine, oh Félix Muñoz? You are cousin to my two daughters, heart and soul. I bid you go with them, deep into Carrión territory, and there see for yourself the estates given to my daughters, and return afterward to make your report to the Campeador."

Said Félix Muñoz: "It pleases me to do so, heart and soul."

Minaya Álvar Fáñez halted before My Cid:

"Let us return, oh Cid, to Valencia of the Many Gates, for if it please God, our father and Creator, we will soon go and see them in the lands of Carrión."

"In God's hands we entrust you both, Doña Elvira and Doña Sol. In all you do, make us proud."

The sons-in-law declared: "God will it so!"

Great were the lamentations at their departure. Father and daughters wept inconsolably, and all the Cid's men along with them.

"Hearken, nephew mine, you, Félix Muñoz! Go by way of Molina, and there spend the night. Send greetings to my friend, the Moor Abengalbón. Bid him show hospitality to my sons-in-law, stinting nothing. Tell him I'm sending my daughters to the lands of Carrión, and to give them whatever they may need, serving them as he sees fit, and thereafter escorting them as far as Medina, for love of me. Tell him that for all he does in this, I will reward him handsomely."

Like fingernail from flesh they parted, as he who was in lucky hour born headed back toward Valencia.

The Scions of Carrión set out, stopping at Santa María de Albarracín along the way. Soon they were in Molina, staying with the Moor Abengalbón. As soon as he heard the news of their coming, the Moor was heartily glad, going out to meet them with great rejoicing. Lord, such hospitality he showed them, gratifying their every wish! [2650]

Next day, he rode out with his guests, ordering an escort of two hundred horsemen to accompany them as they crossed the mountains called Luzón.

The Moor gave his presents to the daughters of the Cid, and fine horses to each of the two Scions of Carrión. Crossing the Arbujuelo Valley and coming to the Jalón, they presently took lodging in the place called Ansarera. All this the Moor did for love of the Cid Campeador.

When they saw the wealth displayed by the Moor, the two brothers immediately began to plot treachery.

"Seeing as how we're ridding ourselves of the Cid's daughters anyway, if we could kill the Moor Abengalbón and get hold of whatever wealth he has with him, it would be as safely in our hands as our property in Carrión. The Cid could never call us to account."

As the two brothers from Carrión schemed this perfidy, a Spanish-speaking Moor, overhearing them, understood what they were up to. Not keeping the secret to himself, he informed Abengalbón.

"Master, watch out for those two. As surely as you are my liege lord, I heard them plot your death, these Scions of Carrión."

The Moor Abengalbón was a most valiant warrior. With the two hundred men accompanying him, he rode, weapons at the ready, to confront the Scions. When they heard what the Moor had to say the Scions were not pleased:

"Tell me, what did I ever do to you, oh Scions of Carrión! Here I am, showing you hospitality with no thought of doing you any harm, and there you are, plotting my death. If I didn't overlook all this for love of My Cid, I would wreak such vengeance on you that the whole world would hear of it. And then I would return the true-hearted Cid's daughters to him, and you two would never get back to Carrión. Here I part from you as from evil, treacherous men. By your leave, Doña Elvira and Doña Sol—I want nothing more to do with these Scions of Carrión. May God ordain and grant, He who is lord over all, that from this marriage some good may yet come to the Campeador."

This the Moor said to them. Wheeling about, arms still at the ready at the crossing of the Jalón, he headed back toward Molina, like the prudent man he was.

Meanwhile the Scions of Carrión set out from Ansarera. Traveling day and night, they passed on the left the town of Atienza, set on a mighty crag. Then, passing Sierra Miedes, they traversed the Montes Claros. Spurring on swiftly, they left behind Griza on the left, a place founded by Alamos—there one may see the caves where Elpha was shut in—and on the right they passed San Esteban, that lies further on.[22]

Then the Scions entered the Oakgrove of Corpes. The trees of the forest were high, their branches reached up to the clouds, while all around prowled wild beasts.

They came to a clearing with a fresh water spring. [2700] There the Scions of Carrión ordered the tent to be set up, and there they spent the night with all their entourage. Taking their brides in their arms, they made passionate love to them.

Little did their love avail the girls when daybreak came!

The Scions ordered the mules loaded up with all the valuables. The tent where they had spent the night was packed up, and the servants were all sent on ahead. The Scions of Carrión gave these orders so that no one, man or woman, would stay behind except their two brides, Doña Elvira and Doña Sol.

The wanted to have their fun with them, with no one to get in the way.

Everyone had gone on ahead. Those four were all by themselves. Such was the malice aforethought of the Scions of Carrión.

"Mark you well, Doña Elvira and Doña Sol: here you will be dishonored, out here in the middle of this wilderness. Today when we leave this place you will be left behind, abandoned by us. You will have no part of the lands of Carrión. News of this will get back to the Cid Campeador. That's how we will get even for the shame of the lion episode."

There and then they stripped the girls of their cloaks and furs, leaving them undressed save for their undershirts and shifts of snow-white cloth. Shod with spurs, the wicked knaves brandished their saddle girths of hard, sturdy leather.

When the ladies beheld this, Doña Sol spoke:

"For God's sake, we beg you, Don Diego and Don Fernando! You have two swords, strong and sharp, the one called

---

22. The poet seems to expect his audience to recognize Griza, Alamos, Elpha, and the caves in which the latter personage is shut in. However, nothing certain is known of any of these places or persons. The geography, like the itinerary, is probably legendary or fictional.

Colada, the other Tizón. Cut off our heads, so we can die like martyrs. Moor and Christian alike will talk of this moment: everyone will say that we were not punished according to our desert. Do not expose us to such ignominy. If we are beaten, you will demean yourselves and be called to account for it in council or at court."

The ladies' entreaties availed them nothing. The Scions began there and then to beat them with the buckled straps—how horribly they hurt them! Hacking at them with their sharp spurs, the Scions inflicted still deeper pain, rending undershirt and flesh alike. The girls' pure blood flowed, staining their snow-white shifts. Both felt agony in their deepest heart of hearts.

How joyous a moment would it have been just then, had it pleased our Creator for the Cid Campeador to appear!

So fiercely did the Scions beat them—for they are pitiless—that the girls' undershirts and shifts were soon blood-drenched. Both Scions quickly grew tired of lashing, as each tried to outdo the other in dealing out blows. Doña Elvira and Doña Sol could no longer speak.

There they were left for dead, there in the Oakgrove of Corpes.

The Scions took with them the fine cloaks and ermine furs, leaving the girls grievously distressed, with nothing but their tunics and their shifts, [2750] at the mercy of birds of prey and fearsome beasts.

The Scions left them for dead, you know, quite sure they were not long for this world.

How joyous a moment would it have been, if then and there the Cid Campeador had appeared!

The Scions of Carrión have left them for dead in the Oakgrove of Corpes, and neither girl can help the other.

Riding away through the mountains, the Scions congratulated themselves:

"Now we've gotten even, good and proper, for those marriages of ours. Why, they weren't even good enough to be our concubines, unless maybe somebody begged us, seeing as how they weren't even fit to be embraced by the likes of us. This is how we're going to get even for the shame of the lion episode."

While the Scions rode along, still congratulating themselves, let me tell you of Félix Muñoz, the Cid Campeador's nephew. They had ordered him to ride on ahead with the others, but he was loath to do so. Riding along the road, he felt heartsick. All at once, leaving all the others, Félix Muñoz headed back through the dense forest, hoping either to see his two cousins coming, or to see what the Scions of Carrión were up to.

He saw the Scions coming toward him, heard them talking. They did not see him, had no inkling he was there. You can be sure that had they seen him, he would not have escaped with his life.

The Scions rode by, heading up the road at full gallop.

Félix Muñoz followed the trail back until he came upon both his cousins, who lay there, beaten to within an inch of their lives.

Crying, "Oh cousins, cousins," he straightaway dismounted, tied up his horse, and ran over to them.

"Oh cousins, my dear cousins, Doña Elvira and Doña Sol, so this is how the Scions of Carrión show their worth! Please God and Saint Mary, they'll get their comeuppance for this!"

He turned the girls over, so badly beaten, both of them, that neither could speak. His heart breaking from sorest grief, he cried out:

"Cousins, cousins, Doña Elvira and Doña Sol! Wake up, oh cousins, for love of the Creator! While it's still daylight and not yet nightfall, before we all get eaten up by wild beasts out here in this wilderness!"

Slowly coming to, Doña Elvira and Doña Sol opened their eyes and looked at Félix Muñoz.

"Pull yourselves together, cousins, for love of the Creator! When the Scions of Carrión see I'm missing, they'll come looking for me in no time. Without God's help, we'll die out here for sure."

Wracked with pain, Doña Sol spoke:

"For love of our father, oh cousin, the Cid Campeador — give us water, the Creator help you!"

With a brand-new hat he had, that he had brought along with him from Valencia, [2800] he scooped up some water and gave it to his cousins. Battered though they were, it refreshed them both. Urging and coaxing, he finally got them to sit up. Comforting and encouraging them until they had recovered somewhat, he picked them up, one by one, and sat them on his horse, covering them both with his own cloak. He took the horse by the reins and led them out of there, all three of them together. Through the Oakgrove of Corpes, traveling day and night, they made their way out of that wilderness, until at last they reached the waters of the Duero, where he left them at La Torre.

To San Esteban went Félix Muñoz, there to find Diego Téllez, one-time vassal of Álvar Fáñez. When Diego Téllez heard the news, he was sick at heart. Taking riding horses and proper clothing, he went out to find Doña Elvira and Doña Sol. Taking them back with him to San Esteban, he gave them lodging, honoring them in every way he could. Those of San Esteban, always well-bred, were stricken at heart on hearing the terrible news. There they cared tenderly for the Cid's daughters, until the girls were better.

Meanwhile, the Scions of Carrión were still congratulating themselves.

As for King Alfonso, this frightful news cut him to the heart.

News of the outrage presently reached Valencia of the Many Gates. When they told My Cid the Campeador, he pondered the matter for a full hour. Raising one hand, he grasped his beard in the other:

"Thanks be to Christ, Lord of all this world, now that the Scions of Carrión have honored me so. By this beard that no one ever pulled, the Scions of Carrión will not have their way. I'll see my daughters well married yet!"

Grief smote My Cid, and all his court, and Álvar Fáñez, heart and soul. Minaya rode out with Pedro Bermúdez, and with Martín Antolínez, the doughty man of Burgos, along with two hundred horsemen, under orders from My Cid, who urgently commanded them to ride day and night, and escort his daughters back to many-gated Valencia.

They do not tarry in obeying their lord's command. Riding swiftly, they traveled day and night, and came to Gormaz, an impregnable castle. There they stayed, mind you, but only one night. Meanwhile the news reached San Esteban that Minaya was coming to bring his two cousins home.

The men of San Esteban, like the stout-hearted fellows they were, received Minaya and all his men. That night they offered Minaya a splendid banquet. He declined, but with heartfelt thanks: [2850]

"Thank you, men of San Esteban. You are most thoughtful, in showing us such honor in this our time of woe. My Cid sends his gratitude to you from Valencia, while I do the same, here in person. Behold, may God in heaven soon reward you most handsomely for your kindness!"

They all thanked him, assuring him it was they who were beholden to him. While his men headed for their quarters to get a good night's rest, Minaya went to see his cousins in their rooms.

When Doña Elvira and Doña Sol set eyes on him, they cried:

"We thank you as if in the presence of the Creator Himself! And you can thank Him that we are alive at all. In a quieter moment, we can tell you all about the misery we've been through."

They all wept bitter tears, the two ladies and Álvar Fáñez.

And Pedro Bermúdez encouraged them:

"Doña Elvira and Doña Sol, be of good cheer! You are safe and sound, and otherwise unharmed. Your good marriages have come to naught, but you'll be given better ones soon enough. And we will yet see the day when we can avenge you."

There they spent that night, amid general rejoicing. The next morning, they set out riding. The men of San Esteban escorted them as far as the River Amor, comforting them as they went. There they took their leave and headed back, while Minaya and the two ladies continued on their way.

They crossed Alcoceva Notch, passing Gormaz on the right. Crossing at the place called King's-Ford, they took lodging at the town of Berlanga. Next morning they set out on the road, staying that night in the place called Medina, and from there to Molina, another day's travel.

Rejoicing in his heart, the Moor Abengalbón went out gladly to meet them. For love of My Cid, he feasted them most bountifully.

From there they headed straight on to Valencia.

When he who was in a lucky hour born received the message, he mounted up immediately and left to go and meet them, joyfully flourishing his weapons as he rode along.

My Cid went up to his daughters and, kissing them both, began to smile.

"Come now, my daughters, God keep you from all harm! I agreed to the marriage, but dared not say anything against it.

Please the Creator, He who dwells on high, that I may yet see you better matched. On those sons-of-law of Carrión, God grant I wreak my vengeance!"

The two daughters kissed their father's hands.

Presenting arms, the company rode into the city.

As the two girls were joyously welcomed back by their mother, Doña Jimena, he who was in happy hour born brooked no delay. Taking counsel with his men, he decided to send a messenger to King Alfonso of Castille. [2900]

"Where art thou, Muño Gustioz, my dauntless vassal? A lucky thing for me, to have brought you up in my court! Take you now this message to Castile, to King Alfonso. Kiss his hand on my behalf, heart and soul, for I am his vassal, and he my lord. Concerning this outrage done to me by the Scions of Carrión, let the good king feel grief in heart and soul. He married my daughters to these men—it was not I who gave them away. Since they have now abandoned my daughters most shamefully, if some dishonor falls on us, most of it, great and small, falls on my lord. My property as well—substantial property— they have also taken from me. That too afflicts me, along with the other dishonor. Let him summon them for me, to meetings, councils, or to court, so I may demand satisfaction of the Scions of Carrión, for great is the umbrage I feel in my heart."

Muño Gustioz rode swiftly, and along with him two knights attending, and with them also two squires of the Cid's household. They left Valencia and traveled as fast as they could, day and night, taking no rest.

Muño Gustioz found the king in Sahagún: the king of Castile and of León, of Asturias as far as Oviedo—as far as Santiago, he is lord of all, for the Galician counts also acknowledge fealty to him.

No sooner had Muño Gustioz dismounted than he knelt down in the church before the saints and prayed to the Creator. He then headed for the palace, where court was being held, and with him the two knights attending him as their lord.

As they entered through the middle of the court, the king saw them, recognizing Muño Gustioz. The king arose and received them warmly.

The noble Muño Gustioz knelt down before the king, and, kissing his feet, declared:

"By your leave, King Alfonso, you who are acknowledged lord of mighty kingdoms! The Campeador kisses your hands and feet. He is your vassal, and you are his lord. You married his daughters to the Scions of Carrión. The marriage was of highest quality because it was you who wished it. By now you know the honor it has brought us. How the Scions of Carrión have shamed us: how they battered the Cid Campeador's daughters and left them, beaten and stripped naked, deeply dishonored, in the Oakgrove of Corpes—fodder for beasts and birds of prey, out there in the wilds. Now, behold his daughters, back safe in Valencia. My Cid therefore kisses your hands, as vassal does to lord, begging you to summon these two to audience, council, or court. My Cid holds himself dishonored, but sees your own disgrace as graver still, [2950] and begs that you yourself take umbrage, you who are most knowledgeable in such matters. May My Cid obtain satisfaction from the Scions of Carrión."

For a full hour the king fell silent, pondering the matter.

"In truth, I tell you, it grieves me in my heart. And you say truly, you, Muño Gustioz, when you remind me that it was I who married the Cid's daughters to the Scions of Carrión. I meant well, and thought it would be an advantageous match for both parties. If only that marriage had never been arranged! The whole affair breaks my own heart as much as it does My Cid's. I will see that he obtains satisfaction, God preserve me! That which I had not thought to do again this season I will do indeed: my messengers will go forth throughout my kingdom, summoning again all my vassals to my court, to be held in Toledo. Let all meet with me there, counts and baronets, and I will command that the Scions of Carrión be there as well, so that they may answer to My Cid, the Campeador, and that he may have no cause for complaint, if I can help it.

"Tell the Campeador, he who was born in a lucky hour, to be ready with his vassals within seven weeks from now and come to me in Toledo—this much time I give him. For love of My Cid, I convene this court. Send my greetings to everyone in Valencia, and bid them be of good cheer: for this disgrace that has befallen them will be set right in due time."

Muño Gustioz took his leave and returned to My Cid.

Just as he had promised, King Alfonso the Castilian—without delay and seeing to it personally—sent his letters to all the lands of León and Santiago, to the Portuguese and Galicians, to the folk of Carrión and to the Castilians, announcing that their honored king would hold court in Toledo, and that they should all assemble there in seven weeks' time. Whoever failed to attend would no longer be considered his vassal. Throughout his many realms, all agreed that none should fail to heed their king's commands.

Now the Scions of Carrión were really worried, because the king was about to convene a court of justice in Toledo. They feared that My Cid the Campeador would attend. Consulting with all their kinsmen, they appealed to the king to exempt them from attending the proceedings.

The king replied:

"I will not, so help me God! For My Cid the Campeador will be there, and you are going to give him satisfaction, for he has lodged a complaint against you. Let whomever refuses to comply and attend my court be banished from my kingdom, for he is no longer in my good graces."

Now the Scions of Carrión saw there was no getting out of it, and took counsel with all their kinsmen. Count García Ordóñez was also involved. My Cid's mortal enemy, who never missed a chance to do him an ill turn: this man was advisor to the Scions of Carrión.

The appointed day was approaching, and everyone attended the court. [3000] Leading the way was good King Alfonso, along with Count Henry and Count Raymond, both of Burgundy—the latter was the father of the good emperor—and Count Froila and Count Beltrán.[23] From Alfonso's kingdom came also many men well versed in the law, the best Castile had to offer. Count García Ordóñez was with the Scions of Carrión, with Ansur González and Gonzalo Ansúrez, and the two of

---

23. Count Henry is a historical personage, grandson of Robert, first Duke of Burgundy, and nephew of Queen Constance, King Alfonso's wife. The historical Count Raymond was Count Henry's cousin, married to Alfonso's daughter Urraca. Froila corresponds to the historical Froila Díaz, the brother of the Cid's wife Jimena. The reference to Beltrán is anachronistic, given that this personage came to prominence years after the Cid's death, inheriting the countship of Carrión in 1117.

them, Diego and Fernando, along with a great company of supporters they brought along to the court with the intention of assaulting the Cid.

From all directions they came to gather there, all but the man born in a lucky hour, who had not yet arrived. Because of this delay, the king was somewhat troubled.

On the fifth day My Cid the Campeador finally arrived. He sent Álvar Fáñez on ahead, telling him to kiss the hands of his lord the king, and let him know that he would be there by nightfall.

When the king heard this, he was very pleased. With a great company attending him the king rode out to welcome the man born in a lucky hour. The Cid came well prepared along with all his vassals—a noble company indeed, to have such a lord as theirs!

As good King Alfonso caught sight of him, My Cid the Campeador jumped down from his horse, intending to do obeisance before his lord and show him honor.

The king, on seeing this, immediately declared:

"By Saint Isidore, I will not hear of it, on such a day as this! Get on your horse, My Cid; otherwise I will be most displeased. Let us greet each other properly, heart and soul. What grieves you distresses me in my very heart. God grant that this court be honored today, on your behalf."

"Amen," answered My Cid, the Campeador.

He kissed the king's hand, and then he kissed him in greeting.

"Thank God I am here to see you, my lord. I bow to you, and to Count Raymond and Count Henry, and all you others who have gathered here. God keep all our friends, and you most of all, my lord! My wife Doña Jimena, a noble lady, likewise kisses your hand, as do both my daughters, and all three beg you commiserate with us for what we have undergone."

The king replied:

"I do indeed, as God is my savior!"

The king was heading back to Toledo, but the Cid preferred not to cross the Tagus that night:

"Now then, my king, a favor, the Creator bless and keep you. You, my lord, go back into the city, while I with my men take lodgings at San Servando. Tonight the rest of my men will get here. I will hold vigil in this holy place, and tomorrow morning I will go into the city [3050] and arrive at court before the midday meal."

The king said in reply:

"I gladly grant you this request."

The king then went into Toledo, while My Cid Ruy Díaz spent the night in San Servando. He ordered candles to be placed on the altar, for he intended to hold vigil in that sanctuary, praying to the Creator and taking secret counsel with his men. Minaya and all the other good men there were agreed on what to do by the time morning came.

As the dawn approached, matins and prime were said.

Mass was done before sunrise, and they had all duly made their offerings.

"You, Minaya Álvar Fáñez, my good right arm, will go with me, and you too, Bishop Jerome, and Pedro Bermúdez, and Muño Gustioz here, and Martín Antolínez, the good man of Burgos, and Álvar Álvarez, Álvar Salvadórez, and Martín Muñoz, born in a lucky hour, and my nephew Félix Muñoz. Mal Anda will also come with me, a man well versed in the law, and Galindo García, the worthy man of Aragon. Along with these, let one hundred more good men of those here present complete our company. Everybody wear padded tunics, the better to wear your armor, and over them, your coats of mail, bright as the sun, and over the coats of mail, ermines and fur cloaks, with the cords tied tight so as not to let your armor show. And under the cloaks, your swords, well-tempered and keen-edged. This is how I want to go to court, to demand my rights and present my case. If the Scions of Carrión are looking for trouble, I'll have nothing to fear with a hundred men like you behind me."

All of them replied:

"We would have it no other way, lord."

Just as the Cid had told them to, they all made ready. Nor did the man born in a lucky hour waste any time. On his legs he wore breeches of finest cloth, and over them shoes of the finest workmanship. He donned a costly linen shirt, as shiny-white as the sun, with all the fastenings of gold and silver, and the cuffs fitting just right, for he had had them made to order. Over it he wore a finely made silk tunic of gold-laced brocade— up and down the length of the garment, the golden threads worked into the fabric shone brightly. Over all this he wore a scarlet cape fringed with gold—the one My Cid always wore.

Covering his hair he wore a cap of the finest linen, gold-embroidered, specially ordered so that nobody could pull the hair of the good Cid Campeador.

His beard he wore long, tied up with a cord. All this he did to protect himself as best he could from any insult. Over it all he wore a magnificent cloak. All those in attendance were bound to mark him well. [3100]

With those hundred of his men that he had ordered to make ready, he rode speedily forth, heading out from San Servando. Thus did the Cid go well prepared to court.

At the outer door he dismounted, as was proper, then cautiously entered the place with all his men—he walked in surrounded by his hundred followers.

As King Alfonso saw him enter, the man born in a lucky hour, the good king rose to his feet, as did Count Henry and Count Raymond, and all the others likewise, you may be sure. They welcomed him with the greatest respect: the man born in a lucky hour.

García Ordóñez—the curly-haired man of Grañón—and all those of the faction of the Scions of Carrión, refused to get to their feet.[24]

The king said to the Cid:

"Come here, sit by me, Campeador, on this same seat that you gave me as a gift. Although it may bother some people to hear me say so, you're a better man than I."

Then the man who won Valencia said many thanks:

"Please do you sit on your throne, as befits our lord and king. I will take my place here with these, my men."

The king was heartily pleased with the Cid's reply.

The Cid then sat down on a finely wrought, high-backed bench, while the hundred men of his guard took their seats around him. Everyone at court was watching My Cid, looking at his long, flowing beard, tied up with a ribbon. He was a manly sight indeed, with all his accouterments. Only the Scions of Carrión, overcome with shame, were unable to look at him.

Then good King Alfonso got to his feet:

---

24. The curly-haired man (*"el Crespo"*) of Grañón was, in fact, the nickname of this historical personage.

"Hear ye, my vassals, as God is your protector. In all my time as king I have never held more than two courts of justice, one in Burgos, the other in Carrión. This third one here in Toledo I have convened today for love of My Cid, the man born in a lucky hour, so that he may obtain justice from the Scions of Carrión. They have done him a great wrong, as all of us are well aware. As judges in this matter I name Count Henry and Count Raymond, and all you other counts who do not side with the Carrión faction: all of you, pay close heed to this matter — you who are so knowledgeable in the law — and make the right finding, for I will brook no wrongful judgment. On both sides, let us be at peace this day. I swear by Saint Isidore, any man who dares disrupt my court will lose my favor and be banished from my kingdom. And now, let My Cid Campeador bring his suit. After that, we will hear what the Scions of Carrión have to say for themselves."

Getting to his feet, My Cid kissed the king's hand:

"Many thanks to you, my king and liege lord, for having convened this court for my sake. This is the claim I bring against the Scions of Carrión: in the matter of their abandonment of my daughters, I feel it is not I who am wronged, but you my lord. For you were the one who married them, my king — you will know only too well what to do about that this day. [3150] But when they took my daughters with them from Valencia of the Many Gates, I showed my love for them, heart and soul — I gave them the swords Colada and Tizón. These I fairly won, in manly fashion, and meant that with them they should do themselves honor and better serve you. When they abandoned my daughters in the Oakgrove of Corpes, they made it clear they wanted nothing further to do with me, and forfeited all further claim to my affections. Let them give me back my swords, since they are no longer my sons-in-law."

The judges found in his favor:

"The claim is entirely fair."

Count García then replied:

"We must confer about this."

Then and there the Scions of Carrión went off to one side with all their kinsmen and all those of their faction who were present. Hastily conferring on the matter, they came to an agreement among themselves:

"The Cid Campeador is still being really nice to us, if he's not calling us to account today for our mistreatment of his daughters. We can quickly come to an agreement with the king. Let's give the Cid back his swords, if that's where he's going to rest his case. When he's got them back, he's sure to depart from the court. Then he's not likely to have any further claim to bring against us."

They went back into the court ready to make this speech:

"Now then, a favor we beg of you, King Alfonso, you, our natural lord! We cannot deny that he gave us these two swords. Seeing as how he asks for them, and is of a mind to get them back, we fully intend to give them to him, with you here as our witness."

They produced the two swords, Colada and Tizón, and handed them over to the king, their lord. As the king drew them from their scabbards, their brightness shone forth throughout the court, for their pommels and hilt-bars were of gold. All the noblemen gathered there were amazed at the sight.

The Cid then accepted the swords, and kissed the king's hands. Then he returned to the bench from which he had gotten up. He held up the swords, looking at them closely. They could never switch swords on him, for the Cid knew these weapons far too well.

His whole body trembled with gladness, and he smiled with heartfelt delight. Raising his hand, he grasped his beard:

"By this my beard, that no man ever tweaked, I declare that Doña Elvira and Doña Sol will soon be avenged!"

Then he called to his nephew Pedro by name, held out his arm, and handed him the sword Tizón:

"Take it, nephew, for now indeed it finds a better lord."

To Martín Antolínez, the doughty man of Burgos, he reached out and handed him the sword Colada:

"Martín Antolínez, my worthy vassal, take Colada. I won it from a most worthy lord, Count Ramón Berenguer, of the great city of Barcelona. I give it to you so that you can take good care of it. I know that if you get the chance, you will win great honor and esteem with it."

Martín kissed the Cid's hand, and took and received the sword.

Then My Cid Campeador arose:

"Thanks be to the Creator, and to you, my lord king. [3200] I am satisfied in the matter of the swords, Colada and Tizón. But now I have another complaint against the Scions of Carrión. When they left Valencia, taking my two daughters with them, I gave them three thousand marks in gold and silver. After I did this, they then carried out their plan. Let them give me back my money, since they are no longer my sons-in-law."

You should have heard them wail, those Scions of Carrión!

Count Raymond spoke out:

"Let's have it: yes or no."

Then the Scions of Carrión replied:

"If we gave the Cid back his swords, it was so he could make no further claim against us, so the matter would be done with."

The judges pronounced:

"If it please the king, this is our finding: that you must satisfy the Cid's demand."

The good king declared:

"I concur with this finding."

The Cid Campeador got to his feet:

"Either give me back the money I gave you, or justify your refusal."

Then the Scions of Carrión went off to one side. They could not agree on what to do, for the sum in question was considerable, and they had already spent it all.

Going back in, they spoke up freely:

"The man who took Valencia is putting us under a lot of pressure, seeing that he is itching to go after our wealth. We will pay him in landed property from our estates in Carrión."

Having heard the defendants' recognition of the debt, the judges replied:

"If the Cid were to agree, we would not disallow it, but our finding in this matter — and this is our ruling — is that you hand the sum over to him here and now, in this court."

To this pronouncement King Alfonso added:

"We are fully aware, concerning this matter, that the Cid is in the right in making his claim. I have two hundred marks from the total sum of three thousand, given to me by the Scions of Carrión. I wish to return this money to them, seeing how hard-pressed they are. Let this sum be returned to My Cid, the man born in a lucky hour. Since they have to pay it back, I no longer want this money."

Fernando González answered:

"We don't have any cash."

Immediately, Count Raymond declared:

"You spent all the gold and silver. Our finding, which we render here in the presence of King Alfonso, is that they repay the Cid in kind, and that the Campeador accept this settlement."

Now indeed did the Scions of Carrión see that there was no getting out of it. You should have seen all the swift horses being led in, all the sleek mules and handsome palfreys, all the fine swords and coats of mail!

My Cid took possession of all this, just as it was all tallied up by the court.

Aside from the two hundred marks that King Alfonso happened to have with him, the Scions of Carrión payed what they owed the man born in a lucky hour. They had to borrow from others, since their own wealth was not enough. You can be sure they came off looking ridiculous from the whole business.

My Cid had taken possession of all these payments in kind. [3250] His men had taken charge of everything and were determined to look after the Cid's goods.

When this matter had been attended to, another was brought up by the Cid:

"A favor, my lord, I pray you. My principal complaint cannot be overlooked. Hear me, all you members of the court, and be moved to pity by my woes. I cannot allow the Scions of Carrión, who have wronged me so grievously, to leave this place unchallenged.

"Tell me, Scions of Carrión, what have I ever done, in earnest or in jest, or in any other way, to deserve this of you? Whatever it is, I will gladly make it up to you, abiding by the judgment of this court.

"Tell me, why did you tear asunder the very fabric of my heart? As you left Valencia I gave my daughters into your safe-keeping, showing you the highest honor and providing you abundant wealth. If you already felt no love for them, why then, you traitorous dogs, did you ever take them from their estates in Valencia? Why did you scourge them with cinches and spurs? You left them abandoned in the Oakgrove of Corpes, to be fodder to wild beasts and birds of prey. For all this that you have done to them, you are liable to the charge of infamy. If you do not give me satisfaction, let the court settle this matter."

Count García then got to his feet:

"Now then, if you please, my king, the greatest monarch in all Spain! My Cid is already experienced in the workings of these courts of justice. He let his beard grow out, and now he wears it long. Some people are downright afraid of him, and others are simply overawed. The Scions of Carrión are members of such a highborn family that they could not be expected to want anything to do with his daughters, even as concubines. And who would ever give these girls to these young men as their equals, as their lawfully wedded wives? These young men did right to desert them. Nothing the Cid says is worthy of consideration."

Then the Campeador declared, taking hold of his beard:

"Thanks be to God, Lord of heaven and earth! If my beard is long, it's because it's been lovingly tended. And what have you got against my beard, Count? For all my life it has been lovingly tended, and no man born of woman has ever tweaked it, and no son of Moor or Christian ever tore so much as a hair from it, the way I did yours, Count, in the Castle of Cabra. When I took Cabra by storm, and you by the beard, there wasn't a lad there who didn't get to tear out a little tuft of his own. Look there, it hasn't grown back where I yanked out my tuft."[25]

Then Fernando González got to his feet—hear him as he speaks out, loud and clear:

"Give up this suit of yours, Cid. You've been paid back all your money and possessions. Let's put an end to this quarrel between us and you. We're of the lineage of the Counts of Carrión. We should be marrying the daughters of kings and emperors. The daughters of petty barons are not suitable wives for us. We only did right, when we left them there. And know this: we think better of ourselves on account of it, not worse." [3300]

My Cid Ruy Díaz looked at Pedro Bermúdez:

---

25. Yet another episode from the Cid's past that the poet expects his audience to be familiar with. García Ordóñez figures in various chronicles, along with the Cid (see Related Texts D and E).

"Speak up, Pedro the Mute, you silent fellow you! They're my daughters, but they're your first cousins. These men are saying these words to me, but you're the one being slapped. If I answer them, you won't get the chance to fight them in the lists yourself."[26]

Pedro Bermúdez started to speak. At first he was a little tongue-tied and could not find the words. But once he got going, you can be sure there was no shutting him up:

"I'll tell you, Cid, you've got some strange habits. You're always calling me 'Pedro the Mute' when we're at court. You know very well I can't talk any better than that. But when it comes to deeds, you know I'll never fail you.

"You lie, Fernando, in everything you've said. Your reputation is a lot better now, thanks to the Campeador. I can tell you all about your little tricks. Remember that day, when we were in combat, near Valencia of the Many Gates? You asked the noble Campeador for permission to strike the first blow. Then you saw a Moor and went to take him on. But even before you got to him, you ran away. If I hadn't helped you, that Moor would have made short work of you. I rode past you and closed with the Moor, and then I defeated him with only a few strokes of the sword. Then I gave you his horse, and kept it a secret. Up to this day, I never told anybody. In front of My Cid and everybody else you bragged how you had killed the Moor and done a warlike deed. Everybody believed you, but they didn't know the truth. So you're handsome enough, but you're a cowardly fellow. You worthless blowhard — how dare you even speak?

"Tell me, Fernando, answer me this: do you recall that time in Valencia, that time with the lion? When My Cid was asleep, and the lion got loose? And you, Fernando, what did you do, being afraid and all? You hid behind the couch of My Cid Campeador! That's where you hid, Fernando, and today your honor is the worse for it. While we surrounded the Cid's couch, watching over our lord, until My Cid woke up — the man who took Valencia! — and rose from his couch, and then went over to the lion. The lion bowed his head and waited for My Cid,

---

26. In Spanish, the name *Bermúdez* invites a play on the word *mudo*, meaning "mute."

then let the Cid take him by the scruff of the neck and put him back in his cage. When the Campeador turned around and saw all his vassals around him, he asked for his sons-in-law. But he couldn't find either of them!

"And now I challenge you, man-to-man, and call you knave and traitor. This I will uphold in combat against you, in the presence of my lord King Alfonso, on behalf of the daughters of the Cid, Doña Elvira and Doña Sol. By abandoning them the way you did, you disgraced yourselves. They are women, and you are men. But in every way, they are more honorable than you. When the fighting starts, please the Creator, you'll own yourself a traitor [3350] and everything I've said will be proven true."

There the matter between these two stood for the time being.

Now hear what Diego González had to say:

"Our lineage is of the noblest and purest blood. These marriages ought never have been arranged, nor should My Cid Don Rodrigo ever have become our father-in-law. Nor do we now, nor shall we ever, regret abandoning his daughters. As long as they live they can sigh and feel sorry for themselves. What we did to them will always be thrown in their faces. This I will uphold in combat, against any man, be he ever so bold: that because we deserted them, we are honored thereby."

Martín Antolínez got to his feet:

"Shut your lying mouth, you traitor! You shouldn't forget that incident with the lion. You ran right out the door and into the yard, and threw yourself under the beam of the wine press. You never again wore that cloak or that tunic! I will uphold this in combat, and I won't have it any other way: that because you deserted the Cid's daughters, their honor is in every way greater than yours. When the fighting's done, you will confess with your own mouth that you are a traitor, and that everything you've said has been a lie."

There the matter stood between these two.

Then Ansur González came strutting into the palace, dragging along an ermine cloak and a tunic. He comes in, his face all red from eating and drinking. What he said did not make much sense:

"My lords, whoever heard such a tale of woe? Who ever heard tell of this My Cid of Vivar? Let him get back to grinding his millstones, back there on the Ubierna River, and collecting his miller's fees, the way he's used to! Whoever told him he could be related by marriage to the Carrión family?"[27]

Then Muño Gustioz got to his feet:

"Shut up, you liar! Wretch! Traitor! You eat before you go to church, and when you kiss people before communion, you belch in their faces![28] You tell the truth to neither friend nor lord. You play everyone false, and especially God. I want no part of any friendship with you. I mean to make you admit that you are everything I say you are."

Then King Alfonso said:

"Enough of this matter for the moment. Those who have issued challenges will get their chance to fight, so help me God!"

Just as they were concluding this matter, two knights came into the hall. One was named Ojarra, representing the Prince of Navarre, and the other Íñigo Jiménez, sent by the Prince of Aragon. Kissing King Alfonso's hands, they asked for the Campeador's daughters in marriage, to be the queens of Navarre and Aragon, and given away in marriage as lawfully wedded wives. [3400]

Having spoken, with the whole court listening, they fell silent.

My Cid the Campeador got to his feet:

"A boon I ask, King Alfonso, of you who are my liege lord! I thank the Creator for this: that the kings of Navarre and Aragon ask for my daughters in marriage. You married them before, not I. Now, here are my daughters: they are in your hands. I will do nothing without your say-so."

---

27. Mills were often under the authority of *infanzones* (nobles of the lowest rank — the official rank of the Cid), who derived a portion of their income from the fees charged for use of the mill.

28. The kiss referred to is that exchanged by worshippers as the blessing known as the Pax Domini ("Peace of the Lord") and is pronounced during mass. The Pax Domini is the last blessing before Holy Communion. According to the rule of the Eucharistic Fast, the worshipper is required to fast before taking communion. In earlier times the period of fasting was three hours or more. The most recent Canon Law stipulates a minimum of one hour. The point with regard to Ansur González is that he is both uncouth and impious.

The king arose then and called for silence in the court.

"I beg you, Cid, renowned Campeador, to agree to this match, and I will approve it. Let this marriage be arranged here today, in this court, for by it you will grow in honor, lands, and estates."

My Cid arose and kissed the king's hands:

"If it please you, my lord, I do consent."

Then the king exclaimed:

"May God reward you well for this! To you, Ojarra, and to you, Íñigo Jiménez, I hereby grant permission to arrange this marriage of the daughters of My Cid, Doña Elvira and Doña Sol, to the princes of Navarre and Aragon. Let these ladies be given to you in marriage, in accordance with all due ceremony."

Ojarra and Íñigo Jiménez then got to their feet and kissed the hands of King Alfonso, and then those of the Cid. They gave their word, and oaths were sworn, that all would be done as they promised, or even better.

Many in the court were pleased at these developments, but the Scions of Carrión were not pleased at all.

Minaya Álvar Fáñez then arose:

"A boon I beg of you, as of my lord and king—and may this in no way trouble the Cid Campeador. I have given everyone plenty of time in this court. Now I would like to say my piece."

The king replied:

"I am heartily glad to grant your request. Speak, Minaya, and say whatever you like."

"Listen to me, I beg you, all you here gathered in this court. For I have a serious grievance against the Scions of Carrión. I gave them my cousins in marriage, at the bidding of King Alfonso. These men accepted the girls to be their lawfully wedded wives. And My Cid the Campeador gave them great amounts of money and goods as a wedding gift. They then deserted these girls, in spite of everything we did for them. I challenge them, man-to-man, as evildoers and traitors. You are of the Vanigómez family, from which have come many renowned and valiant nobles. But we all know these fellows, with their sneaky tricks. For this I give thanks to the Creator above: that the princes of Navarre and Aragon have asked for my cousins Doña Elvira and Doña Sol in marriage. Before they were your equals, to have and to hold. Now you'll kiss their hands, and have to call them 'lady.' [3450] You'll have to serve them, like it or not. Thanks be to God in heaven, and to our king, Don Alfonso, for this way the honor of My Cid the Campeador grows even greater! In every way you are just what I said you are. If there is anyone here who would like to answer me, or give me the lie, then here I am, Álvar Fáñez, ready to face the best of you."

Gómez Peláez then got to his feet:

"What is the point of all this talk, Minaya? Because in this court there are plenty of us ready to face you, and anybody who wants to say different does so at his peril. If God wills it and we come out ahead in this matter, we'll soon see if you're right or wrong."

The king said:

"Enough of this wrangling. Let there be no more allegations, on either side. Let the combat take place tomorrow, when the sun comes up, between the three on each side who have issued challenges before the court."

Immediately, the Scions of Carrión spoke up:

"Give us more time, your majesty, for it cannot be tomorrow. The Campeador and his men are all armed and ready, with their horses and everything. Before we can be ready, we will have to go back to our lands in Carrión."

The king addressed the Campeador:

"Let this combat take place wherever you decide."

To this My Cid replied:

"That is not for me to say, my lord. But I prefer Valencia to the lands of Carrión."

Now the king answered him:

"That goes without saying, Campeador. But entrust your knights to me, with all their weapons and accouterments, and let them go with me now, for I will watch over them. To you I guarantee their safety, as a lord should to a good vassal, and assure you that they will suffer no harm from anyone, whether count or baron. Here and now, in this my court, I do command that three weeks hence, on the plain of Carrión, the combat will take place in my presence. Whoever fails to appear, let him forfeit the judgment, be declared the loser, and be regarded as a traitor."

As the Scions of Carrión accepted this judgment, the Cid, kissing the king's hands, declared:

"I agree, my lord. These three knights of mine are now in your hands. Here and now I commend them to you, as to my king and liege lord. They are all ready to do their duty. Send them back to me in Valencia covered with glory, for love of our Creator."

And the king replied:

"God will it so!"

Then the Cid Campeador took off his cap, white as the sun, and untied his beard, loosening the ribbon. All those there in the court could barely take their eyes off him. Count Henry and Count Raymond headed over to see him. Warmly embracing each one, he invited them all to take of his wealth anything they liked. Likewise all those there who sided with him — one and all, he invited them to take whatever they wished. [3500]

Some there were who accepted his offer, and some there were who did not.

The Cid gave the king back the two hundred marks, while the king also took as much as he felt like from the rest.

"A favor I ask, oh king, for the Creator's sake! Since all these matters have been settled, I kiss your hands and beg your leave, my lord, to head back to Valencia, that I conquered by dint of great struggle."

* * * Gap in manuscript of about fifty lines * * *[29]

The king raised his hand and made the sign of the cross:

"I swear by Saint Isidore of León that there lives no greater man in all our lands."

My Cid, still riding his horse, rode up and kissed the hand of his lord King Alfonso:

"You told me to put Babieca the Charger through his paces. Among Moors or Christians, there is no other to match him. Here, I give him to you as a gift. Order him to be led away, my lord."

Then the king responded:

---

29. A comparison with other accounts of the Cid's adventures suggests that the missing folio chiefly narrates the scene of the Cid's demonstration of his own equestrian skills and of his fabulous steed's abilities.

"This I cannot agree to. If I took your horse away, he would not have so good a master. A horse such as this is made for such as you, to rout Moors in the field and go after them in fierce pursuit. The Creator confound whomever would seek to take him from you, for by you and by your horse do we all grow in fame and honor."

As they took leave of each other, all those present at the court began to go their separate ways. The Campeador, meanwhile, gave wise advice to his champions:

"Now then Martín Antolínez, and you too, Pedro Bermúdez, and Muño Gustioz as well. Hold steady on the field of combat, and fight like men, so that back in Valencia I will hear good things about you."

Martín Antolínez replied:

"Why even say it, my lord? We have accepted this obligation, and now it's for us to fulfill. You may hear news of men killed in battle, but not defeated."

The man born in a lucky hour rejoiced to hear these words. He then took his leave of all those there who were his friends.

And now My Cid set out for Valencia, and the king headed for Carrión. The three weeks' grace period was up, and there were the Cid's champions, arriving on the appointed day and determined to fulfill the obligation that their lord had entrusted to them. They were under the protection of King Alfonso of León.

Two days they waited for the Scions of Carrión.

Then they came, very well equipped with horses and accouterments. And all their kinsmen were with them, planning to see if they could lure the Cid's men into ambush and kill them somewhere out in the countryside, thus dishonoring their lord.

The plot was an evil one, but nothing came of it, for they dreaded the wrath of Alfonso of León.

That night they all kept vigil over their weapons and prayed to the Creator.

Night was coming to an end, and the day was dawning, as many worthy nobles gathered together there, eager to witness the judicial combats. And presiding over them all was King Alfonso, determined to uphold the right and prevent wrongdoing.

Without delay, the Cid's men set about arming themselves for battle. [3550] All three were in agreement, for they served one single lord.

Elsewhere, the Scions of Carrión were likewise arming themselves for battle. There with them was García Ordóñez, haranguing them with advice.

They had a complaint to lodge, and made their case to King Alfonso. They requested that the two keen-edged swords, Colada and Tizón, not be wielded in the forthcoming battle by the champions of the Campeador.

Now the Scions of Carrión really rued the day they ever gave back those weapons.

They made their petition to the king, but he disallowed it:

"You mentioned no such exclusions when we held the court of justice. If the swords you brought with you are good ones, they will serve you well enough. The same will be the case for the Cid's champions. Rise and sally into the field, Scions of Carrión. Now you must fight like men, for you can be sure the Cid's champions will give it their all. If things go well for you in this combat, you will have won great honor for yourselves. If you are beaten, don't blame us, for everybody knows you brought all this on yourselves."

Now indeed did the Scions of Carrión regret what they had done. Now indeed did they truly rue the day. They would have given all their property in Carrión to be able to undo all they had done.

All three of the Cid's champions were armed and ready as the king came to see them.

The Cid's men said:

"We kiss your hand, as our king and lord, and beg you be the field judge today, in this affair between them and us. See justice done for us, for there is no wrongdoing on our side. Here the Scions of Carrión have their whole clan with them, and we don't know what they might or might not be planning. Our lord the Cid put us in your hands. Defend our rights, for love of the Creator!"

The king replied:

"With all my heart and soul!"

And then the horses were led out to them, spirited and swift. They all made the sign of the cross over their saddles, and then leapt astride their mounts. Their shields, all smartly bossed, hung from their necks as they took up their lances, each with a sharp iron point, and each bearing a pennon.

All around were gathered many worthy nobles, as the combatants rode forth into the field set off by the boundary markers. All three of the Cid's men were of one mind: that each should charge forward and smite his opponent with all he had.

On the other side, you should have seen the Scions of Carrión, surrounded by a whole crowd of supporters, for they had many kinsmen.

The king assigned field judges to make fair rulings, no other kind, so that afterward there would be no quibbling about what did or did not happen.

When they were all there, ready on the field of combat, King Alfonso addressed them:

"Listen to what I tell you, Scions of Carrión. This combat should have been held in Toledo, but you would not consent to that. These three knights, vassals of My Cid the Campeador, I have led under my safe conduct to these lands of Carrión. Uphold your cause, but do not try anything wrongful. [3600] For I will subject any man attempting to cheat with the severest punishment: nowhere in my kingdom will he find aid and comfort."

Now the Scions of Carrión were feeling very dejected indeed.

The field judges and the king were showing the combatants the boundaries, and all the onlookers withdrew from the field. All six combatants were carefully shown the marked lines, and were told that whoever crossed them was to be declared the loser. All the spectators were moved back and told not to approach closer than six spear-lengths to the lists. Lots were drawn for positions, and the field judges saw to it that no man would have to face into the sun.

The field judges withdrew from the middle of the lists. The challengers were now face to face.

Then the Cid's men charged toward the Scions of Carrión, and the Scions of Carrión went at the Campeador's champions, each man intent on his particular opponent. They held the shields in front of their chests, lowering their lances, each with a pennon hanging from it. Bending forward over their saddlebows, they struck their horses' flanks with their spurs. Now the earth shook as they hurtled forward, each man having eyes only for his opponent — three against three, joined in battle.

The onlookers thought the combatants would all fall dead to the ground from the encounter. Pedro Bermúdez, he who had issued the first challenge, charged straight at Fernando González. Fearless, they smote each other's shields. Fernando González pierced right through Pedro's shield, but the stroke missed, and the flesh remained unscathed, while Fernando's lance was shattered in two.

Pedro Bermúdez sat up straight in the saddle, keeping his balance, answering the spear thrust with one of his own, smashing the boss of Fernando's shield and splitting the shield down the middle. Pedro's thrust went right through, the blade plunging into his opponent's chest, as Fernando's shield was now useless. It was his three layers of chain mail that saved him: two were punctured, but the third withstood. His shirt and padded tunic, and some of the iron mesh, were driven by the impact a full hand's-breadth into his body. Blood spewed from his mouth, as the saddle girths gave way — they were all useless to him now — and he was driven over the horse's croup and hurled to the ground.

Everybody among the spectators thought he had been fatally wounded.

Pedro dropped his lance and drew his sword.

When Fernando González saw him coming, he recognized the sword Tizón.

Rather than wait for the blow to fall, he declared:

"I am defeated."

The field judges accepted his admission of defeat, and Pedro spared his life.

Martín Antolínez and Diego García struck each other with their lances, both weapons shattering under the force of the impact. Martín Antolínez then took his sword in hand. The weapon's blade, so clean and bright, lit up the whole field. Martín struck Diego a blow from the side, [3650] taking off the upper part of his helmet. Cutting right through the helmet's laces, he hacked off a piece of the chain mail hood and slashed right down to the coif, so that coif and hood were sent flying, and the hairs of Diego's head were shaved, along with a good piece of his scalp. Part of the helmet fell to the ground, the rest stayed on his head.

As Martín struck this blow with the glorious sword Colada, Diego González saw that he would not escape with his life. He reined his horse around to face his opponent.

Martín Antolínez was waiting for him with the sword, and smote Diego with the flat of the weapon, not the edge. Diego González had his own sword in hand, but did nothing with it. Then he cried out in a loud voice:

"God help me! Lord above, most glorious, save me from that sword!"

Tugging at the reins of his horse, to get away from the sword, he crossed the boundary line.

Martín Antolínez remained in the field. The king then said to him:

"Come here and join my company. By all that you have done this day, you have won this battle."

The field judges upheld the king's declaration, confirming that he spoke truly.

And now that the first two have won their battles, I will tell you of Muño Gustioz, and how he dealt with Ansur González.

As they struck mighty blows against each other's shields, Ansur González, strong and brave, drove his lance right through Don Muño Gustioz's shield, piercing his armor. But the lance missed the body, and Muño's flesh was untouched. Muño Gustioz then returned the blow, thrusting through his opponent's shield and piercing his armor right through the middle of the boss, as the shield cracked from the impact. His armor pierced, unable to protect him, Ansur was struck in the side, but away from the heart. Striking clean through Ansur's body, taking the pennon with it, the lance blade stuck out an arm's length on the other side. Giving the lance a twist, Muño lifted Ansur from the saddle, then threw him to the ground as he pulled the weapon out.

The shaft, blade, and pennon all came out red. Everyone thought the wound was a fatal one.

Muño Gustioz took the lance in hand and stood looking down at Ansur.

His father Gonzalo Ansúrez then cried out:

"For God's sake, do not strike him! The field is yours, now that this is over with."

The field judges pronounced:

"We accept this admission of defeat."

The good King Alfonso ordered the field cleared, and he had the weapons remaining on the field gathered up, for they now belonged to him.

Covered with honor, the Cid's champions now departed: they had won the battle, thanks to God the Creator.

Great was the lamentation, throughout the lands of Carrión.

The king sent My Cid's men home at night, so they would have no fear of being ambushed along the way. They traveled day and night, like the prudent men they were, [3700] until they reached Valencia and rejoined My Cid, the Campeador.

They showed the Scions of Carrión to be wrongdoers, and fulfilled the obligation their lord had charged them with. My Cid the Campeador was overjoyed.

And great was the dishonor of the Scions of Carrión. Whoever so mistreats and abandons any noble woman — let him suffer the same or even worse!

But let us now leave the Scions of Carrión and all their dealings, as they groan from the rough treatment they have received, and speak of the man born in a lucky hour.

Great was the rejoicing throughout Valencia of the Many Gates, at the honor won by the Cid's champions.

Grasping his beard, their lord, Ruy Díaz, declared:

"Thanks be to God in Heaven, my daughters are now avenged! Let them be quit of their estates in Carrión. Now I can marry my daughters to anybody I please, with no impediment."[30]

---

30. The Old Spanish reads: "*Agora las ayan quitas heredades de Carrión*" (verse 3715). This is ambiguous. "*Quito*" can mean "rid of," "freed from," and "free and clear of," or it can mean "having the free and clear use of." The former interpretation means that the Cid's daughters are now free from having anything further to do with the estates given to them as wedding presents by the Scions of Carrión. The bad marriage is annulled, and their father can now remarry them without the slightest question of any further connection, impediment, or ambiguity. The second interpretation would mean that the daughters can now enjoy the free use of those estates, which they would be entitled to keep even after the annulment of the marriage, since they were not responsible for the separation. This is the meaning suggested by Montaner (216, note). However, a third interpretation would make the Scions of Carrión the subject of the verb, which would mean something like, "Let the Scions of Carrión now have free use of their estates in Carrión." I

The princes of Navarre and Aragon then began their negotiations, meeting with King Alfonso of León and arranging their marriages to Doña Elvira and Doña Sol. The earlier marriages were excellent, but these new ones were even better: the Cid saw his daughters married much more honorably than the first time.

See how his honor grew, the honor of the man born in a lucky hour! His daughters were now the queens of Navarre and Aragon!

And today, all the kings of Spain are his kinsmen, all gaining in honor through the one born in a lucky hour.

He departed from this life at Pentecost.

May he receive Christ's pardon, and likewise all of us, saint and sinner alike!

Such have been the deeds of My Cid, the Campeador, and here this story comes to its end. [3730]

To him who put this book into writing, may God grant paradise, amen!

Per Abbat wrote it down, in the month of May, in the year 1245 of the Hispanic era.[31]

The story's read, so now give us some wine. If you have no coins, leave something in pawn, and you'll get your money's worth.

The End

---

think this interpretation is plausible, given the Cid's utter contempt for these characters and the fact that earlier in the trial the Scions' offer of payment in landed property was rejected. Moreover, the daughters, now living in Valencia, would have difficulty defending their ownership of the estates in question. My rendering is more or less literal and retains the ambiguity.

31. "Per Abbat" is presumably the name of the copyist of the manuscript (not the author of the work). The "Hispanic era" refers to the old Peninsular dating system, discontinued in the late fourteenth century, that takes as the initial year 38 BC (the supposed date of the foundation of Roman Spain). Thus, the date of the transcription is 1207 CE.

RELATED TEXTS

The following texts offer excerpts from other medieval works about the historical Cid. These selections are taken from chronicles, short poems, a later epic, and a ballad. The purpose is to give the reader a sense of the various — and sometimes contradictory — historical, political, folkloric, and literary perspectives on the Cid.

The Chronicle of Twenty Kings (Crónica de veinte reyes)	CTK
"The Cid and the Moorish King"	CMK
The Epic of the Cid	EC
First General Chronicle (Primera crónica general)	FGC
The History of Rodrigo (Historia Roderici)	HR
The Song of the Campeador (Carmen Campidoctoris)	SC
Treasury of the Excellencies of the Spaniards	TES
The Youthful Deeds of Rodrigo (Mocedades de Rodrigo)	YDR

A. TREASURY OF THE EXCELLENCIES OF THE SPANIARDS

Ibn Bassam (Abu l'Hassan Ali ibn Bassam)
Chronicle composed in Arabic in
the early twelfth century

Born in Santarem (present-day Portugal), Ibn Bassam died in
1147. Various details in his account suggest that he wrote the
following some time in the first decade of the twelfth century;
his work is thus one of the very earliest documents referring to
the Cid.

Ibn Bassam views Rodrigo in a very negative light. This
reminds us that heroism and villainy are very much a question
of viewpoint. The narrator's hero is the other side's villain, and
vice versa. It is thus not surprising that the description of the
Cid by a Muslim portrays the Christian hero as an infidel in-
vader, a marauder, and a perpetrator of atrocities. What is sur-
prising, however, is that even this sworn enemy will
acknowledge admiration for the Campeador's prudence, courage,
and martial accomplishments.[1]

... A certain Abu Tahir[2] lived long enough to witness the down-
fall of all the princes of those petty dynasties of Al-Andalus, and
the calamity that overtook Valencia, a calamity brought about
by that tyrant, the Campeador—God tear him limb from limb!
This Abu Tahir was thrown into prison in the month of Safar
of the year 487.[3] From his prison, he wrote the following letter
to a friend:

---

1. *Le Cid d'après de nouveaux documents*. Reinhart Dozy (Leiden,
1860). Dozy's translation at 13–25.
2. Ruler of the *taifa* kingdom of Murcia from 1063 to 1078; deposed
in the latter year, he went into exile, settled in Valencia, and was
later a witness to the Cid's invasion of that city and kingdom
(Fletcher, *Quest*, 99).
3. March of 1094.

"I write to you in the middle of the month of Safar. We have been imprisoned after a series of misfortunes so disastrous that no man has ever seen the like. If you could only see Valencia (may God favor her again and shed his divine light upon her!), if you could only see what fate has done to her and her people, you would pity her, you would weep for her misfortunes. For calamity has stripped her of her beauty, leaving no trace of her moons and stars! Do not ask me how I suffer, nor how many are my troubles, nor how complete is my despair!

At the moment, I am obliged to buy back my freedom by payment of a ransom, after having faced dangers that almost cost me my life. There remains to me no other hope than in God's goodness, that He has always bestowed on us, and that He in His benevolence has guaranteed us. . . ."

. . . Seeing that we have spoken of Valencia, we must now make known the calamity that overtook her, and say something concerning the war of which this province was the theater — a war whose headlong course lasted only too long for Islam, and which the great and unstinting efforts of justly frightened men were powerless to prevent. We must also set forth an account of all the crimes committed during this war, and of all the woes we Muslims were destined to endure, naming those who trod the path of this war, and also those who entered and left through the gateway of its pitched battles.

. . . later we will say a few words concerning the manner in which Alfonso (whom God tear to pieces!) — that tyrant of the Galicians,[4] that infidel folk — conquered the city of Toledo, the finest pearl of our necklace, Islam's highest tower in this Peninsula. We will then explain how Alfonso came to power in that city, that furnished him so snug a bed, as he so easily manipulated its inhabitants, who ever after resembled so many docile camels once he had established his residence within its high walls. . . .

———

4. *Galicians* (people from the northwestern region of Spain) was the term used by Spanish Muslims to refer to the Castilians and Leonese.

. . . Later, in the year 479,[5] the princes of our country established relations with the Emir of all the Muslims (whom God look upon with favor!)[6] . . . and this man won that glorious victory against the tyrant Alfonso. . . .[7] Alfonso (God curse him!) then returned to his own country, resembling a bird whose wings have been broken, or a sick man who has trouble breathing. . . .

But, as we have already said, the internecine ill will among the Muslim princes grew more poisonous by the day, and mutual calumnies crept stealthily among them. God then permitted the Emir of all the Muslims to thwart their intrigues, to cure the ills that provoked their jealousies, and to deliver all the Muslims from the consequences of their wicked actions and hateful machinations.

This the Emir began to do, as we have indicated, in the year 483. His authority was recognized in all the provinces, and the criers proudly called out his name in public prayers. Through the remainder of the year 483, and throughout the following year, he continued to oust the kinglets from their thrones, in the way that the sun drives the stars before him, causing their brightness to fade away without a trace. . . .

When al-Musta'in[8] — who governs to this day over the province of Saragossa — perceived that the soldiers of the Emir of all the Muslims were charging forth from every mountain pass, and that from every watchtower they were spying out his borders, he set upon them a Galician dog named Rodrigo, nicknamed the Campeador.

This was a man who made a vocation of throwing prisoners into chains. He was the scourge of the country, having engaged the Arab kinglets of the Peninsula in several battles and

---

5. Ibn Bassam, in mentioning the year 479, refers to the Muslim calendar. See Islamic Calendar in the Compendium of Proper Names.

6. Yusuf ibn Tashfin, leader and commander-in-chief of the Almoravids (see the Compendium of Proper Names for entries on Yusuf and Almoravids).

7. The Battle of Sagrajas in 1086.

8. Ahmad ibn Yusuf Al-Musta'in (1085–1110).

inflicted on them every kind of misery. The Banu Hud[9] were the ones who raised him from obscurity; they had made use of his support to carry out their atrocities and put into effect their vile and despicable plans. They had handed over to him various provinces of the Peninsula, enabling him to roam about the plains as a conqueror and to raise his banner over the fairest cities. Thus it was that his power had grown very great indeed, and there was scarcely a country in all of Muslim Spain that he had not plundered.

When therefore this al-Musta'in, of the clan of the Banu Hud, foresaw the fall of his dynasty and feared that his affairs would take a turn for the worse, he sought to put the Campeador between himself and the Emir's advance forces. Accordingly, he provided Rodrigo the occasion of entering Valencian territory, and furnished him money and troops as well. The Campeador then laid siege to Valencia, in which city civil disorder had broken out, and where the inhabitants were divided into several warring factions. . . .

Rodrigo desired more eagerly than ever to take possession of Valencia. He seized upon that city the way a creditor seizes upon a debtor; he loved it the way lovers love the places where they have tasted of love's pleasures. He cut off the city's food supply, killed many of her defenders, caused her all manner of woe, and showed himself to her from every hilltop. How many superb locales — that one could scarcely dream of visiting, places that moon and stars could not hope to rival in their beauty — did that tyrant not overwhelm and profane to their innermost recesses? How many charming girls — their blushing, milk-washed cheeks envied by sun and moon for their beauty; their teeth, like pearls in their mouths, rivaling coral itself for their whiteness — were wedded to his spear-points, crushed beneath the feet of his swaggering mercenaries!

Hunger forced the Valencians to eat the foulest vermin. The qadi Abu Ahmad, not knowing what to do, lost his head and appealed for help to the Emir of the Muslims, despite the fact that the Emir was very far from Valencia. . . . The fate of Valencia greatly concerned the Emir of the Muslims, but because he was far from there, and because destiny had decreed otherwise, he could not come to their aid at that time. . . .

---

9. The ruling clan in Muslim Saragossa from 1039 to 1110.

The tyrant Rodrigo then obtained the accomplishment of his despicable designs. He entered into Valencia in the year 487, by means of trickery, as was usual with him. The qadi had bowed down before him, recognizing the Campeador as his lord and obtaining a treaty from him. But this treaty was not honored for long. Abu Achmed remained by Rodrigo's side for only a little while, before the Campeador tired of his presence and decided to bring about his downfall. . . .

This terrible calamity was a thunderbolt for all the Muslims of the Peninsula, covering all classes of society with misery and shame.

The power of the tyrant grew evermore thereafter, becoming a heavy burden for the high country as well as the lowlands, filling with fear the hearts of noble and commoner alike. . . .

A man once told me that he had heard it said . . . that once upon a time this Peninsula was conquered and taken away from a ruler named Rodrigo, and that another Rodrigo was one day destined to take it back—a prophecy that has filled all hearts with terror, and that has made men feel that what they feared and dreaded most would soon come to pass![10]

And yet this Rodrigo Campeador, this scourge of his time, was, by virtue of his love of glory, his prudent resolution of character, and his heroic courage, one of the Lord's miracles. . . . Victory always followed his banner (God curse him!); he subdued the barbarians; several times he fought against their chiefs . . . chasing their armies before him and killing many of their soldiers with the aid of his little band of warriors.

It is said that books were read aloud in his presence; that tales of the deeds of ancient Arabia's most illustrious warriors were read to him; and that, thrilled and delighted by these tales, he was overcome with admiration . . .

---

10. The ruler named Rodrigo was Roderic, last of the Visigothic kings of Spain, legendarily defeated and killed in 712 in a battle with Muslim invaders.

B. THE HISTORY OF RODRIGO (HISTORIA RODERICI)

Anonymous
Chronicle composed in Latin, sometime
between 1102 and 1238 but probably after 1144

The work's date of composition is a much debated question. The earliest possible date is 1102. The chronicle's penultimate chapter (Chapter 76) refers to the Christian withdrawal from Valencia in that year (the Cid died in 1099). The same chapter also declares that the Muslims, having resettled the city, "have never lost it since that time." Since Valencia was reconquered by James the First of Aragon in 1238, it seems likely that The History of Rodrigo *was written sometime before that year. On the other hand, among several bits of evidence supporting composition after 1144 is the way the chronicle refers in the past tense (Chapter 54) to the Moabites (i.e., the Almoravids). This suggests that the author regards this Berber dynasty as a thing of the past, and that the work was composed after 1144, the year generally taken to mark the end of Almoravid rule in the Peninsula.*

It has been pointed out that one of the things that makes this biography remarkable is that its subject was neither a churchman, nor a member of a royal family, nor of the high nobility. This was very unusual in the early Middle Ages — another indication that the historical Cid made a lasting impression on his contemporaries.[11]

Chapter 1

Unless recorded in the annals of history, the accounts of great deeds that men accomplish in this world, obliterated by the fleeting passage of time, are consigned to certain oblivion. For this reason we have resolved to set down in writing the ancestry of that noblest and most stalwart of warriors, Rodrigo Díaz, and to preserve, under the light of the written word, the record of the wars won by virtue of his manly valor.

---

11. *Chronica Hispana, Sæculi XII,* edited by Emma Falque, Juan Gil, and Antonio Maya (Turnhout, Belgium: Brepols, 1990), 47–98.

Chapter 2

This, then, appears to be the origin of his line. Laín Calvo had several sons, the number of which include Fernán Laínez and Bermudo Laínez . . . [and after several generations] Bermudo Laínez begat Rodrigo Bermúdez, and Laín Fernández begat Nuño Laínez . . . [and] Nuño Laínez . . . sired Laín Núñez. Laín Núñez begat Diego Laínez; Diego Laínez begat Rodrigo Díaz the Campeador from a daughter of Rodrigo Álvarez, the brother of Nuño Álvarez, who held the castle of Amaya and was lord of several other provinces in those regions. Rodrigo Álvarez held the castle of Luna, as well as the provinces of Mormojón, Moradillo, Cellorigo, and Curiel, along with numerous other towns in the plain. . . .

Chapter 4

This Rodrigo Diáz, then, was attentively brought up by Sancho, king of all Castile and overlord of Spain, and received from him the belt of knighthood. When King Sancho went against Saragossa and fought against the king of Aragon at Graus, defeating and slaying him there, he took Rodrigo with him, so that Rodrigo was in the army and was present at Sancho's triumph. After this great victory, King Sancho returned to Castile.

Chapter 5

King Sancho thought so highly of Rodrigo Díaz, with so much affection and such great friendship, that he placed him in command over all his military forces. Rodrigo therefore had great success in the court of King Sancho, becoming the mightiest of warriors and winning the name of Campeador. In all the battles that Sancho fought and won against Alfonso, including Llantada and Golpejera, Rodrigo Díaz bore King Sancho's royal standard, distinguishing himself and gaining ascendancy among all the warriors in the king's army. . . .

Chapter 6

After the death of his lord King Sancho, who had supported him and loved him so much, he was received with all due honor as the vassal of King Alfonso, who retained him as a member of his entourage and showed him great respect and affection.

To Rodrigo Alfonso gave to wife his niece, the lady Jimena, with whom Rodrigo begat sons and daughters.

Chapter 7

Meanwhile, King Alfonso sent Rodrigo as an envoy to the kings of Seville and Cordoba, to collect from them the tribute money they owed Alfonso. At that time, the king of Seville, al-Mutamid, and the king of Granada, Almudafar, were on unfriendly terms. And on the king of Granada's side were García Ordóñez; Fortún Sánchez, the son-in-law of King García of Pamplona; Lope Sánchez, the brother of Fortún Sánchez; and Diego Pérez, one of the great lords of Castile. Each and every one of these came with his own following of knights to do battle with the king of Seville. When Rodrigo Díaz reached the palace of al-Mutamid, he was immediately told that the king of Granada, reinforced by a company of Christians, was advancing against al-Mutamid and his kingdom. Rodrigo then sent letters to the king of Granada, and to the Christians there with him, entreating them, for the sake of their lord, King Alfonso, not to march against the king of Seville, nor enter into his kingdom.

But they, sure of themselves because of their army's great numbers, not only refused to listen to his entreaties, but rejected them with the utmost contempt. They then advanced, laying waste to that whole country, as far as the castle that is called Cabra.

Chapter 8

No sooner had Rodrigo Díaz heard and confirmed the truth of these developments, than he immediately set out with his own forces to confront them, and there joined them in pitiless combat, a combat that kept both sides engaged from the third hour of the day to the sixth. And the greatest carnage and slaughter was done to the king of Granada's army, among Saracens and Christians alike, until at last they fled, routed and thrown into confusion, before Rodrigo Díaz. In this battle, Count García Ordóñez, Lope Sánchez, and Diego Pérez were taken prisoner, along with a great many of their men-at-arms. His victory won, Rodrigo held them prisoner for three days, after which, taking from them all their tents and plunder, he let them go free.

Chapter 9

As for Rodrigo, he returned to Seville, victory in hand. Al-Mutamid remitted to him the tribute payment for his lord King Alfonso, and, in addition to the tribute, many gifts and presents, which Rodrigo brought back to his lord. King Alfonso having received the aforementioned gifts and tribute payments, and the peace between him and King al-Mutamid having been reaffirmed, Rodrigo returned, covered in glory, to Castile and to his lord, King Alfonso.

Jealous at his triumph, and envious of the victory that God had vouchsafed him, many men—both strangers and even some close to him—went and accused him before the king of false and untrue things.

Chapter 10

As Rodrigo returned to Castile crowned with honor, as we have just mentioned, King Alfonso sped without delay, along with his army, to a Saracen country that had risen in revolt against him, determined to subdue that country once and for all, and thereby to enlarge and pacify his kingdom. At that time, Rodrigo, having fallen ill, stayed behind in Castile. The Saracen forces, meanwhile, arriving at a castle called Gormaz, took possession of it and won considerable spoils. When he heard news of this, Rodrigo, enraged and greatly distressed, exclaimed:

"I am going to go after those thieves, and maybe I can catch them."

He therefore assembled his army and, with each company having armed itself appropriately, he plundered the territory of Toledo, ravaged the Saracen country, and took seven thousand prisoners, both men and women, rigorously dispossessing them of all their property and wealth, and then taking everything back home with him.

Chapter 11

When King Alfonso and the principal men of his court heard about Rodrigo's feat of arms, they took it hard and were much vexed. These envious courtiers, seeing that this affair could be used against Rodrigo, said to the king, speaking as one man:

"Your Majesty, it should be obvious to Your Highness that Rodrigo has only done this so that all of us, living and raiding out here in Saracen country, may be slaughtered, dying at the hands of his Saracen friends."

Wrongly persuaded by this envious and underhanded denunciation, the king was stirred to anger and banished Rodrigo from his kingdom.

Chapter 12

Leaving his grieving friends behind, Rodrigo went forth from Castile and made his way to Barcelona. From there he went to Saragossa, where al-Muqtadir reigned as king. . . .

On the death of al-Muqtadir, in that same place, his kingdom was divided between his two sons, al-Mutamin and al-Hayib. The former reigned in Saragossa, and the latter in Denia.

This al-Mutamin thought very highly of Rodrigo, honoring him and exalting him over his whole kingdom and all his lands, and following his advice in all matters.

During this time there arose a baleful and virulent contention between al-Mutamin and his brother al-Hayib, so much so that they set a time and a place for settling the dispute between them by force of arms.

Sancho, the king of Aragon and Pamplona, along with Count Berenguer of Barcelona,[12] allied themselves with al-Hayib and joined forces with him. But Rodrigo Díaz was on al-Mutamin's side, serving him loyally and protecting and watching over his kingdom. For this reason King Sancho and Count Berenguer looked upon Rodrigo with particular ill will, and watched for a chance to take him by surprise.

Chapter 13

Hearing that Rodrigo intended to march from Saragossa to Monzón, King Sancho swore that there was no way Rodrigo would dare do such a thing. As soon as Rodrigo heard about the king's oath, he set out, stirred to anger, with his whole army, and went to set up his camp right under the noses of his foes,

---

12. The same count of Barcelona that figures in the *EC*.

the soldiers of al-Hayib. The next day, right in front of King San-
cho, Rodrigo entered into Monzón, and the king did not dare
go against him.

At this time, al-Mutamin and Rodrigo took counsel on the
matter of restoring and shoring up the defenses of the old cas-
tle known as Almenara. This was done without delay. Then, it
seems, a dispute again broke out between al-Mutamin and his
brother al-Hayib, this time leading them to ready themselves for
outright war.

Chapter 14

But al-Hayib allied himself with Count Berenguer, with the
count of Cerdaña, with the brother of the count of Urgel, and
also with the powerful lords of Besalú, Ampurdán, Rosellón,
and Carcassonne. All of these unanimously resolved to join al-
Hayib in laying siege to this same fortress of Almenara, and this
plan was immediately acted upon. They besieged the place,
therefore, and did battle with its defenders for many days, until
the castle's occupants began to run out of water.

Chapter 15

Rodrigo was then using the castle called Escarp as his base of
operations. Some time before he had taken possession of the
place, located between the rivers Segre and Cinca, at the same
time rigorously taking all its residents prisoner. While abiding
in that place, he sent a messenger to al-Mutamin to inform him
of the distress and hardship that afflicted Almenara, and to tell
him that all the castle's defenders seemed exhausted, worn out,
and reduced to the last extremity. A little while later, Rodrigo,
uneasy in his mind, sent other messengers bearing letters for al-
Mutamin, urging him to come to relieve the fortress that he had
rebuilt. Al-Mutamin then came without delay and found Ro-
drigo at the castle of Tamarite.

As the two of them met there and took counsel together,
al-Mutamin urged Rodrigo to attack the host that was besieg-
ing Almenara. But Rodrigo answered him:

"It would be better to offer him some kind of payment,
and get him to quit storming the castle, than to attempt to do

battle with him, because he has brought with him a great multitude of men-at-arms."

To this proposal al-Mutamin willingly agreed.

Rodrigo accordingly then sent, without delay, a messenger to the aforementioned counts and to al-Hayib, requesting that, on acceptance of a suitable payment, the besiegers lift their siege of the aforementioned castle. But they refused to accede to Rodrigo's proposals and to cease their assault on the castle. The messenger then returned to Rodrigo, conveying to him everything they had told him.

Chapter 16

Stirred to anger, Rodrigo ordered all his men-at-arms to arm themselves and prepare with firmest resolve for war. Quickly he marched with his army to a place where he could see al-Hayib and the counts previously mentioned on one side, and himself and his own forces on the other. Everywhere, amid war cries, the ranks on both sides charged forward, urged on by their leaders, and joined battle. But soon the previously mentioned counts and al-Hayib turned tail in defeat and fled in confusion before Rodrigo.

The majority of the enemy were killed, with only a few escaping. Their spoils, and all their supplies, fell into Rodrigo's hands. Count Berenguer was led away, a prisoner, to the castle of Tamarite, along with his knights. There, after the great victory he had obtained, Rodrigo handed them over to al-Mutamin. Five days later, however, he set them free and allowed them to return to their homeland.

Chapter 17

Rodrigo then returned with al-Mutamin to Saragossa, where he was welcomed by the citizens of the town with the greatest honor and acclaim. Indeed, al-Mutamin, in all his days, exalted and elevated Rodrigo to a place of great dignity and honor, setting him over his own son, over his kingdom, and over the entire country, so that Rodrigo seemed to have sovereignty over every one of al-Mutamin's realms. And he likewise rewarded Rodrigo with many gifts, and innumerable presents of gold and silver. . . .

C. THE SONG OF THE CAMPEADOR (CARMEN CAMPIDOCTORIS)

Anonymous
Ode composed in Latin verse sometime
between the early 1080s and 1190

A number of scholars have favored an early date of composition, possibly even several years before the Cid's death in 1099. Others have pointed to details suggesting a much later date. The varied evidence and its several interpretations are cogently presented by Alberto Montaner and Ángel Escobar in their introduction (see source below, 130–35). They favor a later date between 1181 and 1190; the reader is invited to decide which side's arguments are the more persuasive.

Having said that, I must point out that the work seems animated by an urgent desire to explain who Rodrigo is and to justify glorification of his exploits. This immediacy would seem to suggest a poet writing about a relative newcomer – a subject still living at the time of composition. Details pointing to later dates might result from material inserted by subsequent reworkers of the original version.

What has been said of The History of Rodrigo *– that it was remarkable in its telling the story of a man who was neither churchman, nor royal, nor of the highest nobility – may likewise be said of this panegyric on the martial excellencies of Rodrigo Díaz de Vivar. The tone and style echo Homer and Virgil. The unknown author, perhaps prompted by folklore, is converting the impressive historical man into a larger-than-life figure – a hero.*[13]

---

13. *Carmen Campidoctoris o Poema Latino del Campeador,* edited, translated, and commentary by Alberto Montaner and Ángel Escobar (Madrid: Sociedad Estatal España Nuevo Milenio, 2001), 198–211.

We could tell tales of the glorious deeds of Paris, Pyrrhus, and Aeneas. But these have already been recounted with great praise by many poets—what then would be the point?[14]

To what avail would we sing such deeds of pagans, since they have now lost all meaning, owing to their extreme antiquity? Let us now therefore sing instead the new wars of the great commander, Rodrigo.

What if I sought to recount all the feats of arms of so great a vanquisher? They would not find room in even a thousand books—even if, with utmost care and labor, Homer himself sang of them.

But, inexpert though I be, and although of all the things I should know I have only learned a few, I nonetheless, a fearful mariner, unfurl my sails before the wind.

Come then, all you people, gather around, your hearts filled with joy, and hear this song of the Campeador, and above all let those come forward who have learned to rely upon his might.

Born of a most noble lineage, than which there is no greater in Castile—Seville, and the banks of the Ebro, know full well who Rodrigo is.[15]

His first notable feat of arms was when, still a young man, he vanquished a Navarrese knight in battle. For this reason a new name for him was on the lips of his elders: Campeador.

Already he portended what he would accomplish, destined to overcome counts in battle, treading royal armies under his feat, subduing them with his sword.

King Sancho, king over the land, loved Rodrigo so much, seeing him, so young, scale such heights, that he decided to set him at the head of his royal guard.

Rodrigo showed himself reluctant to accept this honor, so Sancho meant to confer on him an even better one, and would have if he, Sancho, had not soon thereafter faced death, that spares no man.

---

14. Paragraph arrangement roughly approximates the stanza structure of the original.

15. Seville was at that time a great Muslim metropolis of the south, and thus exemplified Al-Andalus as an advanced and prosperous civilization; the Ebro River region meant, among numerous Christian and Muslim states, the emirate of Saragossa, and the powerful Christian realms of Aragon and Catalonia.

After Sancho's treacherous murder, King Alfonso came into possession of the land and from his brother inherited all Castile.[16]

In truth, no less did Alfonso take to loving Rodrigo, wishing to exalt him over all others, until Rodrigo's peers at court began to envy him.

They said to the king: "Lord, what are you doing? You work mischief against yourself, letting Rodrigo be raised up in this way. We find this most worrisome.

"Have no doubt: he will never love you, for he was a member of your brother's court. He will always be devising and carrying out some wickedness against you."

Having heard the words of these talebearers, King Alfonso, heart-struck with suspicion, dreading to lose the seat of honor, for fear's sake, turned all his love to wrath, looking for excuses to confront Rodrigo and charging him, on the grounds of a few things he knew, of other and greater things of which he could know nothing.

The king commanded the baron to be banished from the land. From that moment, Rodrigo began to undo Moors in battle, to devastate all the countries of Spain, to ravage cities.

Hearsay soon reached the king's court, to the effect that the Campeador, gathering together the elite of the Hagaritic tribe,[17] was preparing a trap for the king and his followers.

Furious, the king assembled his cavalry, planning the Campeador's death if he could catch him unawares, and ordering him, if captured, to be executed on the spot.

Against the Campeador the king sent Count García, a proud and prominent man. But then the Campeador doubled his triumph, taking possession of the field.

This, then, was the second battle, in which García was taken prisoner along with many others; that place, where the Campeador's forces also captured García's fortified camp, is called Cabra.

---

16. The treacherous murder of King Sancho by Vellid Adolfo, and events subsequent to it, are described in the *First General Chronicle* (see below, chapters 836 and following).

17. *Agaricae gentis* in the original, "of the Hagaritic tribe." According to tradition, the Arabs were believed to descend from Ishmael, the son of Abraham's concubine Hagar (Gen. 16).

Whence throughout Spain Rodrigo's name is held famous among all kings, who live in dread of him and likewise pay him tribute.

Then he undertook a third battle, which God permitted him to win; putting some to flight and capturing others, he subdued the enemy camp.

Then the Marquis, Count of Barcelona, to whom the Midianites[18] rendered tribute, and with him al-Fagib of Lérida, together with his army, besieged the fortress of Saragossa, which to this day the Moors call Almenara. The Conqueror requested that they yield the place to him and let him replenish his supplies.

Seeing that they spurned his request and denied him free passage in that country, he immediately ordered his men to arm themselves without delay.

And he was the first to put on his cuirass—no man ever saw a finer one—and, belting on his gilded, two-edged sword, wrought by a master hand, he took up the lance of wondrous make, hewn from the ash tree of a noble forest, its point whetted sharp, with hardest iron, by his order.

In his left hand he bore his shield, all shaped in gold, on which a fierce dragon was splendidly painted.

On his head he wore a shining helmet, that the armorer had adorned with silver plates, while fitting the piece all around with bands of electrum.[19]

Rodrigo mounted his horse, brought from across the sea by a barbarian who sold it for a mere thousand gold pieces—an animal that ran swifter than the wind, leapt higher than a deer.

Thus furnished with such splendid weapons and so fine a steed—not Paris, not Hector, in the Trojan war, were ever better than he, nor are any today his equal—he prayed most earnestly . . .

[Manuscript breaks off.]

---

18. *Midianites,* or Arabs. Midian was one of the six sons of Abraham by Keturah, whom the patriarch married after the death of Sarah (Gen. 25:1–6). The people named for him, the Midianites, were traditionally identified with the Bedouin tribes of northern Arabia.

19. *Electrum* is an alloy of gold and silver, pale yellow in color.

D. FIRST GENERAL CHRONICLE (PRIMERA CRÓNICA GENERAL)

Written under the sponsorship and with the
editorial participation of Alfonso X of Castile
Chronicle composed in Old Castilian in
the late thirteenth century

*The work from which the following selection is excerpted is also
known as the* General History (General Historia). *Composed
by the school of chroniclers of Alfonso X (reigned 1252 to 1284),
it was originally conceived as a complete history of the world,
starting with the biblical creation and culminating with the
reign of Fernando III in the mid-thirteenth century.*

*Also known as El Sabio ("the Wise"), Alfonso X was him-
self an accomplished poet and scholar. The law code redacted
under his sponsorship and direction, the* Siete Partidas *("The
Seven Divisions"), is among the earliest promulgated by the
emerging nation states of late-medieval Europe. Composed in
Castilian rather than in Latin, the* Partidas *and the* General
History *greatly contributed to the emergence of Castilian as a
standardized national vernacular.*

The title of First General Chronicle *was given to the work
by the renowned philologist and medievalist Ramón Menéndez
Pidal (1869–1968) in his widely read edition of Alfonso's his-
tory, first published in the early twentieth century and reprinted
several times. Historians and philologists have pointed out in-
consistencies in one of the two manuscripts on which Menén-
dez Pidal principally based his edition. Some parts of this
composite manuscript may date from the time of Alfonso, while
others may be insertions from a later date. The manuscript in
question probably dates from the late fourteenth or early fif-
teenth century.*

*Historians rightly emphasize such issues of dating, au-
thentication, and textual integrity. The medieval chroniclers'
concept of historiography, however, differed greatly from that of
the modern academic discipline of history. Alfonso's monu-
mental account, in the various manuscripts that convey it, bor-
rows from many sources, including versions of* The Epic of

the Cid, *that would be considered anecdotal, fictional, or folkloric by present-day standards. Even if somewhat problematic by today's historiographic standards, Menéndez Pidal's edition — readily available in many university and public libraries, and also from Google Books — presents a readable version of this often novelistic account. The following selection is presented, therefore, not as history but as an extended version of the back story to* The Epic of the Cid *— a background with which the epic narrator assumes his audience is familiar.*

The reader will remark a certain Shakespearean quality to the material. Divisions of kingdoms by old monarchs; murderous sibling rivalry among royal heirs; stalwart heroes and backstabbing courtiers; loyal and disloyal retainers; challenges and feuds; diplomacy and warfare — these are the stuff of pre-Renaissance chronicles, like those of Alfonso X's school, and also like those of Holinshed, on whose work Shakespeare drew so extensively.[20]

Chapter 813

How King Fernando, foreseeing with certainty the day of his death, divided his kingdoms and lands among his sons, and also provided for his daughters.

. . . Fearing that after his death there would be contention and strife among his children, King Fernando divided his kingdom among them in this fashion . . . [H]e gave to Don Sancho, who was the eldest, the lands from the River Pisuerga and beyond, including Castile and Nájera and all the lands this side of the Ebro; he gave to Don Alfonso, the middle son, León and Asturias . . . he gave to the lady Urraca, who was the elder daughter, the Leonese city of Zamora, and all the lands pertaining to it . . . he gave to Doña Elvira, the younger daughter, the town of Toro and its adjacent lands . . . and to Don García, the youngest son, the whole kingdom of Galicia, together with that

---

20. *Primera crónica general de España que mandó componer Alfonso el Sabio y se continuaba bajo Sancho IV en 1289*, edited by Ramón Menéndez Pidal, Antonio G. Solalinde, Manuel Muñoz Cortés, and José Gómez Pérez. 2 vols. (Madrid: Editorial Gredos, 1955).

part of the kingdom of Portugal that he himself, King Fernando, had conquered.

When King Fernando had made this division of his lands among his sons and daughters, Prince Sancho, who was the eldest, disagreed with his father's action and felt much aggrieved by it. And he told his father that he could not do this, for the ancient Goths had agreed among themselves never to divide up the empire of Spain, deciding, rather, that it should always be under the rule of a single lord. For this reason King Fernando should not and could not divide his kingdom among his heirs, since God had seen fit to unite the greater part of Spain into one country. And King Fernando replied that he would not change his mind on that account. Don Sancho then replied:

"You do as you please, but I do not consent to this."

And so matters stood with regard to King Sancho.

A few days later, King Fernando fell sick and had himself conveyed to León, entering into that city on the twenty-fourth of December. There, as was his custom, he knelt down to adore the saints buried in that place, beseeching them to pray for his soul and to ask that the angels carry him to heaven. That same Christmas Eve, the king sang matins with the churchmen, the best he could, although he was sick. At daybreak he called for the bishops, and they sang the high mass for him, whereupon he made his general confession regarding everything he could recall up to that point in his life, down to the least detail. He then received the body of Our Lord Jesus Christ.

At that point he summoned Ruy Díaz, the Cid, who was there at that time, and commended his children into the Cid's safekeeping, bidding him counsel them well and truly, and stand by them whenever they might need help. And he bade his children swear not to do violence to one another, and to live in peace in the domains he had bequeathed them, for they were all well provided for. He also made the brothers swear that they would take nothing from their sisters, but rather look after them. And they all promised him, then and there, that they would comply with his wishes, the Cid vowing to carry out his lord's commands, and the sons and daughters likewise — all save Sancho, who refused to make any public concession regarding the division of the kingdom. On the same occasion, the king admonished all his children to be guided by the counsel of the Cid Ruy Díaz, and to honor their father's testament.

On Christmas day, King Fernando ordered that the bishops and abbots be summoned into his presence, along with all the other clergymen. He had himself conveyed to the church and donned his finest garments, as befits a king. And placing the crown on his head, as he knelt before the body of Saint Isidore, the king cried out to God in these words:

"Lord, Thine is the power and Thine the kingdom, and Thou art king over all kings, ruler over all peoples, and all things are subject to Thy command. Now, oh Lord, I give Thee back the land Thou gavest me. I beseech Thee: have mercy on my soul and grant it may abide in everlasting light."

When King Fernando had spoken these words to God, he stripped himself of the fine garments he wore, snatched off the crown from his head, and dressed himself in haircloth. Praying again to God, he made a complete confession of all the sins he had ever committed, and received absolution from the bishops for all his sins, for they absolved him of all of them. Then he received extreme unction, and covered himself with ashes, living on after that for two more days, weeping contritely the whole while.

On the third day, on the Feast of Saint John the Evangelist, at the sixth hour, having already lived many days, he surrendered his soul, now spotless, to God. And he was buried right next to his father, in that same church of Saint Isidore. . . .

Chapter 814

What King Sancho did at the beginning of his reign.

. . . and according to the division the king their father had made for them, Don Sancho, the eldest brother, was to rule in Castile, and Don Alfonso, the middle son, in León, and Don García, the youngest, in Galicia and Portugal. But . . . King Sancho, as soon as he began to govern and to go about in his assigned kingdom, gave thought to the matter and considered that he was the firstborn and rightful heir, that his father had divided up all the kingdoms that God had seen fit to unite under his rule, and that his father should have left him, the rightful heir, all these kingdoms. Instead he had been bequeathed only a third of his inheritance, and even that was diminished. All this vexed him exceedingly, arousing such anger in him that he could not bear it. And because . . . a lord cannot abide any sharing of lordship within his domain, and even lesser lords refuse to recognize anyone's having authority over them; and, furthermore, because the kings of Spain descended from the fierce blood of the Goths—for it so happened that many times among the Gothic kings brother slew brother over such questions of authority and inheritance—this King Sancho, descendant of the lineage of the Goths and eldest son and heir to King Fernando, was not satisfied with the kingdom of Castile nor with all that he possessed of Navarre. Seeking to recover the lands controlled by his brothers and sisters, and determining that their possession of those lands should be subject to his will and authority, he began to treat them in the most aggressive fashion. Many people died on account of this resolution of his, and much blood came to be shed.

King Fernando had entrusted his daughters Doña Urraca and Doña Elvira to the care of Don Alfonso, his son and their brother, holding the latter to be gentler and more moderate than the other two brothers. And Doña Urraca was a very wise and perceptive lady, and King Alfonso, regarding her almost more as a mother than as a sister, treated her with the greatest respect and was guided by her counsel. . . .

Chapter 817

How Ruy Díaz, My Cid, counseled King Sancho concerning the action Sancho was determined to undertake against his brother King García.

. . . in the third year of King Sancho's reign, as he was dealing with Saragossa, and engaged in the conflict with King Ramiro of Aragon . . . his brother, King García of Portugal, wrested from their sister Urraca half the territory bequeathed to her by their father, King Fernando.

Learning of this, she fell to weeping bitterly, and cried out:

"Oh, King Fernando! In an evil hour did you divide your kingdom! . . . for now all Spain will fall into ruin on our account. King García, my younger brother, is the one who has disinherited me, rather than either of the other two, who are older. He has violated the oath he swore to his father, disobeying the king's command and ignoring the mandate that he himself promised to uphold. I pray to God that he be disinherited in this world and the next."

King Sancho, whose relations with his brothers were already strained, was much vexed when he heard this news and considered that his sister had been greatly wronged. But, at the same time, he was pleased, for he considered that this situation offered him the pretext and ready means by which he might proceed against his brothers. He said:

"Now then, since my brother King García has violated the oath he swore to our father, I am going to take his kingdom away from him, for in this I shall be in no way more perjured than he is, considering the offense he has committed against our sister Doña Urraca."

And right after this he sent his highest-ranking nobles, along with a company of knights, chosen from among his most trusted vassals, bidding them tell his brother King García to cease from acting so wrongly and violently against their sister Doña Urraca, depriving her of her rightful inheritance. Rather he should restore her lands, as was only right, and remember what he and his brothers had promised their father King Fernando, solemnly swearing to hold to the division imposed by him. Sancho told them to determine if King García intended to do as his brother King Sancho asked, and, if not, to inform King García that he, Sancho, would do what he saw fit regarding this matter.

Thus did King Sancho hold audience regarding this affair, consulting in private with his most valued and trusted vassals. Speaking to them more for show than for any other motive, he reasoned thusly:

"My good lords, you know how my father left me and my brothers in a very quarrelsome situation, for the kingdom that should have been mine was divided by him into five parts. And I, the eldest and by rights the sole heir to the whole kingdom, do not enjoy possession of it and am thereby greatly wronged. I therefore pray you, as my good and faithful vassals, to counsel me as to how I might go against my brothers while avoiding the charge of treachery. For I will die if I do not become king of Portugal and León."

Thereupon Count García arose and said to him:

"My lord, who could ever advise you in an affair such as this? For I know of no man anywhere who could rightly counsel you in any attempt to trespass against the will and oath of your father, who declared that anyone who went against what he had established should be considered a traitor."

When King Sancho heard this, he was stirred to wrath against Count García, and angrily declared:

"Remove yourself from my presence! For I can no longer look to you for wise counsel."

Then, taking the Cid by the hand and leading him off to one side, King Sancho said to him:

"I pray you to advise me as to how to proceed in this matter, and to remember now what my father told you as he was about to die: that the man who let himself be guided by you would not be ill advised. For this reason I gave you a county within my domains. And now, if I cannot look to you for help, I cannot rely on anybody else in this world."

Whereupon the Cid replied:

"My lord, it does not seem appropriate to me to advise you to go against your father's will and testament. For you know quite well that when I came to Cabezón, your father had already divided up the kingdom. And when I came into his presence, he made me swear, holding my hands in his, to advise his sons the very best I could and to the best of my knowledge, and never give bad advice. And as long as I am able, I will do exactly as I promised."

King Sancho then replied to the Cid:

"Cid, I don't consider myself to be going against my father's will, for he had no right to divide up the kingdom, nor did I give my consent when he did so. I was never happy with his decision, and immediately declared my opposition to his plan. And I therefore wish you to advise me how I might restore the land to the way it was in my father's day: one united kingdom."

The Cid, when he saw that the king was not to be dissuaded from his objective, and that there was no way for him, the Cid, to rightly remain silent on the matter, gave Sancho the following advice. He should, with all brotherly affection, ask his brother Don Alfonso for free passage through his kingdom. If he could not obtain this favor, the Cid advised, Sancho should renounce his plan.

Then King Sancho considered that the Cid had given him good advice and immediately sent letters to his brother King Alfonso, asking to meet with him in Sahagún. And King Alfonso, as soon as he read his brother's letters, wondered what this request might be about, but replied nonetheless that he would be pleased to meet with his brother. Soon after, the two kings met in Sahagún on the appointed day.

There King Sancho told his brother King Alfonso, as they sat together talking, of the reason why they were meeting there:

"Don Alfonso, our father left us, sinners that we are, a realm badly divided. He gave King García the greater share of the kingdom, while you ended up the most disinherited of us all, with the least portion of land. For this reason I think it proper to deprive and dispossess King García of the land our father gave him."

King Alfonso said, then and there, that he would on no account do such a thing, nor would he in any way go against their father's will, for he was quite content with what he had.

To these words King Sancho replied:

"Brother, grant me free passage through your kingdom, and I will take his away from him. And all that I win there I will divide between us, equally."

This conversation being concluded in the manner just described, King Sancho, because he did not feel that he had obtained a straight answer from King Alfonso, requested yet another meeting. Concerning this they set a day on which to meet a second time. And they presented, on each side, trustworthy vassals to stand surety for what they agreed upon, twenty from León, twenty from Castile, to insure they would hold to whatever pact they made there. And when this business was concluded, each of the two kings went back to his own country.

Chapter 818

How King Sancho sent to challenge his brother King García.

King Sancho then gathered together, to go against his brother King García, a great host of Castilians, Leonese, Asturians, Navarese, Biscayans, and Extremadurans, and along with these many stout knights from Aragon. And he thereupon summoned Álvar Fáñez, a noble knight who was nephew to the Cid, and spoke thus to him:

"Álvar Fáñez, go and tell my brother King García to hand over Galicia to me, and if he refuses, tell him that I challenge him to single combat."

Although it troubled him greatly to be the one to convey such a message to King García, his lord's brother, Álvar Fáñez was bound to carry out the orders of King Sancho, his natural lord. And appearing before King García he declared:

"King Sancho, your brother, sends me to tell you to hand over Galicia, and if not, to inform you that he challenges you to single combat."

When King García heard this, he was troubled in his heart and deeply distressed. Plaintively he cried out to God:

"Jesus Christ, our Lord: remember the pledge and oath we made to our father King Fernando, to the effect that whoever should disobey his command, and go against his brother, should be held a traitor on that account, and be subject to his wrath and God's. And, base sinner that I am, I was the first to overstep, in taking away from my sister Urraca the inheritance our father had bequeathed her."

After uttering these words he said to Álvar Fáñez:

"Go and tell my brother King Sancho that he should not seek to violate his father's will and testament. But if he chooses to disregard my warning, I will be ready to defend myself as best I can."

After this, Álvar Fáñez took his leave of King García and went back to King Sancho. King García then summoned an Asturian knight named Ruy Jiménez, telling him to go to his brother King Alfonso and inform him that their brother King Sancho had challenged García and was seeking to deprive him, García, of his kingdom. And he earnestly entreated his brother King Alfonso to take pity on him in this plight and to deny their brother passage through his kingdom. The knight immediately traveled to the court of King Alfonso and conveyed the whole message, just as his lord had told him to.

When King Alfonso heard this message, he responded thus to the knight:

"Tell my brother King García that I will neither help nor hinder our brother, and that if he, García, manages to defend himself, I will be pleased."

The knight returned with this answer to King García and declared to him:

"My lord, to my way of thinking you must look to fortify yourself as best you can, for you can in no way rely on your brother King Alfonso for any help whatsoever."

Chapter 819

How King García's knights abandoned him.

This king García, although the youngest of the three brothers, was, according to the histories, very resolute of character. When he heard the message his brother King Sancho sent to him, he immediately sought to gather together an army to go against the invader. And in that time King García had in his service a certain advisor, by whom he was guided in all things and to whom he entrusted all his dealings and secrets. And this advisor was at odds with all the nobles of the kingdom, opposing them in everything they sought to accomplish. The nobles, seeing the great harm that came to them from this man's contrary attitude, begged the king, out of consideration for them, to dismiss the man from his service. But the king, ignoring all their demands, would have none of it.

When they saw the harm and mischief that they were subjected to on account of this man, they killed him, right in front of the king. The king became enraged at this and was exceedingly vexed, considering himself highly dishonored by the way they killed his advisor right in front of him. Angrily confronting them, he rebuked them bitterly and began to interfere with them in their affairs, much more persistently than he had ever done before, and warned them that they would never again be in his good graces nor enjoy his affection. And they, fearing his threats and resenting the indignities he subjected them to, began one by one to depart his court and abandon his service. . . .

Chapter 820

How King Sancho and King García warred against each other, and how King Sancho first vanquished King García.

. . . and King Sancho, seeing himself at the head of a numerous army, went against Galicia. And finding the king his brother estranged from the great nobles of his kingdom, in the way we have described in the previous chapter, King Sancho entered the land and easily took possession of it, sending out his raiding parties and pillaging the countryside all around.

Responding to all this, King García quickly sent out his couriers and criers, telling them to go throughout the land urgently summoning to his aid every able-bodied knight and footman capable of bearing arms. Thus he gathered a numerous host in Villafranca de Valcárcel. Meanwhile, the counts Nuño de Lara, Enzón, and García de Cabra, in the vanguard of King Sancho's army, approached with a numerous force of cavalry.

King García sallied forth intrepidly to meet them, and the combat they engaged in there was a great and hard-fought one, so that fully three hundred of King Sancho's knights were killed, and more than twice as many on the other side. And, as the history of these matters tells us, what Arias Gonzalo had foretold came to pass: that brother would kill brother, and kinsman would kill kinsman, over who should rule those kingdoms.

When King Sancho learned of the casualties suffered by his vassals, he rode forth as quickly as he could, with all the forces he could muster, to come to their aid. But King García, as he saw King Sancho coming, did not tarry to wait for him but rather took flight. And King Sancho sped after him in hot pursuit, all the way to Portugal, never stopping once.

Chapter 822

How King García captured King Sancho, and how Sancho was set free by Álvar Fáñez, one of his knights.

. . . King García was at that time in Portugal, in the town called Santa Aren, and King Sancho launched an all-out attack against the place . . . and as they all took the field, with battle ranks forming and both sides eager to fight, King García exhorted his followers in these words:

"Friends and vassals, you all see the great wrong that my brother King Sancho does me in seeking to wrest from me the land my father gave me. I pray you therefore grieve at my distress and come to my aid, for you know well that ever since I have been king, I have shared everything I have with you: property, horses, weapons. And I have cherished you for just such an occasion, and just such a day, as this."

And they, to show their heartfelt love for him . . . declared:

"Lord, you have shared most generously and given us much wealth. And today you will be very well rewarded, as much as is in our power."

Thereupon, as the opposing forces were ready to join battle against each other, the knight called Álvar Fáñez, whom we mentioned earlier, appeared before King Sancho, and called out to him:

"I have lost the horse and weapons I had. And if it please your highness to provide me with a horse and weapons, I will fight for you in today's battle like six knights, and if not, regard me as a traitor."

And Count García said to the king:

"My lord, give him what he asks of you."

And King Sancho accordingly replied:

"I am pleased, and will gladly do so."

And he ordered Álvar Fáñez to be immediately provided with horse and weapons.

Then the battle began, up and down the line, and many knights died, along with other men-at-arms, on both sides . . . and the Castilians were getting the worst of it . . . and King Sancho was thrown to the ground from his horse, taken prisoner by his brother King García, and placed in the keeping of six knights. . . .

And King Sancho said to the six knights who held him under guard:

"My lords, let me go, and I will leave this kingdom of yours and never again do you any further harm or mischief. What's more, I will share everything I have with you."

They declared they would not do this under any circumstances, but that they would hold him there under guard, leaving him otherwise unharmed until King García arrived.

And while they were thus engaged, Álvar Fáñez arrived, the knight whom King Sancho had provided with a horse and weapons as the battle was about to begin. He cried out to the knights who held the king:

"Let King Sancho go, you traitors!"

Saying this he charged right into them, knocking two of them down and driving away the others. Taking possession of the horses of the two knights he had overcome, he gave one to King Sancho, who immediately leapt into the saddle, and kept the other for himself. . . . and King Sancho was thus set free at that time. . . . [Álvar Fáñez] then led his lord to a hilltop, where a number of Sancho's knights were gathered.

Addressing them, he cried out:

"My lords, behold your king and lord, Don Sancho. Be mindful now of the renown you Castilians have always enjoyed, and look to see that it remains untarnished."

At this point four hundred knights arrived, of those who had just been defeated in battle. And while they were gathered there, they saw the Cid arrive with three hundred knights, for it chanced that he had not yet gotten there by the time the battle had begun . . . and when Sancho saw that it was Ruy Díaz, My Cid, who had just arrived with reinforcements, he rejoiced at the sight of him, and declared to his vassals:

"Friends, let us now go down from here, out into the plain, for My Cid is come. Have no fear, for now we shall surely prevail."

And he went to meet the Cid, welcoming him warmly, saying to him:

"You are most welcome, Cid, you lucky man! Never did a vassal come in more timely fashion to the aid of his lord, than you do here and now, for me."

Then the Cid replied:

"Believe me, my lord, I'll see you get even and win the field today, or die trying."

Chapter 823

How King Sancho, fighting for a second time against his brother King García, captured him, threw him in irons, and imprisoned him in the castle of Luna.

As King Sancho and the Cid were thus occupied, King García was still engaged in the pursuit he had undertaken. He was in the highest spirits as they rode along, telling his knights, in lavish detail, how he had vanquished King Sancho and now held him prisoner. And as he thus made his way, a message arrived for him, informing him of King Sancho's escape, how the prisoner had been forcibly rescued from the custody of the six knights King García had assigned to guard him, and how his brother was now determined to resume the fight.

When King García heard this, he was sick at heart, but there was nothing he could do. Soon thereafter the battle began anew, and was even more hard-fought than the first one. Both sides contended fiercely, but in the end the Portuguese abandoned King García and took flight . . . and Ruy Díaz, My Cid, took King García prisoner and handed him over to his lord, King Sancho. And King Sancho ordered King García to be thrown into irons and conveyed to Luna, a well-fortified castle, and García remained a prisoner in that castle for nineteen years.

Chapter 824

How King Sancho of Castile and his brother King Alfonso of León warred against each other . . . and how King Alfonso was vanquished.

After King Sancho had accomplished the things we have related, he immediately attacked his brother Don Alfonso, marauding throughout his realm. When King Alfonso saw what was happening, he straightaway undertook to defend himself against his brother. They agreed to a time and place in which to meet and do battle, with the winner to take over the kingdom of the loser.

And they came on the day set aside to the place called Llantada, and both sides fought there. And thus it was that King Sancho prevailed, and pursued his brother King Alfonso, although many perished on both sides. And in this battle Ruy Díaz, My Cid, fought most valiantly. And the fate so frequent among the Moors, that of brothers killing brothers, fell this time to the lot of the Christians. And King Alfonso, vanquished, retreated to León. Soon after, he and King Sancho agreed to do battle once again, with the loser to relinquish his kingdom, without further contention, to the winner.

Chapter 825

How King Alfonso and King Sancho fought for a second time, this time in Golpejera, and how both were captured and taken prisoner, and how King Sancho was rescued by Ruy Díaz, My Cid.

. . . the history tells how King Sancho and King Alonso met yet again in Golpejera, near the river Carrión, and how many on both sides fought and died there. In the end, King Sancho, vanquished, fled the field. King Alfonso, taking pity on his fellow Christians, ordered his men to leave off the pursuit and to refrain from any further killing.

When that noble and most valiant knight, Ruy Díaz My Cid Campeador, saw his lord a beaten man, he bade him take heart, and spoke to him in these words:

"My lord, the Leonese are now with your brother King Alfonso, safe at home and thinking you pose no threat to them. Have your men turn back, the ones who have fled, and gather them all around you. And tomorrow at dawn strike that host of Leonese and Asturians and take them by surprise. For they and the Galicians are used to boasting when things go well for them. They swagger, and show off, and make fun of their enemies. They'll spend the whole night bragging about the day's doings, and by morning they'll all be sound asleep."

Things turned out just as the Cid had predicted. King Sancho and his forces attacked them just at the time the Cid had advised, killing many, taking many others prisoner, and putting the rest to flight. King Alfonso himself was captured in the church of Santa María of Carrión.

When the Leonese saw that their lord had been captured, they turned and, charging fiercely into the ranks of King Sancho's army, took him prisoner as well. When the Cid saw his lord captured and carried off by fourteen Leonese knights, he rode after them, crying out:

"Knights of King Alfonso, give me back my lord, and I will give you back yours."

They answered him:

"We are all Christians, and we have no desire to do you harm, Don Ruy Díaz. So turn back and go in peace, otherwise we will take you prisoner along with your lord."

Thereupon the Cid replied:

"Let one of you give me a lance, for I don't have one with me. You will see how, with God's help, I will rescue my lord from you all by myself, against the fourteen of you."

And the knights, scorning the chances of one knight against fourteen, gave him a lance. And the Cid fought all of them, handling himself so deftly in the give-and-take of combat that he slew them all—all save one who gave up, exhausted. Ruy Díaz, My Cid, spared this one's life.

And thus, as we have related, the Cid freed his lord and returned with him to the Castilian host. At the same time, they took King Alfonso, still a prisoner, back with them to Burgos.

In Chapters 826 and 827, Doña Urraca persuades Sancho to release Alfonso, on condition that the latter become a monk in the monastery of Sahagún. Alfonso escapes from the monastery and goes into exile at the court of al-Ma'mun, the Moorish king of Toledo, where he is treated as an honored guest. Both Alfonso and his host overhear two of the latter's Moorish subjects discuss a dream that seems to foretell Alfonso's eventual conquest of Toledo. Urged by his counselors to put Alfonso to death, the Moorish king refuses, but requires his guest to swear never to harm al-Ma'mun or his family. Alfonso swears a solemn oath, and the two men become fast friends.

In the following two chapters, Sancho takes possession of the kingdom of León and has himself crowned king. Soon Urraca hears that Sancho intends to take her kingdom of Zamora away from her, and the town of Toro from their sister Elvira as well. Proceeding against Toro, Sancho conquers the town, disinheriting Elvira. He then sends word to Urraca, commanding her to surrender Zamora to him. At the same time, he promises to provide handsomely for her for the rest of her days. She replies that she will never surrender the kingdom bequeathed to her by their father, King Fernando. Sancho, on the advice of his counselors, decides to winter in Burgos, waiting until the following summer to undertake the siege of Zamora.

Chapter 830

How King Sancho besieged Zamora.

In the seventh year of the reign of Don Sancho, king of Castile, León, Galicia, and Portugal . . . with many of his followers gathered in Sahagún, on the day he had ordered them to appear, King Sancho was much pleased to hear that his command had been obeyed. In his delight at this, as the history tells us, he raised his hands up to God and twice exclaimed:

"Praise be to Thee, oh Lord! Praise be to Thee! For you have delivered to me the kingdoms that were my father's."

When he had spoken these words, he ordered it to be proclaimed throughout the city of Burgos that everyone should go out from the town and await his signal . . . and the king went to Sahagún, where his host was waiting for him. There he camped outside the town. And that night, at the end of the first hour, he ordered the entire host to move out. They traveled so quickly that on the third day they reached Zamora and camped there on the banks of the Duero.

The king ordered it to be proclaimed throughout the host that everyone was to remain calm and at peace, and to refrain from attacking anyone until he gave the order. After that, the king rode with the vassals closest to him, all around the city. He saw how it was built on a steep crag, with massive walls and high towers likewise fortified with very thick walls. On one side, the waters of the Duero came right up to the foot of the walls.

The king said to the men who accompanied him:

"Now see how strongly built this town is. I don't think it could be attacked by Moors or Christians. If I could get this place away from my sister, either paying for it or by some kind of trade, I would become the lord of all Spain."

Now we will tell what King Sancho did next.

Chapter 831

How King Sancho sent a message to his sister Doña Urraca, ordering her to surrender Zamora to him.

After King Sancho had looked the city over and spoken to his vassals in the manner just described, he returned to his encampment. Having sent for the Cid, he said to him:

"Cid, you know how my father brought you up in his own household, in the most honorable fashion, and how he himself knighted you and placed you in charge of his residence in Coimbra, after he took that place from the Moors. And on his deathbed, in Cabezón, he entrusted you with the safekeeping of all his children, just as we all swore to him that we would look after you. I made you the lord and majordomo of my household, and gave you a portion of my lands bigger even than a county. And now I most urgently beseech you, as my friend and faithful vassal, to go to Zamora and tell my sister Doña Urraca, yet again, to hand over Zamora to me, either in exchange for some payment in property, or by making some kind of trade. The trade I propose is this: I will give her Medina de Rioseco, with all its dependencies, from Villalpando to Valladolid, and even Tiedra, which is a very fine castle. I will swear to her, before twelve of my vassals, never again to break my oath to her, nor any other agreement that I ever make with her. And if she refuses this offer, tell her that I will take the place from her by force."

Then the Cid kissed King Sancho's hand, saying:

"My lord, for any other this would be a most grievous task to undertake, but one appropriate for me, since I was brought up in Zamora, where your father sent me to be raised, along with Doña Urraca, in the house of Don Arias Gonzalo. I know Don Arias and all his children, and therefore I will gladly do what you command me to."

The Cid then took his leave of King Sancho and went in to Zamora with fifteen of his knights. As he approached the town, he called out to the guards stationed in the towers, telling them not to shoot their arrows at him and his men, since he was Ruy Díaz, the Cid, sent with a message from King Sancho for his sister, Doña Urraca. He bade them go and ask her if she gave permission for the Cid to come in to the city.

A knight came out, a nephew of Don Arias Gonzalo who was stationed on guard at the gate. He invited the Cid to come in, and told him he would arrange suitable lodgings for him while he went to ask the lady Urraca if she would grant an audience. The Cid told him that this proposal was quite acceptable, and agreed to do as the man suggested.

The knight went to see the lady Urraca and told her that the Cid was in the town, having come with a message from her brother, King Sancho. And she declared that she would be pleased to meet with him, telling the man to conduct the Cid into her presence, so that she could hear what he had to say. She ordered Don Arias Gonzalo to go and welcome the Cid, accompanied by all the knights there in attendance.

And when the Cid came in to the palace, the lady Urraca greeted him warmly, telling him that he was most welcome. As the two of them sat down, the lady Urraca spoke out, before any other words were spoken:

"Cid, you know that we were brought up together, here in the house of Arias Gonzalo. You remember how my father,

King Fernando, on his deathbed, charged you with advising his children, to the best of your knowledge and ability. I therefore pray you tell me what King Sancho intends to do. For I see him here, having gathered all of Spain around him, and any other country it might have occurred to him to go to."

Then the Cid replied to her:

"Lady Urraca, he who bears a message should remain unharmed. If you grant me leave to speak freely, I will convey the message your brother King Sancho has sent me to tell you."

She told him then that she would do whatever Don Arias Gonzalo told her to. And Don Arias told her that it was well to listen to the message her brother had sent to her:

"For if perchance he intends to go against the Moors and wants to ask you for help, it would be well for you to do so. I would send him fifteen of my sons, well equipped with horses, weapons, and supplies, even for as many as ten years."

The lady Urraca then told the Cid to speak freely and say what he had to say. My Cid spoke thus:

"King Sancho, your brother, sends greetings to you and tells you to hand Zamora over to him, either in exchange for some payment of money, or in trade for something else. He offers you by way of trade Villalpando, as far as Valladolid, and in addition, Medina de Rioseco, with all its dependencies, and Tiedra, a fine and well-built castle. He will swear to you, with twelve of his barons standing witness, that this is a firm offer, and that he will never play you false regarding it. And if you refuse to give him what he wants, he says to tell you he will take it from you."

Now we will tell what the princess did.

Chapter 832

Concerning the discussion between the lady Urraca and the inhabitants of Zamora as to whether she should surrender the town to King Sancho.

When the lady Urraca had listened to this ultimatum from King Sancho, she was very apprehensive and sick at heart. She exclaimed, weeping bitter tears:

"Oh, woe is me! What am I going to do, with all this bad news I keep hearing, ever since my father died? My brother

Sancho has wrested our brother García's lands from him, taken him prisoner, and thrown him in irons. There he lies, even now, punished as if he were a thief, some ordinary felon. Sancho has also wrested Alfonso's kingdom from him, driving him from the land and into Moorish country, as if he were a traitor. He would not allow anyone to accompany him, and Alfonso would be alone if it weren't for Pedro Ansúrez and his brothers, whom I sent to be with him. From my sister the lady Elvira he has taken Toro, against her will, and now he wants to take Zamora away from me. Let the earth now open up and swallow me down, that I may not endure so many woes."

Overcome with rage, it is said that she spoke these words against her brother King Sancho:

"I am just a woman, and he knows full well that I can't fight with him. But I can have him killed, either secretly or out in public."

Don Arias Gonzalo then got up and spoke before all the good men of Zamora and all members of the town council summoned to assembly there by the lady Urraca:

"Lady Urraca, you gain nothing by complaining and bemoaning your fate, for the best and most sensible thing to do is to take counsel in time of gravest trouble and choose the best course of action. Let us now do this: order all the townsfolk of Zamora to meet in council in the Plaza of San Salvador, and let us determine if they want to stand by you, seeing that your father left them under your authority. And if they should indeed wish to stand by you and defend the town, do not hand it over for anything, neither for money nor in exchange for some other place. And if they do not want to do this, we should all immediately take our leave and head for Toledo, to live among the Moors, like your brother King Alfonso."

The lady Urraca, like the shrewd and sensible woman she was, did as her one-time guardian advised her, and immediately ordered proclamation to be made throughout the town, to the effect that all the townsfolk should gather in the Plaza of San Salvador. And when they were all gathered there together, the lady Urraca addressed them:

"Friends and vassals, I have come here before you to make known to you how my brother King Sancho has sent to tell me to hand over the town to him, for money or in exchange for another place. If I do not agree, he intends to take the town by force. And if you all are determined to stand firm and defend the place, like good and faithful vassals, I will not surrender. I ask you now to give me your answer."

At that moment, an elder named Nuño, one of the town's most respected residents, got to his feet. With the consent of the town council and the encouragement of all, he declared:

"Lady, God bless you for wishing to honor us in coming to our meeting. We are your vassals, and we will never forsake you, as long as we live. And standing with you, we will eat up all the food there is here rather then hand over the city without your consent."

When princess Urraca heard this reply from the town council of Zamora, she rejoiced in her heart. She said to the Cid:

"Cid, now you have heard what my loyal councilmen of Zamora have to say to this ultimatum, and with the agreement of all the townsfolk. Go and tell my brother that I would sooner die here with all the folk in Zamora than hand over the town, whether in a trade or for money."

The Cid then took his leave and returned to tell King Sancho exactly how things stood, namely, that Urraca and her subjects would on no account hand over the town to him.

Now we will tell you what happened after this.

Chapter 833

How King Sancho flew into a rage and ordered the Cid to leave his kingdom, and how he then changed his mind and sent for him.

Returning with the answer to the king's ultimatum, the Cid told King Sancho what the lady Urraca and her subjects had said, to the effect that they would never, on any account, hand over the city. The king, when he heard this reply and saw that they would never surrender, flew into a rage against the Cid and said to him:

"You advised my sister to do this, because you were brought up with her in this town. And if it weren't for the fact that my father commended me to you, I would have you killed for this, right here and now. And I order you now to be gone from my land, within nine days' time, so that I may never again find you anywhere within my kingdom."

The Cid went immediately to his tent, asking for his vassals, his attendants, and his friends, and left that very night to take lodging in Castro Nuño. And he decided to go into Moorish country, in Toledo, where King Alfonso had gone into exile.

When all the counts and principal barons of the king's host learned of this, they went straight to King Sancho and declared:

"Your majesty, you must not even think of losing a vassal such as the Cid, not on any account. Send for him, we beg you, and do not send him from you, for your cause will be very greatly weakened if you do."

The king, seeing that they were in the right, summoned a knight named Diego Ordóñez, who was the son of Count Ordoño and the nephew of Count García, nicknamed the curly-haired man of Grañón.[21]

The king said to Diego:

"Go quickly, and tell the Cid that I ask him to return to me, and if he does so it will be as my good and faithful vassal, and that I will give to him, from my lands, yet another county and will exalt him over all other members of my household."

Diego Ordóñez rode out speedily, and caught up with the Cid as quickly as he could. When the Cid saw him, he greeted him warmly, asking why he had come. To this Diego replied:

"The king sends to tell you that he wishes you to come back to him, and that he will give you, in addition to the lands you already have, yet another county within his kingdom. He promises always to treat you right, and to exalt you over all others in his household. What he said to you before, telling you to be gone from the land, was only because he was furious with his sister, the lady Urraca."

The Cid then replied to Diego Ordóñez that he would consult with his vassals and do as they advised him to.

The Cid immediately called together his friends and vassals and told them the message Diego Ordóñez had brought from the king. His vassals advised him to return to the king, since Sancho had sent for him. For it was better to remain with

---

21. This is the same personage, nicknamed "Curly-Head," who figures in the *EC*. See also below, *FGC*, chapter 838.

his lord, and in his rightful place, than to go into exile among the Moors in foreign lands.

The Cid considered that his vassals had given him good advice. He summoned Don Diego and told him that he wanted to do as his lord commanded. And Don Diego immediately sent word on ahead to the king. The king rode out two leagues' distance, with a company of five hundred knights, to welcome the Cid. And when the Cid saw the king, he jumped down from his horse and went to kiss the king's hand, asking him to please grant the favor that he, the king, had promised when he sent Diego Ordóñez to bring him back. And the king granted this request, then and there before all those assembled knights, and assured the Cid that ever afterward he would always be treated very well.

Then the king returned to his host, and everyone rejoiced along with the Cid, and kept him company . . .

Chapter 834

How King Sancho warred against Zamora, and how Don Arias Gonzalo gave the lady Urraca certain advice.

After all these doings, the king held council with his principal barons and others who were there, concerning how to conduct the war against Zamora. He ordered it proclaimed throughout the host that all should prepare themselves to attack the city on the following day.

And then they stormed the town furiously for three days and three nights. The moats, which were very deep, were quickly filled up with earth and stones, and the fill tamped down flat. They pulled down the outer watchtowers, while both defenders and besiegers smote one another furiously with their swords. So many were killed there, on both sides, that the waters of the Duero, downstream from the city, ran red with the blood of the dead.

When Count García de Cabra saw this, he was sick at heart to see so many men lost, Christians all of them, on both sides. Going to King Sancho, he kissed his hand and said:

"My lord, may it please your highness: order the assault on the city to cease. For you are losing many of your men. Lay siege to the place instead, for you will soon starve them out."

The king then ordered his men to cease the assault. He ordered them to count the dead. They counted them up and determined that there were thirteen hundred deaths. Greatly distressed by this report, Sancho ordered the town to be immediately surrounded . . . every day the town was subjected to fierce attacks, as the siege went on for a long time . . . and the inhabitants soon suffered from hunger.

And when Don Arias Gonzalo saw how grievously the people suffered from hunger, and how many of them were dying, he said to Princess Urraca:

"My lady, I ask you to please assemble everyone in the town, and that you bid them hand over the town to King Sancho within nine days. For they have suffered greatly and endured great privation out of loyalty to you. You and I, meanwhile, can go and live in Moorish country with your brother King Alfonso. For if I have my way, you will never dwell in Zamora with King Sancho."

Princess Urraca did as he suggested, summoning the inhabitants of Zamora and addressing them thus:

"Friends, you have been very good and very loyal. You have endured much pain and suffering, and lost many friends and kinsmen, out of loyalty to me. And because I consider that you have done more than enough, I bid you surrender the town to King Sancho in nine days' time. I will go to Toledo to be with my brother Don Alfonso."

The people of Zamora, when they heard this, were deeply saddened, because they had held out against the siege for so long, and now, after everything that had happened, they were going to end up surrendering the town anyway. Most of them agreed to accompany the princess into exile and not remain in the town.

And now we will tell you what came of all these developments.

Chapter 835

How King Sancho received as his vassal Vellid Adolfo, and how the Zamorans warned the king to beware of this man.

When Princess Urraca had addressed the Zamorans in this fashion, a certain knight called Vellid Adolfo, who was in attendance, after listening to things said by the princess and by the council members, spoke up in this way:

"My Lady, I came to Zamora with three hundred knights, all of them my vassals. They and I have served you well for a long time now, praise God. I have asked you to reward me in whatever way you could, and you have never gotten around to doing so. And now, by your leave, I will rid Zamora of King Sancho and lift the siege."

The lady Urraca replied:

"Vellid Adolfo, I will remind you of the wise man's words: that beggars can't be choosers. That's the way it must be between us. I don't order you to do anything about any evil ideas you might have contrived. But I tell you that any man who would rid Zamora of my brother and lift the siege would receive from me anything he asked for."

When Vellid Adolfo heard this, he kissed the lady Urraca's hand, saying nothing further to her. He went right to the city gate and spoke with the gatekeeper, and told him that if he should see Vellid in distress, to open the gate for him right away. And he gave the fellow the cloak he was wearing at the time.

Then he went to his lodgings and armed himself. Mounting his horse and riding to the house of Arias Gonzalo, he addressed the latter:

"We all know it's because you're having an affair with the lady Urraca that you won't make any kind of a deal or exchange with her brother."

When Arias Gonzalo heard these words, he was sore at heart. He said:

"In an evil day indeed was I born, if that's the way people talk to me, and no one around to take revenge on the one who talks to me that way."

All his sons were immediately up in arms and went in pursuit of Vellid Adolfo, who was now fleeing in the direction of the city gate. No sooner had the gatekeeper seen him coming than he opened up the gate for him, just as they had agreed earlier.

This Vellid Adolfo then went out from the town, and, going before King Sancho, kissed his hand. He then spoke these false and lying words:

"My lord, because I recommended to the town council of Zamora that they hand over the city to you, the sons of Arias Gonzalo tried to kill me. Now I have come to you and declare myself your vassal. I will see to it that Zamora is handed over to you within a few days, if God wills. And if I don't do just as I have said, let me be killed for it."

Believing what he said, the king received him as his vassal and treated him most honorably. And all the while, Vellid Adolfo became the king's most intimate confidant.

Next day, in the morning, a Cordoban knight of the town went and stood on the wall overlooking the siege tower, and cried out in a loud voice so that everybody in the besieging army could hear him:

"King Sancho, pay close heed to what I tell you! I am a knight of noble lineage; my fathers and grandfathers prided themselves on their loyalty. I wish to undeceive you and tell you the truth, if you will listen to me. I tell you that a traitor has just left this town, one called Vellid Adolfo. He's coming to kill you—watch out for him! And I tell you this so that if, by some mischance, something should happen to you, no one in Spain can ever say thereafter that you were not warned beforehand."

. . . when Vellid Adolfo heard these words, he went straight to the king and declared:

"My lord, that old Arias Gonzalo is very shrewd. Because he knows I intend to see you gain possession of Zamora, he has ordered somebody to make these accusations."

As soon as he said this to the king, Vellid Adolfo asked for his horse, making as if to leave and go somewhere else because he was so upset by what had been said about him. But the king took him then by the hand, saying:

"My friend and vassal, pay no attention to that calumny. For I tell you: if I win Zamora, I intend to make you the first and foremost man over that city, in the same way that Don Arias Gonzalo is now."

Vellid Adolfo kissed the king's hand then, wishing that God would grant the king long life and health with which to keep his promise.

But though the traitor spoke thus, he planned something else entirely in his heart. . . .

Chapter 836

How Vellid Adolfo slew King Sancho, and what Ruy Díaz, My Cid Campeador, did about it.

After the events just described, Vellid Adolfo, eager to carry out the treachery rooted in his heart, took King Sancho aside and said to him:

"My lord, if you think it a good idea, let us ride out together, just the two of us, and go all around Zamora, so that you may see the tunnels you ordered to be dug. And I will show you the entry the Zamorans call the Gate of the Sandpit. By means of this we will gain entry into the town, for this gate is never locked. And as soon as night falls, you will give me one hundred noble knights to go with me, and we will all be armed and go on foot. Since the Zamorans are weak from suffering and hunger, they will be unable to stop us from overpowering them. That way we can open the door and go inside, and keep it open so your entire host can come through—in this way, you will take the town."

The king believed him and told him the plan was an excellent one. And the two of them rode out. As they rode around the outskirts of the town, far away from where the army was camped, the king observed the tunnels that had been dug and considered how quickly they might conquer the town. Then the traitor showed him the gate that was to be their means of gaining entry.

And as soon as they had gone all around the town, the king felt like going down to the banks of the Duero, to find there some diversion. He carried in his hand a small gilded throwing spear, such as kings in those days often used to have with them. And he gave it to Vellid Adolfo to hold for him while he went aside to answer the call of nature, that no man can deny. And Vellid Adolfo followed him, and when he saw him exposed in that way, he hurled the spear at him so that it struck him in the back and, coming out the other side, stuck out from his chest.

As soon as he had speared him in this way, the traitor wheeled his horse around and rode as fast as he could for the gate he had shown the king, the one that was to be the means of taking the city. . . .

Ruy Díaz, the Cid, seeing him take flight like that, called out to ask him what he was running from. And Vellid Adolfo refused to answer, saying nothing. The Cid understood then that he had worked some mischief, or even that a man running away like that might have slain the king. For Vellid had become the king's favorite and closest confidant, and the two were inseparable. The Cid asked for a horse to be brought right away, and while they were bringing it to him, Vellid Adolfo was getting away.

Very concerned about his lord, the Cid quickly took a spear and headed off after Vellid as fast as a horse can gallop who does not even wait for the spurs to be applied.

Meanwhile, Vellid gave up on reaching the Gate of the Sandpit and made instead for the main gate of the town. There, the histories tell us, the Cid overtook Vellid as he entered through the gate of the town, striking him with the spear and pushing him halfway through the doorway. There, they say, the Cid killed Vellid's horse and would have killed the rider too, if he, the Cid, had been wearing spurs. . . . And of all the great feats of arms engaged in by the Cid, this was the only one in which any man could ever find anything to hold against him: in that he failed to go in through the door after the traitor, and failed to kill Vellid after he had caught up with him. But the Cid did not act on this occasion from anything remotely approaching cowardice, nor from any fear of death or imprisonment. It was, rather, an oversight on his part, to have set out in pursuit without remembering to put on his spurs as he should have.

Chapter 837

How Vellid Adolfo was captured.

As soon as Vellid Adolfo found himself inside Zamora, he ran in terror to Princess Urraca, taking refuge under her cloak. Then Don Arias Gonzalo said to the lady Urraca:

"Lady, I beg of you, for God's sake, to hand that traitor over to the Castilians. If not, great harm will come to us, for they will surely accuse all Zamora, and after that, you will be unable to do the city any good."

The lady Urraca answered him:

"Don Arias Gonzalo, advise me as to what I should do with this man, in such a way that he does not die for what he has done."

Don Arias replied:

"Lady, hand him over to me, and I will have him placed under guard for three weeks or so. If the Castilians call us to account for the crime, we will hand him over to them. And if during that time they fail to bring charges against us, we will throw him out of the city and see to it he never again shows his face among us."

Princess Urraca, feeling obliged to go along with Arias Gonzalo's recommendation, let him take Vellid Adolfo away. And Arias Gonzalo took Vellid and ordered him shackled with two sets of irons and kept under close guard.

Chapter 838

The death of King Sancho.

As Vellid Adolfo was thus being taken in charge, the Castilians went looking for their lord. They found him on the banks of the Duero, mortally wounded but still able to talk. He still had the spear in his body, thrust into his back and sticking out from his chest. They did not dare try to take it out, for fear he might lose the power of speech and die without ever getting it back. And a battle surgeon arrived there, one who traveled with the host, who told them to saw off the shaft of the spear on both sides of the body, so that the king would not lose the power of speech.

Then Count García of Cabra, the one they called the curly-haired man of Grañón, spoke to the king:

"My lord, look to your soul, for you are gravely wounded."

The king then replied:

"God bless you, Count, for speaking so frankly. For I know quite well I am a dead man. It was that traitor Vellid Adolfo who killed me. The one who made himself my vassal. I truly believe that all this is on account of my sins and the wrong I have done my brothers and sisters. I broke the promise I made my father and the oath I swore, to never seek to take away anything of theirs from any of my brothers."

As the king finished speaking, the Cid, Ruy Díaz, arrived. Kneeling down before the king, he said:

"My lord, I am lost and helpless, more than any other of your vassals. When your father, King Fernando, divided up his kingdoms, he commended me to you, and to all your brothers and sisters, so that you would do right by me. I came to serve you, and have done or tried to do them great harm, according to their view of the matter. They now hold me a real grudge. Now it is no longer possible for me to go out among the Moors, there where your brother Don Alfonso is, nor to remain among the Christians, with your sister the lady Urraca. Both of them think that all the harm you did them was done because I advised it. And you well know, my lord, that I always advised you as a loyal vassal should advise his lord, and I never counseled any wrongdoing, nor gave you bad advice. And I beg your highness to please think of me before you die."

The king then ordered them to place him in his bed. All around him were counts, barons, archbishops, and bishops. And he spoke to them thus:

"Friends and vassals, in all the Cid has said regarding his having counseled me well and faithfully, he speaks nothing but the truth. Never in any of this business did he advise me to do anybody any harm. And I therefore pray Count García, here present, as my good and faithful vassal, to ask my brother Don Alfonso when he gets back from Moorish country—I believe he will be here presently, as soon as he hears of my death—to do right by the Cid, and receive him as his own vassal."

Then the count kissed his hand and promised to carry out his wish.

The king then said:

"I pray you all, as my good and faithful friends and vassals, to speak to my brother Don Alfonso, earnestly beseeching him to forgive all the wrongs I did him. And all of you pray to God to have mercy on my soul."

When he was done speaking, as he asked for a candle, his soul departed his body. And all his vassals greatly mourned his passing, and all his other subjects too. Then . . . most of the host immediately scattered, most of them fleeing in every direction, leaving everything behind, while some were killed or captured, amid the uproar and confusion occasioned by the king's death, by those who bore them a grudge. . . . But a party composed of the principal barons of the host, together with the bishops, conveyed King Sancho's body to the monastery of San Salvador de Oña, where he was buried with all due honors, as befits a king. . . .

In Chapter 839, the Castilians agree that because the Zamorans have given sanctuary to Vellid after the death of King Sancho, Urraca and her people are to be held accountable, one and all. The Castilians send as their challenger Diego Ordóñez. The latter's accusation is answered by Arias Gonzalo, who offers to defend against the charges in single combat. They agree to a truce while both sides prepare for the trial. Chapter 840 tells how Alfonso, learning of his brother's murder, returns from Toledo, having renewed his pledge to his host, King Al-Ma'mun, never to harm him or his family.

In Chapter 841, all the inhabitants of Zamora, responding to the charges of treason leveled against the whole town, assemble in the town square. All solemnly swear that none had anything to do with Vellid's murder of King Sancho. Arias Gonzalo then picks five of his own sons to fight against Diego Ordóñez, the plaintiffs' champion, in the upcoming combat. In Chapters 842 through 844, Arias Gonzalo's sons Pedro, Diego, and Rodrigo are slain in judicial combat by Diego Ordóñez.

Chapter 845

How the Leonese and Castilians came before King Alfonso, welcoming him as their lord, and how the Cid made Alfonso swear an oath.

And the history tells us that, as soon as Alfonso arrived in Zamora, he set up his camp outside the city, in the place called Santiago's Field. Then he went to see his sister, Princess Urraca, taking counsel with her concerning how he might best proceed with the business at hand. And Princess Urraca, according to the histories, was a very astute lady. King Alfonso, having conferred with her, sent out his proclamations, throughout the land, summoning all his subjects to come there and swear fealty to him.

When the Leonese, the Galicians, and the Asturians learned that King Alfonso had come, they rejoiced at his arrival and went to Zamora without delay. There they all accepted him as their king and lord, and there, without hesitation, swore fealty to him, solemnly promising to uphold their allegiance.

After that, the Castilians and Navarrese arrived. They also accepted Alfonso as their lord, provided that he swear under oath that he, Alfonso, had had nothing to do with King Sancho's death. However, no one under those circumstances was willing to take his oath, even though King Alfonso was willing to give it.

Only the Cid Ruy Díaz would agree to do so. But he stipulated that he would on no account receive Alfonso as his lord, nor kiss his hand, until Alfonso solemnly swore that he had nothing to do with the death of King Sancho. . . .

And the histories tell us that when King Alfonso saw that the Cid Ruy Díaz refused to kiss his hand in sign of fealty, as all the other great lords and prelates and royal advisors had done, he addressed the assembled company in these words:

"Friends, since all of you here have received me as your lord, and you have consented to give me control of cities and castles and all the rest, and to concede that the kingdom is mine, I would like you to inquire of My Cid Ruy Díaz why he has refused to kiss my hand. For I would gladly show him favor, just as I promised my father King Fernando when he commended the Cid to me and to my brothers and sisters."

After King Alfonso had spoken these words before the assembly, My Cid Ruy Díaz, who had been listening, arose and said:

"My lord, all the men you see here before you—although none dares say it to you—suspect you of being involved in the death of King Sancho. And I therefore say to you that, if you do not clear yourself of this suspicion, as is only proper, I will never kiss your hand in fealty."

To this the king replied:

"Cid, I am very pleased at what you say. And here and now I agree to swear, to God and Holy Mary and to you, that I never ordered such a thing, nor was I involved in any way, nor was I in any way pleased when I learned of my brother's death, even though he did drive me from the land. I therefore pray you tell me, as my loyal vassals, how I may be cleared of this suspicion."

His principal barons then urged him to swear before twelve knights, in the church of Santa Gadea in Burgos. In this way he would be absolved of blame.

The king was much pleased with this judgment, as they rode toward Burgos with the purpose of putting this acquittal into effect. When they had arrived, My Cid Ruy Díaz took up the book of the Gospels and placed it on the altar of Santa Gadea. And as King Alfonso placed his hands on the book, the Cid began to take his oath in this manner:

"King Alfonso, do you now swear to me that you had nothing to do with the death of my lord King Sancho?"

And King Alfonso responded:

"I do."

The Cid declared:

"If you swear falsely, please God that you be slain by a treacherous vassal, just as Vellid Adolfo was to my lord King Sancho."

King Alfonso replied:

"Amen."

And as he said this, he blushed, so that his face turned all red.

The Cid continued:

"King Alfonso, do you swear to me that in the matter of your brother King Sancho's death, you neither took part in planning it, nor ordered him to be killed?"

King Alfonso replied to this:

"I do."

"And if you swear falsely, may a vassal of yours slay you, deceitfully and with perfidy, just as Vellid Adolfo slew my lord King Sancho."

King Alfonso again replied, "Amen," and again his face turned red.

The Cid made him swear yet again. And King Alfonso swore just as the Cid charged him to, and the twelve knights stood witness.

And when the oaths had been sworn and duly witnessed, the Cid Ruy Díaz sought to kiss King Alfonso's hand in fealty.

But the king held back his hand, according to the history. Rather he told the Cid that henceforth he would never be in the king's good graces, no matter how daring and hardy the Cid might be.

Afterward, however, they were reunited, sometimes amicably and sometimes not, until the time the king sent the Cid into exile. But in the end, they remained friends, and the Cid showed himself worthy of the king's goodwill. . . .

E. THE CHRONICLE OF TWENTY KINGS (CRÓNICA DE VEINTE REYES)

Anonymous
Chronicle composed in Old Castilian in
the late thirteenth century

*This chronicle, regarded by some scholars as perhaps older and
more representative of the Alphonsine school than the* First
General Chronicle, *has long been noted for its reliance on a
version of* The Epic of the Cid *very similar to the one we know.
A number of editors have used it to fill in the gaps represented
by* The Epic *manuscript's missing folios.*

*This selection tells of events occurring just before the open-
ing of* The Epic *as we know it, events possibly referred to in the
manuscript's missing first folio.*[22]

Book X, Chapter VII

Concerning how the Cid vanquished King Almudafar of
Granada, along with the great lords of Castile who were Al-
mudafar's allies, when he, the Cid, went to collect tribute pay-
ments from the king of Seville.

Four years into the reign of King Alfonso, the king sent Ruy
Díaz, the Cid, to collect the tribute monies payable each year by
the kings of Cordoba and Seville. Al-Mutamid, king of Seville,
was at that time the great enemy of the king of Granada. The
two kings hated each other mortally. . . .
. . . and all these Christian lords, along with their respec-
tive followers, joined their forces with those of Almudafar in at-
tacking al-Mutamid of Seville. Ruy Díaz, the Cid, when he
learned that they were about to attack the king of Seville, the
vassal and tributary of King Alfonso, his lord, was much vexed,

---

22. *Crónica de veinte reyes* (Burgos: Excelentísimo Ayuntamiento de
Burgos, 1991).

considering that they were entirely in the wrong. He sent letters to all of them, entreating them to desist from their attack on the king of Seville, and beseeching them to refrain from laying waste to his lands, out of consideration for their obligations toward King Alfonso. For should they attempt any other action, they should be assured that the king would have no choice but to come to the aid of his tributary.

The king of Granada and his allies the great lords, scornfully disregarding the Cid's letters, invaded the Sevillan king's realm with all their forces, ravaging his country as far as the castle of Cabra. When the Cid Ruy Díaz saw what they were doing, he gathered together all the forces he could, both Christian and Moorish, and went against the king of Granada, determined to expel him from the king of Seville's territory. And when the king of Granada, along with his Christian allies, heard that the Cid was coming against them in this way, he sent to inform the Cid that they were not about to turn back and leave the country on his account.

The Cid Ruy Díaz, when he heard this reply, felt that he had no choice but to attack them immediately. He accordingly set out and went against them on the battlefield. The encounter lasted from the third hour of the day until noon, with a great many fatalities, both Moorish and Christian, on the side of the king of Granada. As the Cid routed them and chased them from the field, he captured Count García Ordóñez, yanking out a tuft of this great lord's beard. He also captured Lope Sánchez, Diego Pérez, and many other knights, along with countless others, holding them prisoner for three days and afterward releasing them.

While he held them prisoner, he ordered his men to gather up all the captured goods and plunder remaining on the battlefield. After this, the Cid returned, with all his captured loot and all his men, to King al-Mutamid of Seville, handing over to them all the spoils they considered to be rightfully theirs, and even anything of the rest that they might wish to take. From that moment on, both Moors and Christians called Ruy Díaz of Vivar "The Cid Campeador," which means "The Battler."

Al-Mutamid then gave him many gifts, along with King Alfonso's tribute payments for which the Cid had come. The pact between King Alfonso and King al-Mutamid was then reaffirmed, and the Cid returned with all the tribute monies due to his lord, King Alfonso. And the king welcomed him back and was much pleased with him, and very content with all the Cid had accomplished in the south.

For this reason, many there were who begrudged him his success. Seeking to do him any harm they could, they were determined to estrange him from the king.

Book X, Chapter VIII

How Ruy Díaz, the Cid Campeador, was banished from the land.

As the Cid had returned to King Alfonso, the king had already gathered together a great host in order to carry out a raiding expedition into Moorish territory. . . . the Cid wanted to go with the king but fell gravely ill and could not go with his lord. The king then left the Cid in charge of the country.

King Alfonso led his forces into Moorish country, ravaging much of their territory and causing them considerable damage. As the king was busy there in Al-Andalus, accomplishing what he had set out to do, a great force of Moors came together between where he was and his homeland back in Castile. Entering into his kingdom, they surrounded and laid siege to the castle of Gormaz, attacking it with everything they had, while ravaging the countryside all around.

While all this was going on, the Cid was recovering. When he heard about what the Moors were doing in the country around San Esteban, he gathered together all the forces available and headed into Moorish territory, raiding and laying waste all the country around Toledo, and capturing some seven thousand Moors, both men and women. After that he returned to Castile, a wealthy man crowned with glory and in possession of great plunder.

When King Alfonso heard about this, he was very sore at heart. Seeing the king's distress, the great lords in his company, exceedingly envious of the Cid's accomplishments, spoke ill of him and sought to poison the king's mind against him.

They said:

"Lord, the Cid Ruy Díaz, who has broken the peace that you have established and confirmed with the Moors, did what he has done only to make sure that the Moors kill us all."

The king, full of anger and harboring wrath against the Cid, readily believed them, the more so for the oath the Cid had exacted from him in Burgos, on the matter of his brother King Sancho's death. . . .

He then sent letters to the Cid, ordering him to be gone from the land. The Cid, as soon as he had read these letters, despite being much distressed at these developments, decided to comply without delay, for he had no more than nine days in which to leave the kingdom. . . .

F. THE YOUTHFUL DEEDS
OF RODRIGO
(MOCEDADES DE RODRIGO)

Anonymous
Epic poem composed in Castilian in the
latter half of the fourteenth century

*Written down a century and a half or more after the previous
selections, this work is what we would nowadays call a "pre-
quel." It recounts the exploits and adventures of the young Ro-
drigo Díaz de Vivar. The prodigious warrior and respected
leader of those earlier versions dominates his world, but performs
deeds within the bounds of credibility. And he is a grown man:
a prudent vassal and responsible lord, a dutiful husband, father,
and kinsman. This version's once and future Cid — not quite
thirteen at the time of his first fabulous exploit — is a precursor
of modern superheroes. Headstrong, impulsive, defiant of au-
thority, this adolescent Rodrigo is in some ways a rebel, a trou-
blemaker. But his preternatural martial prowess and uncanny
wisdom serve transcendent causes: the upholding of justice and
the defense of the realm.*

*Another important difference, with respect to earlier Cid-
ian narratives, is the depiction of Jimena. Instead of the exem-
plary wife and mother of* The Epic of the Cid *we have here a
precociously resolute and self-possessed young woman who
brings her own suit before the king, makes her own marriage,
and seeks to bring peace to the kingdom. Although it may seem
odd to say so to present-day readers, her proposal of marriage
to her father's slayer could be seen as fourteenth-century femi-
nism. The traditional woman would be expected to pursue, or
at least support, clannish vengeance. Instead, Jimena comes up
with a diplomatic solution to the conflict between families, and
a very pragmatic way to deal with her dilemma as an orphaned
daughter.*[23]

---

23. *Las Mocedades de Rodrigo: estudios críticos, manuscrito y edición,*
edited by Matthew Bailey (London: King's College Center for Late
Antique and Medieval Studies, 1999), 189–216.

. . . The land was at peace, for there was no war in any part of the country.

Count Gómez de Gormaz wronged Diego Laínez, maltreating Diego's shepherds and stealing his cattle.

Diego Laínez came to Vivar, answering the call to arms. Sending word to his brothers to meet him, he rode forth without delay.

They went out to raid Gormaz as the sun was rising. Setting fire to the outer buildings, they broke through the town walls.

Diego captured Gómez's vassals and everything they were carrying with them, and took back with him all the cattle grazing in the fields. And he captured, to their great shame, the laundry-maids working on the river bank.

Count Gómez rode after them, along with a hundred wellborn knights, challenging in a loud voice the son of Laín Calvo:

"Let my laundry-maids go, you son-of-a-town-judge![24] For your forces cannot match mine!"

Thus he spoke, for he was flushed with rage.

Ruy Laínez — the lord of Haro that he was — then replied:

"We'll be there to face you, a hundred against a hundred, ready for action, toe-to-toe!"

They all gave their word to be there on the day agreed upon.

Diego and his men sent back some of the laundry-maids and the count's vassals, but not the cattle. For they wanted to keep the livestock to compensate for what the count had stolen.

As the ninth day came around, they all rode swiftly forth.

Rodrigo, the son of Diego and grandson of Laín Calvo and Nuño Álvarez de Amaya, and great-grandson of the king of León — he was twelve years old, not yet even thirteen. Never had he found himself in battle, and now he was bursting to join in the fray. He joined the ranks of the other hundred warriors, whether his father wished it or not.

---

24. In many cultures, small-town magistrates are proverbially depicted as meddlesome, grasping, ambitious, pedantic; the comparison is not a compliment.

As he and Count Gómez strike the first blows between the two of them, the battle lines are drawn, and everyone begins to join battle.

Rodrigo killed the count, for the latter could not stave off the young man's attack.

The count's hundred men charged forth, determined to do battle. Rodrigo rode after them, showing them no mercy. He captured two of the count's sons, much to their chagrin—Fernando Gómez and Alfonso Gómez—and took them back to Vivar.

The count had three daughters, each one of them of marriageable age:

The eldest was Elvira Gómez, and the middle one Aldonza Gómez.

And the other was named Jimena Gómez, the youngest.

When they learned that their brothers had been captured and their father killed, they wore brown-colored clothes and veils everywhere they went. Back then such colors were worn in mourning; nowadays they are worn to rejoice.

The three daughters left Gormaz and headed for Vivar.

Don Diego saw them coming and went out to welcome them.

"Where are these nuns, who've come to ask something of me?"

"We will tell you, lord, for we have no reason not to speak freely. We are daughters of Count Gormaz, and you ordered him to be killed. You have captured our brothers and are holding them here. We are only women, and now there is no one to watch over us."

Then Don Diego replied:

"You must not blame me. Ask Rodrigo for your brothers, and see if he will be willing to release them to you. As Christ is my witness, I will not mind at all."

Rodrigo heard this and spoke out:

"You have done wrong, my lord, in disavowing your authority. For I am still your son and my mother's. For charity's sake, think of what people will say. The daughters cannot be blamed for what their father did. Give their brothers back to them, for they have great need of them. Toward these ladies you should show forbearance."

Then Don Diego replied:

"Son, order them to be handed over to these young women."

The brothers are set free and handed over to the ladies.

When the brothers saw themselves out in the clear, safe and sound, they fell to talking.

They gave Rodrigo and his father two weeks' respite:

"Let's come back at night and burn them out of their houses in Vivar."

Jimena, the youngest girl, then spoke:

"Calm yourselves, brothers, for charity's sake. I will go to Zamora to state our grievance before King Fernando. You will be safer this way, and he will do right by you."

Then Jimena Gómez rode forth, accompanied by three young ladies and by several squires assigned to protect her.

She arrived in Zamora, where the king holds court.

Weeping tears from her eyes, she begs him to take pity on her:

"Your majesty, I am a wretched woman — take pity on me. At an early age I was bereft of the countess, my mother. Now a son of Diego Laínez has greatly wronged me. He took my brothers prisoner and killed my father. I come before you now, my king, to state my grievance. My lord, I beseech you: order to be righted this wrong that has been done me."

The king was greatly grieved and began to speak:

"My kingdoms are greatly troubled at this moment. Castile is likely to rise up against me, and if the Castilians rise up against me, they will make a lot of trouble for me."

When Jimena Gómez heard this, she stepped forward to kiss the king's hands.

"If it please you, sire, do not take my claim amiss. I will show you how to bring peace to Castile, and likewise to all your kingdoms. Give me Rodrigo as my husband: the very one who killed my father."

When Count Osorio, King Fernando's guardian and counselor, heard this, he took the king by the hand and led him aside:

"What do you think of this boon that she asks of you? Indeed, you should thank the Almighty Father himself! My lord, send immediately for Rodrigo and his father."

Quickly they write the letters, for they do not want to put it off. They give the letters to the messenger, who sets out on his way.

When the messenger arrived in Vivar, Don Diego was resting.

The messenger said:

"I bow before you, my lord, for I bring you good news. Our good King Fernando sends for you and for your son. Behold these letters I bring you, signed by the king himself. For if it be God's will, Rodrigo will soon be raised to the highest rank."

Don Diego looked over the letters, then turned pale. He suspected that the king wanted to kill him over the count's death.

"Hear me, my son. Pay heed to this. I have a bad feeling about these letters, which seem full of deceit. When it comes to this kind of business, kings are very wicked in their ways. Any king you serve, serve him faithfully, no tricks. But watch out for him, as if he were a mortal enemy. Now then, my son, go to Haro, where your uncle Ruy Laínez dwells. Meanwhile I will go to the court, where the good king resides. And if perchance the king should kill me, you and your uncles can avenge me."

To this Rodrigo replied:

"That would not be right. Whatever you go through, I will go through also. Even though you are my father, I wish to advise you. Take with you a full three hundred knights. As we enter Zamora, my lord, put me in charge of them."

Then Don Diego said:

"Well then, let's ride out."

They set out on the way, heading for Zamora.

At the entrance to Zamora, where the Duero River flows, the three hundred men take up their weapons, and Rodrigo does likewise.

As soon as he saw them armed and ready, he began to address them:

"Hear me," he said, "friends, kinsmen, and vassals of my father. Watch over your lord, with no false dealing or trickery. If you see that the bailiff is trying to arrest him, kill the bailiff as quick as you can. May the king have as dark a day as the rest of the men there with him. They can't call you traitors for killing the king, since we're not his vassals, and God forbid we ever should be. The king would be more of a traitor if he killed my father, than I was for killing my enemy in a fair fight on the battlefield."

Enraged, he heads for the court, where good King Fernando was in residence.

Everyone declared:

"Look! It's the one who killed the noble count!"

As Rodrigo turned his eyes toward them, they all scattered. They were very much afraid of him and looked at him in awe.

Diego Laínez went forward to kiss the king's hand. Seeing this, Rodrigo refused at first to kiss the king's hand; then, kneeling down, he made to kiss his hand. The sword he wore was a long one; the king, alarmed, cried out in a loud voice:

"Remove that devil from my presence!"

Then Don Rodrigo said:

"I'd sooner have a doornail for a lord than you. I would never be your vassal. It makes me sick to see my father kiss your hand."

At that moment, the king said to Don Osorio, his childhood guardian and counselor:

"Bring that damsel here, and let's get this young buck betrothed."

Still unable to believe what he had been told, Don Diego remained very apprehensive.

The damsel came forward, Count Osorio leading her by the hand. Directing her gaze toward Rodrigo, she looked intently at him, then said:

"My lord, many thanks, for this is indeed the nobleman I am asking for."

There and then Doña Jimena Gómez and Rodrigo the Castilian were betrothed.

Rodrigo, very irate, turned and said to the king of Castile:

"My lord, you have betrothed me, more against my will than with my consent. But I swear to Christ that I will never either kiss your hand, or be with her in town or open country, until such time as I have prevailed five times in fair combat on the battlefield."

When the king had heard this, he was astonished and said:

"This is no ordinary man—he has the look of a devil about him."

Count Osorio replied:

"I will soon show you. When the Moors come raiding into Castile, let no living man come to his aid. We'll see then if he's speaking in earnest or just bragging."

Then father and son took their leave, setting out on the road. Rodrigo went to Vivar, to San Pedro de Cardeña, to dwell there for the summer.

The dauntless Moor, Burgos of Ayllón, came raiding, and with him the most honorable sheik Bulcor of Sepúlveda, and his brother Tosios, the sheik of Olmedo, very rich and well-off. All in all there were five thousand Moors on horseback. They went raiding into Castile, and got as far as Belorado, setting fire to Redecilla and Grañón, from one end to the other.

The call-to-arms reached Rodrigo as he was taking his siesta. As Rodrigo forbade anyone to even dare wake up his father, they armed themselves and rode out at full speed. Three hundred of his father's knights went with him, at his orders, along with other folk from Castile who also joined up with him.

Meanwhile, the Moors were pillaging the countryside, doing great harm. Their forces were very numerous, as they took away with them droves of stolen cattle and many Christian captives—God curse them!

At Nava del Grillo, in the place called Lerma—that was where Rodrigo overtook them. Chasing after them, he fought with the marauders but not with the herdsmen who drove the stolen cattle. Some he killed, and the others he sent running in all directions.

Through the countryside of Gomiel, and as far as Yoda they came, there where the enemy forces were getting away with all their plunder.

There Rodrigo fought a fair fight with them, there on the battlefield. A day and a night, until noon of the following day, the battle hung in the balance, and the fray was a tangled skein. But Rodrigo won the battle, praise God!

As far as Peña Falcón, to the place called Peñafiel, they roiled the waters of the Duero. As they neared Fuentedueña, the melee was renewed. Rodrigo killed the two sheiks, took the noble Moor Burgos prisoner. He then led away the pagans toward Tudela de Duero, as well as the stolen cattle and the captive men and women: all these the Castilian brought back with him.

The news reached Zamora, where good King Fernando was in residence.

When the king heard these tidings, he was glad and very pleased. Lord, how the king of Castile rejoiced!

The good king rode forth, and with him many counts and knights and other high-born men. He went to Tudela de Duero, where the cattle were grazing.

As he saw the king coming, Rodrigo welcomed him without delay.

"Behold, good king," he said. "See what I bring you, even though I am not your vassal. Of the five battles I promised you on the day you betrothed me, I have now won the first. Now I will look to winning the other four."

Then the good king replied:

"May you be pardoned for everything, as long as you give me a fifth of all you've won here."

Then Rodrigo said:

"Let there be no thought of that! I will give it instead to the poor, who lead a life of suffering and deprivation. I will give the tithe-gatherers their share, for I would not have their curse upon me. And from my own share I will give their pay to all those who have followed me into battle."

Then the good king replied:

"Give me then that proud Moor."

Rodrigo answered:

"Let there be no thought of that, not for as much as I am worth. For when one nobleman takes another nobleman prisoner, he must not dishonor him. Of the rest of this loot, I will only give you a fifth of the money in coin. The rest I am giving to my vassals, for they have gone through a lot in serving me."

They took their leave of the king and kissed his hand.

Three hundred knights in all were those gathered there together. When Rodrigo saw this, he quickly turned to the Moors:

"Hear me, Burgos of Ayllon, valiant Moorish king that you are! I would never capture a king, nor would it be fitting that I do such a thing. But I asked you to come with me, and you willingly did so. Go now, back to your kingdom, safe and sound. Would that as long as I live you have nothing to fear from any king, Moor or Christian. And all the possessions of those sheiks I killed, are now bequeathed to you, if they'll open up their towns to you; if not, send me a message, and I'll see to it that they open up for you out of fear, if not of their own free will."

When the noble Moor Burgos of Ayllon saw how things were, he knelt down before Rodrigo and kissed his hand, giving voice to these words:

"You I now call my lord, and I am your vassal. And I will give you the fifth part of all I have, and your tribute payments, every year from now on."

The Moor went away happy, and the Castilian also went home happy. The valiant Moorish king of Ayllon paid him tribute thereafter, so that in less than four years Rodrigo became rich and well-off. . . .

G. "THE CID AND THE MOORISH KING"

Anonymous
Romance ("ballad") composed in Castilian
verse in the late fifteenth or early sixteenth century

The word for ballad in Spanish is romance. *The Iberian Penin-sula, like the British Isles, has a long and voluminous ballad tra-dition going back at least as far as the fifteenth century, but probably having oral antecedents from much earlier times. The Spanish ballad tradition, the* romancero, *includes many folk songs about the Cid. It has long been recognized that many of these songs seem to paraphrase or even excerpt scenes and episodes from epics and chronicles. The relationship between the romances and earlier written works is very complex and con-troversial. What is certain is that the Cid of the* romancero *is even further removed from the hero of* The Epic of the Cid *and the chronicles than the Rodrigo of* The Youthful Deeds. *This is partly due to the narrative form of ballads, which are short poems that present a scene, a brief episode, and a few snippets of dialog. Ballads are terse and elliptical; they assume the audi-ence knows the folklore, popular history, and singing tradition behind any given poem. Another reason for the difference be-tween the earlier and later Cid is the change in popular taste. Ballads eschew politics, making everything personal. So the siege and occupation of Valencia, in the following romance, are merely a backdrop to the face-to-face confrontation at center stage. The Cid of this ballad is a bit picaresque. He actually asks his daugh-ter to flirt with the Moor in order to distract him—a ruse that would be unimaginable in* The Epic of the Cid.

The original is in the traditional Spanish ballad meter, an eight-syllable line with assonanced rhyme. The ballad is here rendered in prose.[25]

---

25. *Spanish Ballads,* edited by Colin Smith (Oxford and New York: Pergamon Press, 1964), 100–103.

There he goes, there he goes, riding down the road: a Moor mounted on a bay mare. His boots were of Moroccan leather, of beaten gold his spurs. In one hand he holds a shield, in the other a Moorish lance.

He beheld Valencia: how nearby she was!

"Oh, Valencia, Valencia, may you burn in hellfire! You belonged to the Moors before the Christians took you. If my lance tells me no lie, to the Moors you will be returned. I will seize that dog the Cid by his beard; his wife Doña Jimena will be my captive, and his daughter Urraca Hernando will be my sweetheart. When I'm tired of her, I'll hand her over to my men."[26] The good Cid was not too far away — he overheard all the Moor was saying.

"Come here, my daughter, my daughter, Doña Urraca. Take off your everyday clothes and put on your Sunday best. You keep that Moorish son-of-a-dog busy with sweet words, while I saddle Babieca and gird on my sword."

The beautiful damsel leaned out her window; no sooner did the Moor catch sight of her than he spoke to her these words:

"Allah keep you, lady, my lady Doña Urraca!"

"Likewise, my lord, and be you most welcome here! For seven years already, my king, full seven years have I been sweet on you."

"For as many years, my lady, I have held you in my heart!"

As these two were thus occupied, the good Cid appeared.

"Farewell, farewell, my lady, my sweetheart oh so fair. For I clearly hear the sound of the horse Babieca's hooves!"

Wherever the mare puts her hoof, Babieca plants his own.

Then the horse himself spoke up — listen close to what he said:

"Cursed be the mother who won't wait up for her son!"

Seven times round the rock-rose bush they ran. The mare was swift, and gained a good lead. She reached the river bank, where a boat was tied up.

---

26. The historical Cid's daughters were Cristina and María. *The Epic* refers to them as Elvira and Sol. This ballad presents yet another name, Urraca.

As soon as the Moor saw it, he was right glad it was there. He shouts out to the boatman, bidding him row closer. Responding with alacrity, the boatman had the boat ready for him. Quickly the Moor got aboard, he tarried not an instant.

With the Moor now aboard the boat, the Cid reached the river. Seeing the Moor had gotten away safe and sound, the Cid was stricken with chagrin. But with the fury he felt, he hurled a lance at the Moor and cried:

"Pick up the lance, dear son-in-law, pick up that lance for me! Perchance a time will come when I will want it back!"

COMPENDIUM OF
PROPER NAMES

Entries figuring prominently in *The Epic of the Cid* and Related Texts are accompanied by one or more parenthetical abbreviations (see abbreviations at the beginning of Related Texts, p. 107). Examples: FERNANDO, KING *(FGC)*; GRANADA *(HR, CTK)*.

ABENGALBÓN *(EC)*. The historical personage who corresponds is probably Ibn Ghalbun, the *alcaide* (governor) of the castle of Molina de Aragón in the days of the historical Cid (late eleventh century). In the epic he is shown to be the steadfast friend and ally of the Cid. Although there is little or no historical evidence of such a friendship, it is very possible that the real Cid maintained such affiliations with some Muslims.

AL-ANDALUS. The Arabic name for the areas in the IBERIAN PENINSULA, in what is now southern France, that were controlled by Muslims in the early Middle Ages. The Muslim conquest and colonization of Iberia and other parts of southern Europe began in 711, the year in which a relatively small army of Muslims undertook a surprisingly rapid conquest of Visigothic Spain (see VISIGOTHS). From the early eighth to the end of the eleventh century, Al-Andalus was the most powerful and prosperous country in Europe. Its power and influence as an independent polity came to an end in 1031 (see CALIPHATE OF CORDOBA), when Muslim Spain fragmented into a number of independent kingdoms and emirates (see TAIFA STATES; BERBERS). The name Al-Andalus is the origin of the modern name Andalusia (Sp. *Andalucía*), referring to the present-day autonomous community[1] of Andalucía, and, more generally, to the southern region of Spain.

---

1. *Autonomous community* ("comunidad autónoma") is a first-level political-administrative division of contemporary Spain, above the level of province.

ALCOCER (*EC*). Probably corresponds to the present-day Castejón de las Armas (Michael, *Poema de Mio Cid,* n. to l. 553), a municipality in the province of Saragossa, in the present-day autonomous community of ARAGON.

ALFONSO, KING (*EC, FGC*). Alfonso VI of history (1040–1109). Surnamed "The Brave." The second son of Fernando I (see FERNANDO, KING), he received the kingdom of LEÓN (1065) when his father divided the kingdom among his three sons. After a war with his elder brother Sancho II (see SANCHO, KING), he ascended the throne of CASTILE (1072), unifying the two kingdoms. After conquering the Muslim kingdom of TOLEDO in 1085, he took over the kingdom of GALICIA from his younger brother García on the latter's death (1090). Reducing the strategic Muslim kingdom of SEVILLE to the status of a tributary state (1069), he embarked upon a campaign to reconquer southern Spain. With the support of the CLUNY and of Pope Gregory VII, Alfonso, now married to CONSTANCE OF BURGUNDY and aided by a force of Burgundian knights, besieged and conquered Toledo (1085). The loss of the latter kingdom, regarded as one of the jewels of Islam, was a shock to the entire Muslim world. Alarmed, the Spanish Muslims appealed for help to the ALMORAVIDS, who, crossing the Strait of Gibraltar, defeated Alfonso at the Battle of Sagrajas (1086). Failing to pursue the advantage seemingly gained from the latter battle, the Almoravids never managed to quell the ongoing Christian resistance to Islam that came to be symbolized by the leadership and successes of the Cid.

Alfonso VI is one of the most important medieval Spanish Christian monarchs. He is credited not only with extending Christian influence in an early phase of the RECONQUEST but also with unifying León, Castile, and Galicia; with promoting the influence of reformed French monasticism in the Peninsula (see CLUNY); and with replacing the old liturgy of the MOZARABS with the Roman (see ISIDORE, SAINT).

ALMOHADS. A BERBER dynasty that dominated the MAGHREB and AL-ANDALUS from 1147 to 1269. Beginning, like their predecessors the ALMORAVIDS, as a puritanical Muslim sect, the Almohads, led by their founder the reformer Muhammad ibn Tûmart, were organized as a militant fundamentalist community in the High Atlas (see ATLAS MOUN-

TAINS). Succeeding to leadership after the death of ibn Tû-mart, Abd al-Mumin lead the Almohads to victory over the Almoravids in the MAGHREB and in Al-Andalus. Inflicting a resounding victory against Alfonso VIII at Alarcos (1195), the Almohads, whose intolerant policies toward non-Muslims drove many Jews and Christians to emigrate to the Christian kingdoms of the Peninsula, eventually succumbed to a Christian coalition led by Alfonso VIII at the battle of Las Navas de Tolosa (1212). The latter defeat marked the end of Almohad ascendancy and opened the way to the systematic Christian reconquest of Al-Andalus over the next several decades.

With its capital in Marrakesh (present-day Morocco), and extending at its height from northern Al-Andalus to present-day Libya, the Almohad Empire became an important patron of architecture, literature, science, and technology. Maintaining extensive international trade networks, the Almohad dynasty was also a vital link between the Christian and Muslim worlds.

ALMORAVIDS. A North African Muslim dynasty that began as a puritanical religious movement among the nomadic BERBERS who roamed between present-day Senegal and the southern part of present-day MOROCCO. In the mid-1100s, these nomads united under the leadership of the preacher Abdallah ibn Yasin. Succeeding to leadership after Ibn Yasin's death in combat in 1059, Abu-Bakr founded the city of Marrakesh (1061), led Almoravid resistance to aggressors from the present-day Algeria, and sought to make peace among warring Berber tribes to the south. Left in charge of the MAGHREB in Abu-Bakr's absence, Yusuf ibn Tashfin (see YUSUF) assumed power. Conquering Fez in 1075 and Tlemcen in 1080, Ibn Tashfin founded the kingdom of Tlemcen, which included present-day Morocco and part of western Algeria. In 1086, invited by the TAIFA STATES of AL-ANDALUS, who sought his help against ALFONSO VI, Ibn Tashfin led a Muslim coalition against the Christians, winning a triumphant victory at Sagrajas. Seeing the Spanish Muslims quarreling amongst themselves and engaged in conspiracies against him, Ibn Tashfin, supported by many local Muslim clerics, conquered all of Muslim Spain between 1090 and 1094. When Ibn Tashfin died in 1106, at the age of 100, he left behind a thriving empire that was to continue to dominate Muslim Spain and the Maghreb for the next two decades. After a period of conflict and internal dissension, the weakened Almoravid Empire finally came to an end in 1147, with the entry of the triumphant ALMOHADS into Marrakesh.

ÁLVAR FÁÑEZ, MINAYA (*EC, FGC*).[2] A historical person (d. 1114), the vassal of ALFONSO VI and one of the latter's principal commanders. He was lord of Zorita and governor of TOLEDO. The *EC*'s portrayal of him as the Cid's chief lieutenant and closest companion in exile is largely fictional. The nickname "Minaya" given to him in the *EC* probably derives from the Spanish possessive *mi* ("my") and the Basque *anai* ("brother").

ÁLVAR SALVADÓREZ (*EC*). The name of a historical person. Mentioned in the *EC* as a loyal vassal of the Cid.

ANSUR GONZÁLEZ (*EC*). Elder brother of the SCIONS OF CARRIÓN.

ARABY, THREE KINGS OF (*EC*). Melchior, Caspar, Balthasar: the three kings or Magi of the New Testament (Matt. 2:1–12).

ARAGON. A region and kingdom of northern Spain, bordered to the north by France, to the east by CATALONIA and VALENCIA, to the west by CASTILE, and to the south by NEW CASTILE. The present-day autonomous community of the same name includes the provinces of HUESCA, SARAGOSSA, and TERUEL.

Conquered in the fifth century by the VISIGOTHS, Aragon was incorporated into the kingdom founded by that Germanic people. At the time of the MUSLIM INVASION of the early eighth century, some Christians took refuge in the mountains of Aragon, making this region one of the staging points of the

---

2. What seem to be last names in *The Epic of the Cid* are patronymics. They literally mean "son of." Thus, RODRIGO DÍAZ = "Rodrigo, Son of Diego", DIEGO GONZÁLEZ = "Diego, Son of Gonzalo." Medievalists generally list such names by given name, not by the patronymic. Similarly, for an edition of the *Iliad* in English a translator would index the hero under ACHILLES, SON OF PELEUS, rather than under PELEUS'S SON, ACHILLES.

early RECONQUEST. Its chief city, SARAGOSSA, was conquered by Muslims in 714, and remained an important Moorish kingdom until conquered by Christians in the twelfth century. A dependency of NAVARRE in its earliest history, the Christian kingdom of Aragon attained independence under Ramiro I in 1035. During the following centuries it grew steadily, partly by reconquering Moorish territories in the EBRO RIVER basin, and partly by absorbing Catalonia, Valencia, the eastern PYRENEES, and eventually the Balearic Islands. The marriage of Ferdinand of Aragon and Isabel of Castile in 1474 resulted in the unification of Christian Spain.

ARBUJUELO VALLEY (*EC*). A valley lying to the southeast of Medinaceli (see MEDINA), in the present-day province of Soria.

ARLANZÓN RIVER (*EC*). The stream on whose banks the city of BURGOS is located.

ASTURIAS (*EC, FGC*). A region and kingdom of northwestern Spain, bounded to the north by the Cantabrian Sea (see CANTABRIA), by GALICIA to the west, by OLD CASTILE to the east, and by LEÓN to the south. The land of the ancient Astures, a people who resisted Roman rule until the time of the emperor Augustus in the first century BC, Asturias eventually became one of the nine provinces of Visigothic Spain. Soon after the MUSLIM INVASION in 711, Asturians and VISIGOTHS took refuge in the mountains of Asturias. Pelagius (Sp. *Pelayo*), the semilegendary founder of the Asturian kingdom, is traditionally credited with defeating the Muslim invaders at Covadonga in 718. He is thus also regarded as the initiator of the RECONQUEST. When the Asturian Christians came to control the kingdom of León during the ninth century, the two realms united as the Asturian-Leonese kingdom, which included Galicia, much of the Basque country (see BASQUES), and from about 1028, Old Castile, as a result of the marriage of Fernando I (see FERNANDO, KING) to Doña Sancha, the sister of the Leonese king.

ATLAS MOUNTAINS. A mountain range in northwestern Africa, extending about 2,500 kilometers from southwest to northeast, and traversing all three of the present-day countries occupying the MAGHREB (MOROCCO, Algeria, and Tunisia).

The highest peak is the Toubkal Mountain in southwestern Morocco, with an altitude of 4,167 meters (13,671 feet). See also MONTES CLAROS.

BABIECA *(EC, CMK)*. The Cid's legendary warhorse.

BARCELONA *(EC, HR, SC)*. The second-biggest city in Spain, after Madrid; the chief port; and most important financial and industrial city of present-day Spain, Barcelona was probably founded in the third century BC. A port city under the Romans and VISIGOTHS, it was captured by the Muslims in 715 CE, then retaken in 801 by Christians of the CAROLINGIAN EMPIRE. It was the capital of the SPANISH MARCH. Beginning in the latter half of the eleventh century it became the principal city of an independent county, and afterward the capital of the kingdom of CATALONIA.

BASQUES. An ancient people of northern Spain and southwestern France. Basque, unrelated to any known language, is the only living representative of the many tribal languages spoken in Iberia before the coming of the Romans in the third century BC. Occupying the lands along the eastern Atlantic coast of the IBERIAN PENINSULA and on both sides of the western PYRENEES, the Basques have traditionally been fiercely independent. Many Christian settlers of unoccupied or Moorish-occupied territories in the western-central and north-central parts of the Peninsula in the early centuries of the RECONQUEST (especially OLD CASTILE) probably came from the Basque Country (*País Vasco*).

BERBERS. A native African people, speaking a number of affiliated dialects and occupying since ancient times a zone between the Atlantic Ocean and western Egypt, and the area between the Mediterranean Sea and the central Sahara. Converted to Islam around the turn of the seventh century, Berbers were an important factor in the Muslim expansion into the MAGHREB. The majority of the Muslim invaders of Spain in the early eighth century were Berbers (i.e., not Arabs). For several centuries after the MUSLIM INVASION, Berbers continued to constitute the majority of Muslim settlers in most areas of AL-ANDALUS.

BÚCAR, KING (*EC*). A Moorish chieftain; possibly correspon-ding to the historical Almoravid ruler Abu-Bakr Ibn-Umar (died 1087).

BURGOS (*EC, FGC, CTK*). The principal city of CASTILE. Founded in 884 as an outpost and staging point for Christian resettlement on the frontier, the city became the seat of the newly independent county of Castile around 930. In 1038 Bur-gos was made the capital of the unified kingdom of León-Castile, retaining that honor until ALFONSO VI's conquest of TOLEDO in 1085, when the latter city became the new Castil-ian capital (see also LEÓN).

CABRA, CASTLE OF (*EC, FGC*). Located in the present-day province of CORDOBA, this fortress was the site of the histor-ical Battle of Cabra (1079), in which the Cid defeated the com-bined forces of Count GARCÍA ORDÓÑEZ and the emir of GRANADA.

CALATAYUD (*EC*). A town on the JALÓN RIVER in the pres-ent-day province of SARAGOSSA, strategically situated be-tween the central plateau of the Iberian Peninsula and the EBRO RIVER valley.

CALIPHATE OF CORDOBA. Established when Abd al-Rah-man III, the descendent of Abd al-Rahman I, the founder of the Spanish UMAYYAD dynasty, declared himself Caliph in 929. Around 950, Abd al-Rahman III, his military forces augmented and reorganized, extended his influence into the MAGHREB, controlling the zone between Tangiers and Algiers. Under the first Spanish Umayyad caliph and his successor, al-Hakam II (961–976), the Caliphate's territories were expanded and the realm's prosperity increased. At its height, the Cordoban caliphate controlled 80 percent of the IBERIAN PENINSULA. Sometimes at war with Spanish Christian kingdoms, other times at peace, the Umayyads occasionally intervened on behalf of one Christian kingdom or another. The capital, meanwhile, benefited from the Umayyads' sponsorship of architecture and urban beautification. Cordoba's population of half a million made it the most populous city in Europe. A famous center of patronage for the arts and sciences, the Umayyad capital was one of the most important seats of learning in the Europe of its day, with its great library attracting Christian and Muslim scholars from many countries.

During the early years of the Caliphate of Cordoba, a general policy of tolerance toward Jews and Christians was observed. This changed under Hicham II, whose grand vizier, the formidable Almanzor, persecuted Jews and Christians within AL-ANDALUS, while launching a holy war against the Peninsular Christian kingdoms, carrying out destructive raids against BARCELONA (985) and SANTIAGO DE COMPOSTELA (997). After Almanzor's death in 1002, the Caliphate under Hicham II (976–1013) was beset by dynastic struggles, civil wars, and factional strife among Arabs and Berbers. Finally, in 1031, the realm was divided into twenty-three independent kingdoms or city states (see TAIFA STATES).

CANTABRIA. A historic region, situated in the north-central part of the IBERIAN PENINSULA. It is bordered to the east by the BASQUE country; to the west by ASTURIAS; to the south by OLD CASTILE; to the north by the Cantabrian Sea (part of the Atlantic).

CAROLINGIAN EMPIRE. The domain of a Frankish dynasty that took its name from Charles Martel (in Latin, Carolus Martellus, "Charles the Hammer"), the victor against the invading Muslims at the Battle of Poitiers (732). Its most prominent ruler was Charlemagne ("Charles the Great"), king of the FRANKS from 768, and self-styled Emperor of the Romans from 800 until his death in 814. Among the campaigns undertaken by Charlemagne early in his career was an attempted invasion of northern Spain, which ended with his withdrawal into southern France. During the retreat his rear guard was famously overrun by BASQUE guerrillas in the Battle of Roncevaux (August 778). See SPANISH MARCH.

CARRIÓN (*EC*). The present-day Carrión de los Condes. A town in the present-day autonomous community of Castile and León, sixty-five kilometers from the city of Palencia. Known in history as the ancestral home of the VANIGÓMEZ, the clan of the SCIONS OF CARRIÓN (see DIEGO GONZÁLEZ; FERNANDO GONZÁLEZ).

CASTEJÓN (*EC*). A town (in modern Spanish, Castejón de Henares) on the banks of the Henares River in the present-day province of Guadalajara, in the autonomous community of Castile and León.

CASTEJÓN *(EC)*. A seaport (in modern Spanish, Castellón de la Plana) located on the Mediterranean coast sixty-five kilometers northeast of VALENCIA; the capital of the present-day province of Castellón.

CASTILE (Sp. *Castilla;* from *castillo,* "castle"). An area in north-central Spain, at first a militarized buffer zone between the Christians of ASTURIAS and LEÓN and northern AL-AN-DALUS, then constituted as a county in the mid-ninth century. Although the county of Castile achieved a de facto independence from León under the semilegendary Count Fernán González (910–970), it technically remained a Leonese dependency until Fernando I (see FERNANDO, KING) merged León and Castile into a single kingdom (1037). The newly unified realm was greatly expanded under ALFONSO VI (1065–1109) and Alfonso VII (1126–1157).

CATALONIA. A region and old kingdom of northeastern Spain, whose borders are the Mediterranean Sea to the east, ARAGON to the west, France to the north, and VALENCIA to the south. Attaining its independence in the ninth century, Catalonia extended, in its earlier history, into the southern part of present-day France. The language of the region, Catalán, is a separate Romance tongue related to the Occitanian dialects of southern France. Its principal city has always been BAR-CELONA, which became the seat of a powerful independent county of the same name. In the twelfth century the county of Barcelona merged with the kingdom of Aragon, with the unified realms thereafter governed by a single ruler. See also RAYMOND, COUNT OF BARCELONA.

CHARLEMAGNE. See CAROLINGIAN EMPIRE.

CID, EL. See RODRIGO DÍAZ DE VIVAR.

CLUNY, ABBEY OF. A famous French monastery located in east-central France, Cluny was the origin of an influential reform movement in the Benedictine Order, and one of the chief cultural and intellectual centers of Christian Europe from the tenth through the twelfth centuries. The site of an important library, Cluny benefited from the leadership of a line of highly effective abbots. ALFONSO VI, and his father Fernando I (see FERNANDO, KING) before him, were major contributors to the abbey's activities and supported the expansion of Clunaic influence in Christian Spain.

COLADA (*EC*). One of the two swords legendarily belonging to the Cid (see also TIZÓN). In the *EC*, the Cid wins the sword in battle from the Count of Barcelona.

CONSTANCE OF BURGUNDY (1046–1093). The daughter of Duke Robert I of Burgundy and of Hélie de Semur-en-Brionnais, she married ALFONSO VI of León and Castile in 1079. Of their several children, the only one to survive beyond infancy was URRACA OF LEÓN AND CASTILE.

CORDOBA. An Andalusian city, founded in ancient times and one of the principal political, cultural, and economic centers of Spanish history. A Roman provincial capital, it retained its importance during the Visigothic period (fifth through seventh centuries; see VISIGOTHS). Conquered by Muslims in the early eighth century, it became the capital of an emirate (755–929), then of a caliphate (929–1031; see CALIPHATE OF CORDOBA). After its reconquest in 1236, it continued to be an important Spanish city, although eclipsed by SEVILLE in the later Middle Ages and in the colonial era.

CORPES, OAKGROVE OF (*EC*). A town called Robledo de Corpes ("Oakgrove of Corpes") exists in the present-day province of Guadalajara. In so far as we can deduce the route taken by the SCIONS OF CARRIÓN on their way home to CARRIÓN, the town is located in the area where the *EC* shows the Scions' misdeed was committed. However, controversy surrounds attempts to identify the location of any real forest with that of the grove described in the epic (see Michael, n. to l. 2697).

CURLY-HAIRED MAN OF GRAÑÓN (*EC*). See GARCÍA ORDÓÑEZ.

DAROCA (*EC*). A Muslim town for four centuries, eventually conquered by the Christians in 1120.

DENIA *(EC, HR)*. A city founded in Roman times, situated on the north coast of the province of Alicante. The capital of a *taifa* of the same name, established in the early eleventh century, Denia became one of the most powerful kingdoms in eastern Al-Andalus. Annexed by the *taifa* of Saragossa in 1076, it was conquered by the ALMORAVIDS in 1091 and remained in Muslim hands until its conquest by Christians in 1244.

DIEGO GONZÁLEZ *(EC)*. One of the two SCIONS OF CARRIÓN.

DIEGO TÉLLEZ *(EC)*. Probably corresponds to the historical Diego Téllez, governor of the Castilian town of Sepúlveda.

DUERO RIVER *(EC, FGC, YDR)*. One of the principal Spanish rivers, flowing west across the north-central Peninsula and emptying into the Atlantic at the Portuguese city of Porto. During the early days of the RECONQUEST period, it marked the boundary between Christian and Muslim territory. See EXTREMADURA.

EBRO RIVER *(SC, FGC)*. The most voluminous river on the IBERIAN PENINSULA, flowing into the Mediterranean Sea in the province of Tarragona.

ELVIRA, DOÑA *(EC)*. One of the two daughters of the Cid in the epic. Possibly corresponds to Cristina, the elder daughter of the historical Cid.

ELVIRA OF TORO *(FGC)*. Younger daughter of Fernando I of Castile (see FERNANDO, KING).

EXTREMADURA *(FGC)*. A historical region in west central Spain whose name derives from a Latin phrase meaning "beyond the Duero" (because the latter river long marked the boundary between Christian and Muslim territory). A frontier zone and important area of Christian occupation and settlement during the earlier part of the Reconquest. Its chief cities are Mérida (the Roman Emerita Augusta), Badajoz, and Cáceres.

FÁRIZ (*EC*). A fictional Moorish chieftain. See also GALVE.

FÉLIX MUÑOZ (*EC*). Fictional character, the Cid's nephew in the epic.

FERNANDO GONZÁLEZ (*EC*). One of the two SCIONS OF CARRIÓN.

FERNANDO, KING (*FGC, YDR*). Fernando I, the Great (1016–1065). The son of Sancho III of NAVARRE and Munia Mayor of CASTILE, Fernando married Sancha, the sister of King Bermudo III of LEÓN. In 1037, he defeated his brother-in-law's army and laid claim to the Leonese throne, invoking his wife's right of succession. In 1054 he won a victory over the armies of Navarre, killing his brother García IV of Navarre during the battle. This victory allowed him to further expand his realm. Fernando I was also known for his victorious campaigns against the Moors, taking Coimbra in 1064 and making SEVILLE a vassal state.

Fernando's five children were URRACA OF ZAMORA; SANCHO II of Castile; ELVIRA OF TORO; ALFONSO VI of León and Castile; and GARCÍA II of GALICIA. Shortly before his death, Fernando divided his kingdoms among his three sons, with Sancho receiving Castile, Alfonso León, and García Galicia, a partition leading to a period of fratricidal warfare from which Alfonso emerged victorious.

FRANKS (*EC*). A western Germanic people who came to settle and eventually conquer most of Roman Gaul in the sixth century CE. Within Spain, the name *Franks* was also applied to the peoples of Barcelona and Catalonia, because of the historical association of those areas with the SPANISH MARCH (see also CAROLINGIAN EMPIRE).

FROILA, COUNT (*EC*). A historical character, Froila Díaz, one of the most prominent nobles in the court of ALFONSO VI, and the majordomo of RAYMOND, COUNT, the governor of GALICIA during the later reign of Alfonso VI.

GABRIEL, ARCHANGEL (*EC*). Mentioned in Luke 1:10–20. Regarded as the special messenger of God in both Christian and Muslim traditions.

GALICIA *(TES, FGC)*. A historic region and ancient kingdom in the extreme northwest of the IBERIAN PENINSULA. Roughly corresponding to the Roman province of Gallaecia, and known since ancient times for its mineral wealth, it was a county in the ninth and tenth centuries, then became a kingdom in the eleventh (see FERNANDO, KING). Since the Middle Ages it has been best known for its legendary association with Saint James the Greater (see SANTIAGO) and as the site of SANTIAGO DE COMPOSTELA.

GALINDO GARCÍA *(EC)*. Identified in the poem as Aragonese; possibly corresponding to a historical knight who collaborated with the Cid in the defense of VALENCIA.

GALVE *(EC)*. A fictional Moorish chieftain. See also FÁRIZ.

GARCÍA *(FGC)*. García II of Galicia. Youngest son of Fernando I (see FERNANDO, KING).

GARCÍA ORDÓÑEZ *(EC, FGC)*. A historical personage (d. 1108), the Count of Nájera, one of the most important nobles in the kingdom of ALFONSO VI. Depicted in the *EC* as the archrival of the Cid, he was also known as "the curly-haired man of Grañón."

GONZALO ANSÚREZ *(EC)*. A count; father of the SCIONS OF CARRIÓN.

GORMAZ, CASTLE OF *(EC, HR, CTK, YDR)*. Strategically situated on a hill north of the DUERO RIVER in what is now the province of Soria, this fortress, built by Muslims in the 800s, was the largest fortification in Europe in the tenth and eleventh centuries. After changing hands several times, it was definitively taken by Christian forces in 1060. See SAN ESTEBAN DE GORMAZ.

GRANADA *(HR, CTK)*. Founded in pre-Roman times as a fortified town, Granada was of minor importance in imperial times, and largely depopulated during the early Muslim period. Not until the era of the TAIFA STATES did it become one of the principal cities of AL-ANDALUS. Famous for its fortified palace and residence known as the Alhambra (constructed in the mid-fourteenth century), it remained an independent Muslim state after the main phase of the RECONQUEST was completed in the middle of the thirteenth century. The Muslim kingdom of Granada came to an end in 1492, when, after a ten-year war, the city surrendered to Isabel and Ferdinand.

HENRY, COUNT (*EC*). The historical Henry of Burgundy. A nephew of Robert, first duke of Burgundy, and of CONSTANCE OF BURGUNDY, Henry became the Count of PORTUGAL in 1093, when he married Teresa, Countess of Portugal, the illegitimate daughter of ALFONSO VI.

HISPANIA. The ancient Roman name for the IBERIAN PENINSULA.

HUESCA (*EC*). A town in the northeastern IBERIAN PENINSULA, located in the present-day autonomous community of ARAGON. Founded in pre-Roman times, it was important during the imperial and Visigothic periods. After the fall of the CALIPHATE OF CORDOBA, it became subject to the *taifa* kingdom of SARAGOSSA.

IBERIAN PENINSULA. Derived from ancient Greek and Latin names for the EBRO RIVER (Greek *Ibēros*, Lat. *Ibērus* or *Hibērus*), the name is used to refer to the land mass of the Peninsula, as opposed to any of the political divisions within it (e.g., PORTUGAL, CASTILE). See also HISPANIA; SPAIN.

ISIDORE, SAINT (*EC*). Saint Isidore of SEVILLE (Sp. *San Isidro* or *San Isidoro*; c. 560–636 CE; canonized in 1598). The archbishop of Seville, Isidore was the most prominent theologian and scholar of Visigothic Spain. Regarded by some as the last great thinker and writer of antiquity, he exerted a lasting influence not only in Spain but throughout Christian Europe. His most famous work, the *Etymologies*, a kind of encyclopedia, was widely read until the Renaissance.

ISLAMIC CALENDAR. Also known as the Hijri Calendar, this dating system takes as its starting point the year of the migration (*Hegira*) of the Islamic prophet Muhammad and his followers from Mecca to Medina (622 AD). The abbreviation that corresponds to AD (*anno Domini*, "in the year of our lord") of the Christian calendar is AH (*anno Hegirae*, "in the year of the Hegira").

JALÓN RIVER (*EC*). A river in northeastern Spain, a principal tributary of the EBRO RIVER.

JÁTIVA (*EC*). A town founded in pre-Roman times, located in the southern part of the present-day province of VALENCIA. After the fall of the CALIPHATE OF CORDOBA, it was subject to a succession of TAIFA STATES (TOLEDO, CORDOBA, DENIA).

JÉRICA (*EC*). A TAIFA STATE founded in 1010. The first such state to declare independence from the disintegrating CALIPHATE OF CORDOBA, it was conquered in 1076 by the *taifa* of SARAGOSSA.

JEROME, BISHOP (*EC*). The historical Jerome, originally from the province of Périgord, France, was made bishop of the newly conquered VALENCIA in 1097–1098, remaining in that office until the Christian withdrawal from Valencia in 1102. He died c. 1120.

JILOCA RIVER (*EC*). A river in ARAGON; a tributary of the JALÓN RIVER.

JIMENA, DOÑA (*EC, FGC, YDR*). The historical Jimena Díaz (born probably before 1046; died around 1115). Married to the Cid in 1074, Jimena bore him three children: Cristina (b. 1075), called DOÑA ELVIRA in the *EC*; María (1077–1105), called DOÑA SOL in the *EC*. The *EC* does not mention a son, Diego (1076–1097), killed at the age of nineteen in the Battle of Consuegra. After the Cid's death in 1099, Jimena stayed in VALENCIA, leading the city's resistance to Muslim attacks. But in 1102, Jimena and the other Christians living in the city were forced to withdraw. She ended her days in the monastery of SAN PEDRO DE CARDEÑA.

JÚCAR (*EC*). A river in eastern Spain, flowing 509 kilometers eastward from its source in the Sierra de Tragacete, in the present-day province of Cuenca, and emptying into the Mediterranean near the town of Cullera, in the province of VALENCIA.

LEÓN. A city in the northwestern IBERIAN PENINSULA, founded in Roman times. Conquered from the Muslim city in the middle of the eighth century, the town became the capital of an independent kingdom of the same name in the early tenth century. The most important Christian kingdom in the Peninsula during the tenth and early eleventh centuries, León was briefly controlled by NAVARRE in the 1020s, before becoming part of the combined kingdom of León-Castile under Fernando I (from 1037 until his death in 1065; see FERNANDO, KING).

LONGINUS (*EC*). The name given in medieval Christian tradition to the Roman soldier (unnamed in the Gospels) who, at the crucifixion, pierced Jesus' side with a lance (John 19:34). The same medieval tradition identified Longinus as the centurion who declared that Jesus was indeed the son of God (Matt. 27:54; Mark 15:39).

MAGHREB. The name (Arabic, "place of the setting sun") given to the northwestern part of Africa. The region is occupied by several countries: MOROCCO, Mauritania, Algeria, Tunisia, and Libya.

MAL ANDA (*EC*). A character unknown to history, probably fictional. A legal expert, supporter of the Cid.

MARTÍN ANTOLÍNEZ (*EC*). A knight of Burgos, unknown to history. In the epic, a staunch supporter of the Cid.

MARTÍN MUÑOZ (*EC*). A historical person, the governor, under ALFONSO VI, of what is now the Portuguese town of Montemor-o-Velho (called "Montemayor" in the *EC*). Later named the Count of Coimbra, he could not have accompanied the historical Cid into exile.

MEDINA (*EC*). Identified with Medinaceli, a strategically important frontier town located in the present-day province of Soria, at the confluence of the JALÓN and ARBUJUELO valleys.

MOHAMMED (*EC*). The founder of the religion of Islam (570–632).

MOLINA (*EC*). Probably the present-day Molina de Aragón.

MONREAL (*EC*). A town corresponding to the modern Monreal del Campo, located in the present-day province of TERUEL, in the autonomous community of ARAGON.

MONTES CLAROS (*EC*). A name used in the *EC* as another name for the ATLAS MOUNTAINS. It is also the name of a range traversed by the SCIONS OF CARRIÓN and their brides. Michael (n. to l. 2693) points out the difficulty of identifying these mountains with any known range.

MONZÓN (*EC*). A town and fortress, founded by Muslims in the tenth century, located in the present-day province of HUESCA.

MOOR. In traditional Spanish usage (and in the *EC*): an inhabitant of the MAGHREB or of AL-ANDALUS, of Berber, Arab, or Black African descent; or a Muslim.

MOROCCO (*EC*). The country situated in the northwest corner of Africa, bordered on the west by the Atlantic Ocean, by the Strait of Gibraltar and the Mediterranean Sea to the north, by Algeria to the east, and by the Sahara to the south. Conquered by Arabs and converted to Islam at the end of the seventh century, the BERBERS of Morocco constituted the majority of the Muslim forces that carried out the MUSLIM INVASION of Spain. See also BERBERS; MUSLIM INVASION.

MOZARABS (Sp. *mozárabes*; from the Arabic *musta'rib*, meaning "arabicized"). A term referring to Christian inhabitants of AL-ANDALUS, practicing the Christian religion according to their own rite, speaking a variety of related Romance dialects, and generally granted a certain degree of communal and legal autonomy under Muslim law. During the RECONQUEST period, owing to increasing persecution of non-Muslims in Al-Andalus, many Mozarabs emigrated to the Christian kingdoms of the northern Peninsula, retaining their characteristic liturgy, customs, and language.

MULADÍ. Term referring to the Christians of AL-ANDALUS who converted to Islam, and to their descendants. Also refers to those of mixed Muslim and Christian parentage.

MUÑO GUSTIOZ *(EC)*. Vassal of the Cid and brother-in-law of Doña Jimena.

MURVIEDRO *(EC)*. The modern Sagunto (a readopted form of the ancient name, Saguntum), a town on the Mediterranean coast thirty kilometers north of the city of VALENCIA. Held by Muslims from the early eighth century until its conquest by Jaume I in 1238.

MUSLIM INVASION (of Spain). Initiated in 711 CE and completed within eight years, this conquest toppled the Visigothic kingdom that had lasted 250 years and initiated the long Islamic period in Peninsular history. The period came to a gradual close with the advance of the RECONQUEST in the eleventh through mid-thirteenth centuries, followed by two and a half centuries during which GRANADA lingered as an independent Muslim state, finally conquered in 1492. The Muslim era could be said to have finally come to a close in 1609, with the expulsion of the Moriscos (descendants of Spanish Muslims who converted to Christianity). See also AL-ANDALUS; CALIPHATE OF CORDOBA.

NAVARRE *(EC, SC, FGC)*. A region in the extreme north-central part of the IBERIAN PENINSULA. Never fully subjugated by the VISIGOTHS or by the Muslims, Navarre, with its capital Pamplona, became an independent kingdom in the early Middle Ages. Under Sancho III (992–1035) it was the most powerful Christian kingdom of the Peninsula, claiming authority over CASTILE and attempting to unite the Spanish Christians. Sancho's division of his realm among his sons shortly before his death undid the unity he had fostered. Navarre, although surviving for six centuries as an independent monarchy, was never again to enjoy the same power and prestige.

NEW CASTILE (Sp. *Castilla la Nueva*). The name of an historical region to the south of CASTILE (see also OLD CASTILE) and originally comprising the provinces of Ciudad Real, Cuenca, Guadalajara, Madrid, and TOLEDO. The designation distinguished Castile proper, or Old Castile, from newly reconquered and resettled territories pertaining to the Castilian crown and forming an extension of the original kingdom.

OJARRA *(EC)*. A character unknown to history, probably fictional.

OLD CASTILE. The name of an historical region, more or less coinciding with the original kingdom of CASTILE. It comprised the provinces of Santander (now Cantabria), Logroño (now La Rioja), BURGOS, Palencia, VALLADOLID, Soria, Segovia, and Ávila. The name emerged to differentiate the older part of the Castilian kingdom from its reconquered and assimilated territories to the south (see NEW CASTILE).

PER ABBAT *(EC)*. The name of the copyist (probably not of the author) of the only extant manuscript of *The Epic of the Cid*. Little is known concerning the identity of this scribe.

PEDRO BERMÚDEZ *(EC)*. Probably a historical person, about whom little is known. In the *EC*, the nephew, standard-bearer, and trusted vassal of the Cid.

PETER, SAINT *(EC)*. One of the twelve apostles. Venerated by all Christians as a leader of early Christianity and by the Catholic Church as its first pope. The patron saint of the monastery of SAN PEDRO DE CARDEÑA.

PORTUGAL *(FGC)*. The present-day country of the same name had its beginnings during the reign of ALFONSO VI as a county made up of reconquered territory to the south of GALICIA. This county was given by Alfonso to his son-in-law, COUNT HENRY, in 1093.

PYRENEES. A mountain range running from west to east and extending approximately 430 kilometers between the Bay of Biscay and the Mediterranean Sea. The range forms a natural barrier separating the IBERIAN PENINSULA from the rest of continental Europe. The highest elevation is Pico d'Aneto (11,168 feet, or 3,404 meters).

RAQUEL AND VIDAS *(EC)*. Moneylenders, probably fictional. Some have suggested that these characters are Jewish. However, there is no indication of their ethnicity in the text; moreover, usurers could come from any religious group.

RAYMOND, COUNT OF BARCELONA (*EC, HR*). A historical person, Count Berenguer Ramón II (1050s to 1090s), surnamed "The Fratricide" because public opinion blamed him for the murder of his twin brother and co-ruler Ramón Berenguer II.

RAYMOND, COUNT (*EC*). Count Raymond of Amoux (in Burgundy), the son of William I, Count of Burgundy, and the cousin of COUNT HENRY. The governor of GALICIA under ALFONSO VI, he married URRACA OF LEÓN AND CASTILE, the daughter of Alfonso and eventual heir to his throne.

RECONQUEST (Sp. *Reconquista*). The term used to refer to the long period during which AL-ANDALUS was conquered by Christian kingdoms. A Spanish Christian concept, promulgated since the twelfth century, sees the beginning of the Reconquest in the victory of Pelayo over Muslim forces at the Battle of Covadonga in 722. Another more objective historical perspective sees an earlier phase of several centuries of generally peaceful coexistence, punctuated by frequent warlike episodes that varied in scale, intensity, and duration. Throughout this earlier period, both sides knew setbacks and triumphs, as places and territories were lost, then retaken, then lost again. The balance of power favored the Islamic side, while permitting Christian autonomy and initiative.

The collapse of the CALIPHATE OF CORDOBA in 1031 was the watershed moment that changed all this. Ever after, the Christian kingdoms tended more and more toward collaboration, consolidation, and unification, while the Muslim *taifas* became ever more prone to rivalry, dissension, and disunity. On the Christian side, during the first century or so after the breakup of the Cordoban Caliphate, there was as yet no systematic sense of a Christian *Re*-conquest. Conquest was conquest, plain and simple, as it had always been. The propagandistic *re-*, implying the taking back of something that had always rightfully belonged to the Christians in the first place, was only added, mainly in the twelfth and thirteenth centuries, by apologists and fomenters of religious crusade and territorial expansion. The epic Cid's notion of conquest is prepolitical, prepropagandistic. He needs no ideological justification: he conquers because he wants to and because he can. The epic shows no sense of his furthering any agendas but his own.

RODRIGO DÍAZ DE VIVAR (*EC* and all Related Texts). The full name of the man known to history and folklore as "the Cid" or "My Cid." Born in VIVAR, near BURGOS, c. 1040 (though some have argued for other dates between that year and 1050); died in VALENCIA, 1099. The son of Diego Laínez, an *infanzón* ("baron") of BURGOS, and of a mother, given name unknown, with the family name of Rodríguez. The vassal and close collaborator of KING SANCHO II, then, after the Sancho's death, the vassal and confidante of Sancho's brother and successor, ALFONSO VI. Estrangement between Rodrigo and Alfonso led to a period of exile (c. 108 –c. 1087), during which Rodrigo served the *taifa* kingdom of SARAGOSSA. A reconciliation with Alfonso, apparently prompted by Alfonso's fear of Almoravid invasion, was followed by another period of exile and a period of independent campaigns in the eastern-central part of the Peninsula. These culminated in Rodrigo's famous siege and conquest of the great Muslim city of Valencia in 1094. Dying peacefully in 1099, he was later buried at the monastery of SAN PEDRO DE CARDEÑA.

ROMANCE LANGUAGES. The languages of western Europe that descend from regional dialects of vulgar Latin spoken in the Roman Empire. In the IBERIAN PENINSULA these include Castilian (i.e., Spanish, the official national language of the modern Spanish nation-state), Galician, Portuguese, Catalan, and several regional dialects. Other Romance languages include French; the Occitanian dialects (Provençal, Limousin); Italian and its several dialects; Sardinian; and Romanian.

RUY. A short form of the proper name "Rodrigo" (see RODRIGO DÍAZ DE VIVAR).

SAHAGÚN (*EC*). A town in the southeastern section of the present-day province of LEÓN.

SAINT JAMES THE APOSTLE (*EC*). See SANTIAGO.

SAN ESTEBAN (*EC*). A town situated near the banks of the DUERO RIVER, close to the Castle of Gormaz (see GORMAZ, CASTLE OF).

SAN PEDRO DE CARDEÑA (*EC*). A Benedictine monastery located eight kilometers southeast of BURGOS. Founded in 899, it became one of the most important shrines in the era of the *Camino de Santiago* ("Way of Saint James"; see SANTIAGO DE COMPOSTELA). Historically associated with the Cid, it was the site where his remains were originally buried before their subsequent removal to the Burgos cathedral.

SANCHO, KING (*FGC, HR, SC, CTK*). Sancho II of Castile. Second-born child and eldest son of Fernando I (see FERNANDO, KING).

SANTA MARÍA (*EC*). The cathedral of BURGOS.

SANTA MARÍA (*EC*). The cathedral of VALENCIA.

SANTIAGO (*EC*). Saint James the Greater, the son of Zebedee; one of the Twelve Apostles and the patron saint of Spain. "Santiago" was the traditional Christian battle cry in the era of the RECONQUEST. Peninsular Christian tradition believed that this saint preached in Roman Spain as well as in the Holy Land; that his body was conveyed to Spain after his martyrdom at the hands of Herod Agrippa (Acts 12:1–2); that his remains were buried in GALICIA; that he miraculously appeared to fight alongside Spanish Christians in their wars against the Muslims — hence his nickname, Matamoros ("Moor-slayer").

SANTIAGO DE COMPOSTELA (*EC*). A town in GALICIA: the legendary burial site of Saint James the Greater (see SANTIAGO); one of the three principal pilgrimage destinations of Christian Europe (along with Rome and Jerusalem); and the end point of the famous pilgrimage route, the WAY OF SAINT JAMES (*Camino de Santiago*).

SARAGOSSA (Sp. *Zaragoza; EC, HR, TES*). Principal city of the former kingdom of ARAGON, located on the EBRO RIVER. Founded in 14 BC during the reign of the Emperor Augustus, and named Caesaraugusta in his honor, the city has been important both commercially and militarily since its foundation. The capital of the powerful TAIFA STATE of Saraqusta, it was reconquered by the Christians in 1118 and became the capital of the Aragonese kingdom.

SCIONS OF CARRIÓN (*EC*). (Sp. *Infantes de Carrión*, "noble heirs of Carrión."*) DIEGO and FERNANDO GONZÁLEZ were historical persons and members of the powerful Leonese family of the VANIGÓMEZ, whose ancestral lands were located near CARRIÓN. Members of the court of KING ALFONSO VI. There is no historical evidence of their having married the daughters of the Cid.

SEVILLE (*HR, SC, CTK*). One of the oldest Spanish cities, founded over two thousand years ago on the banks of the Guadalquivir River. Important in Roman times, it became an important Visigothic town in the mid-sixth century, and, after the MUSLIM INVASION, one of the principal cities of AL-ANDALUS. After the breakup of the CALIPHATE OF COR-DOBA, Muslim Seville became the seat of one of the most important TAIFA STATES. Reduced to the status of a tribute state by Fernando I (see FERNANDO, KING) and then by his son ALFONSO VI, Muslim Seville looked for help to the AL-MORAVIDS. After several expeditions in supposed relief of the Spanish Muslims, the Almoravids mounted an all-out invasion of Al-Andalus in 1090, and remained in control of Al-Andalus until their overthrow by the ALMOHADS in the middle of the twelfth century. Prospering under the Almohads, Seville was reconquered by Fernando III in 1248.

SOL, DOÑA (*EC*). Probably corresponds to the historical María, younger daughter of the Cid.

SPAIN (Sp. *España; EC*). In the medieval context, a regional name referring either to the entire IBERIAN PENINSULA or — occasionally — Muslim Spain (i.e., AL-ANDALUS).

SPANISH MARCH (*Marca Hispánica*). A buffer zone between northern AL-ANDALUS and the Frankish lands, created by CHARLEMAGNE in the late eighth century on the Spanish side of the PYRENEES. Its southern boundary was the EBRO RIVER. The several counties and lordships of which it consisted, including Pamplona and BARCELONA, at first paid allegiance to the Frankish monarchs, but gradually attained independence. See also CAROLINGIAN EMPIRE.

TAGUS RIVER (*EC*). At 1,038 kilometers, the longest river in the IBERIAN PENINULA. Of its length 716 kilometers are in Spain and the remainder in PORTUGAL, where it flows into the Atlantic at Lisbon.

TAIFA STATES. When the CALIPHATE OF CORDOBA collapsed in 1031, the once unified and powerful AL-ANDALUS broke up into a number of independent kingdoms and principalities. The cities and towns of the old Caliphate (e.g., SEVILLE, CORDOBA, GRANADA, TOLEDO, VALENCIA, and SARAGOSSA) became the urban nuclei and administrative centers of their respective areas. The Arabic word *taifa*, from which these states take their collective name, means "faction" or "party." The term aptly characterizes these petty realms, whose rulers competed among themselves, both militarily and culturally, recruiting mercenaries and palace guards while patronizing scholars, poets, musicians, and artists. This fragmented environment of kinglets and city-states constituted the political map of Al-Andalus in the historical Cid's day (latter half of the eleventh century). The disunity of the situation insured the constant vulnerability of the *taifa* states to domination, exploitation, and conquest by both Christians from the northern Peninsula and by Muslim powers (such as the Berber AL-MORAVIDS) from the MAGHREB.

TARANZ, THICKETS OF (*EC*). The area called Campo Taranza in present-day Spain is an area of uncultivated scrubland, probably densely forested in the Middle Ages, located in the modern provinces of Guadalajara and Soria.

TERUEL (*EC*). A town in ARAGON, the capital of the present-day province of the same name.

THREE KINGS OF ARABY (*EC*). See ARABY, THREE KINGS OF.

TIZÓN (*EC*). The second of the Cid's famous swords, won by the hero in battle from the emir of MOROCCO.

TOLEDO (*EC, TES, HR*). Founded by the Romans in 192 BC, and strategically situated in the center of the Peninsula, Toledo has been an important Spanish town throughout its history. It was the capital of the Visigothic kingdom, the seat of a TAIFA STATE, and one of the principal Christian cities after its conquest by ALFONSO VI in 1085.

UMAYYADS. A dynasty of Caliphs that ruled the Muslim world from 661 to 750. Their name comes from an ancestor, Umayya, the great-uncle of Mohammed. In the lifetime of the prophet, they controlled the region around Mecca. Their caliphate, with its capital in the Syrian city of Damascus, was, in terms of territorial extent, the greatest Muslim state in history. Overthrown in 750, the Umayyads relocated to AL-ANDALUS, where, under the leadership of Abd al-Rahman I (756–788), they established an independent emirate. Abd al-Rahman III (c. 890–961), assuming the title of caliph in 929, presided over the most powerful and prosperous country in tenth-century Europe (see CALIPHATE OF CORDOBA).

URRACA OF ZAMORA (*FGC*). Eldest child of Fernando I of Castile (see FERNANDO, KING).

URRACA OF LEÓN AND CASTILE (1079–1126). The eldest surviving child of ALFONSO VI, she succeeded her father as queen of LEÓN, CASTILE, and GALICIA, and in 1109 assumed the title of "Empress of All the Spains."

VALENCIA (*EC*). A Roman military colony, then an important port in the late-imperial and Visigothic eras, Valencia became one of the principal cities of AL-ANDALUS. The Cid's conquest and occupation was a brief interlude (1094–1102), as Muslims retook the city after the withdrawal, in 1102, of JIMENA, Bishop JEROME, and most of the other Christian residents. The city remained in Muslim hands until 1238.

VALLADOLID (*EC, FGC*). A historic city of OLD CASTILE, situated at the confluence of the Pisuerga and Esgueva Rivers. From the time of ALFONSO VI, one of the most important towns of the RECONQUEST era.

VANIGÓMEZ (or Beni-gómez; *EC*). Noble family whose ancestral estates were located near the town of CARRIÓN; the SCIONS OF CARRIÓN were members of this family.

VELLID ADOLFO (*FGC*). The legendary assassin of King SANCHO II during the latter's siege of ZAMORA.

VISIGOTHS. A Germanic people who immigrated into the western Roman Empire in the early fifth century. Obtaining control of southern Gaul (present-day France) by means of a pact with the Roman emperor, they entered HISPANIA in 414 as allies of Rome. Making TOLEDO their capital in the sixth century, they consolidated their realm, seizing control of the northwestern area of the Peninsula (GALICIA and ASTURIAS) from a rival Germanic people (late sixth century).

After the collapse of the western Roman Empire in 476, the Visigoths played an important military, political, and cultural role in western Europe. Latin speakers by the time of their settling in the Peninsula, they were admirers and inheritors of Roman civilization. They established law codes, fostered trade and commerce, sponsored literature and the arts, especially architecture, and encouraged the expansion of Christianity. Theirs was perhaps the most prestigious of the so-called Germanic successor states that were the direct heirs of the western Roman Empire.

Invaded in 711 by a Muslim army of between 10,000 and 15,000 soldiers, consisting mostly of BERBERS recently converted to Islam, the Visigothic kingdom was subdued after an eight-year campaign. Only mountainous regions in the extreme northwest (GALICIA and ASTURIAS) and in the BASQUE country remained unconquered.

The relative rapidity and completeness of Visigothic Spain's conquest by the Muslims in the early eighth century is attributed to internal tensions and disunity within the Germanic kingdom; to its harsh treatment of Peninsular Jews; to the regime's persistent identity as an exploitative warrior elite rather than an assimilating minority, and its consequent failure to win the hearts and minds of the Hispano-Roman population.

VIVAR (*EC*). A village in OLD CASTILE, ten kilometers north of BURGOS.

YUSUF (*EC, TES*). A historical person, Yusuf ibn Tashfin (1009?–1106), the leader of the ALMORAVIDS from 1061 until his death. The commander-in-chief of Almoravid forces in the Muslim coalition (including the *taifas* of SEVILLE, GRENADA,

Malaga) that defeated ALFONSO VI and his forces at the Battle of Sagrajas (1086). Afterward, between 1090 and 1094, he conquered a disunited AL-ANDALUS for the ALMORAVIDS, who stayed in power until 1147.

ZAMORA (*FGC*). A city in the northwest part of the IBERIAN PENINSULA, the capital of the present-day province of the same name. One of the most important Christian fortified towns in the early years of the RECONQUEST. Famous for being bequeathed to URRACA OF ZAMORA by King Fernando I (see FERNANDO, KING), and as the site of SANCHO II's legendary assassination by VELLID ADOLFO in 1072.

INDEX

711, year of Islamic invasion of
Iberian Peninsula, ix
1031, year of final collapse of
Cordoban Caliphate, xi
1085, year of Alfonso VI's con-
quest of Toledo, xi

Abd al-Mumin (Almohad
leader), 181
Abd al-Rahman I (founder of
Spanish Umayyad dynasty),
185
Abd al-Rahman III (founder of
Cordoban caliphate), 185
Abengalbón, 43–45, 75–76, 81
Abraham (biblical patriarch),
125 (n. 17)
Abu Achmed (qadi of Valencia),
113
Abu Tahir (Muslim ruler of
Murcia), 109
Abu-Bakr (Almoravid leader),
181, 185
Achilles, 182 (n. 2)
Aeneas, 124
Aeneid (Latin epic), xviii, xix
Africa, xviii
Agaricae gentis ("of the Hagaritic
tribe"), 125 (n. 17)
AH (abbreviation of anno
Hegirae, "in the year of the
Hegira"), 192
Ahmad, Abu (qadi of Valencia),
112
Al-Andalus, xi–xii, 109, 163; as
caliphate (912–1031), ix; as in-
dependent emirate (756–712),
ix
al-Hakam II (Spanish Umayyad
caliph), 185
Alamos, 76

Alarcos, Battle of, 181
Albarracín, xi, 43
Alcalá (town), 15, 16
Alcañiz, 27
Alcarria River, 17
Alcobiella, 14
Alcocer (town), 18, 19–20, 25–26
Alcoceva Notch, 81
Aldonza Gómez (YDR; middle
daughter of Count Gómez de
Gormaz), 167
Alfonso Gómez (son of Count
Gómez de Gormaz), 167
Alfonso, King (Alfonso VI of
Castile and León), xi–xii, 3–4,
14, 16–17, 20, 24, 26, 32, 37,
39, 40–41, 51–52, 53–59, 61–
63, 80, 82–85, 87–91, 94–97,
99–101, 103, 105, 116–118,
125, 128, 130–131, 134, 136,
140–142, 146, 148, 150, 156–
159, 161–163; mentioned by
Ibn Bassam, 111; his decree
banishing the Cid, 5; his
wrath against Cid, 6
Alfonso VII, 187
Alfonso VIII, xi
Alfonso X (king of Castile), 127
Algeria, 181, 194, 195
Algiers, 185
Alhama, 17
Alhambra (Moorish palace in
Granada), 191
Alilón, 14
Almanzor (Cordoban grand
vizier under Hicham II), 186
Almenara, 33, 39, 120, 126
Almohads, xi
Almoravids, xi–xii, 115
Almudafar (Moorish king of
Granada), 117, 161

Alphonsine school of historians, 161
Álvar Álvarez, 23, 49, 56–57, 86
Álvar Díaz, 58
Álvar Fáñez, Minaya, 13, 15–17, 19–21, 23–25, 26–28, 32, 34, 37–39, 40–42, 44–46, 49–55, 61, 63–64, 68, 70, 72–73, 75, 80–81, 85–86, 96–97, 135, 137–139
Álvar Salvadórez, 15, 23, 48–49, 56, 86
Amor, River, 81
Ampurdán, lord of (ally of Count of Barcelona), 120
Andalusia, 179
Andros (place name), 56
Anguita, Caves of, 17
Ansarera, 76
Ansur González (elder brother of Scions of Carrión), 62, 66, 94–95
Araby, kings of (mentioned in Jimena's prayer), 12
Aragon, xii, 57, 105, 124; allied with Sancho II, 134
Aragon, prince of (suitor of Cid's daughter), 95–96
Arbujuelo Valley, 43, 45, 75
Arias Gonzalo, 137, 144, 145, 146, 149, 150, 151, 152, 154, 155, 157
Arlanzón River, 5, 9
Arlanzón Bridge, 11
assembly convened by Alfonso, 56–57
Astures (ancient Iberian people), 183
Asturians, 134, 141, 158
Asturias, kingdom of, xi, 82, 128
Ateca, 17–18, 19–20, 25
Athena (in Homeric epic), xxi
Atienza, 76
Atlantic Ocean, 184, 186, 189, 195
Atlas Mountains, 35

Audience of epic poetry, implied, xii
Augustus (Roman emperor), 200
authorship of EC, xx
Ávila (Spanish town and province), 196

Babieca, 45–46, 49–50, 61, 69, 98–99, 176
Badajoz, 189
Bailey, Matthew (editor of Mocedades de Rodrigo), 165 (n. 23)
Balearic Islands, 183
ballads, xiv; characteristics of, 175
Balthasar (one of the Magi), 12
bandits in folklore and history, xvii
banishment of hero, 3
Banu Hud (ruling clan in Saragossa), 112
Barcelona, xi–xii, 119; county, 29
Barcelona, Count of. See Raymond (Count of Barcelona)
bard, folkloric, xx
beard, symbolic and folkloric significance of, 30, 58, 92
Belorado, 171
Beltrán, Count, 84
Benedictine Order, 187
Benicadell, 35, 39
Beowulf (Old English epic), xviii
Berbers, xi
Berlanga, 81
Bermúdez, punning significance of name, 93 (n. 26)
Bermudo III (king of León), 189
Bermudo Laínez (ancestor of Cid; HR), 116
Besalú, lord of, 120
Bethlehem, 12
Biscayans, 134
breeches, as gift, 9
Bronchales, 43
Bubierca, 17

Búcar (King of Morocco), 67, 69–72
Bulcor of Sepúlveda (Moorish sheik; *YDR*), 171
Burgos, xi, xii, 4–6, 10, 25, 43–44, 56, 80, 88, 142–143, 159, 199
Burgos of Ayllon (Moorish chieftain; *YDR*), 171–173
Burriana, 33
Cabezón, 133, 143
Cabra, castle of, 92, 117, 125, 137; Battle of, 185
Cáceres, 189
Calatayud, 18–20, 23, 25–26
Caliphate of Cordoba, xi, 186
Calvary, 12
Camino de Santiago. *See* Way of Saint James
Campeador (meaning of epithetic title), xxi, xxiii–xxiv
Campidoctor (epithetic Latin title of Cid), xiii, xxiii
Campo Taranza, 202
Canon Law, 95 (n. 28)
Cantabrian Sea, 183
cantar ("song"; medieval Spanish term for epic poem), ix, xxi
Cantar de Mio Cid (Spanish title of *EC*), ix
Carcassone, lord of, 120
Carmen Campidoctoris (Latin title of *SC*), 123 (n. 13)
Carrión, 39, 67, 71, 73–76, 88–90, 99, 104; de los Condes (present-day Spanish town), 186; plain of, 97; River, 141; counts of, 40, 73
Caspar (one of the Magi), 12
Castejón (modern Castejón de Henares), 15–17, 186
Castejón (modern Castellón de la Plana, Catalonian city), 39, 187
Castejón de las Armas, 180
Castile, xii, 3, 8–9, 11, 14, 21, 25–26, 28, 37, 44, 51, 74, 82, 116, 124, 128, 131, 134, 163, 168, 171
Castilians, 56, 84, 134, 138, 139, 158
castles, wooden, used in mock warfare, 64
Castro Nuño, 148
Catalan (Romance language), 199
Catalonia, 124
Catholic Kings (Ferdinand and Isabella, so-called), xi
cavallero, meaning of in *EC*, xii–xxiii
Cebolla, 34, 39
Cella de Canal, 20, 26, 35
Cellorigo (province), 116
Cetina, 17
chansons de geste (French epic genre), xix
Charlemagne, 29 (n. 10)
Charles Martel (founder of Carolingian dynasty), 186
chests, used to trick moneylenders, 6–8
chivalry, xxiii
Christina (daughter of historical Cid), xii, 176 (n. 26), 193
Chronicle of Twenty Kings (*Crónica de veinte reyes*), 3, 67 (n. 20), 161
Cid, the. *See* Rodrigo Díaz de Vivar
"Cid and the Moorish King, The" (ballad), 175
Cid poet, xix
Cinca River, 120
Ciudad Real, 196
Coimbra (Portuguese city), 190, 143, 194
Colada, 30, 70, 74, 78, 88–90, 100, 102
combat, judicial, 65 (n. 19), 101–103
composition of epic, methods of, xxi

concordance of verbal tenses, inconsistency of in *EC*, xii
Constance, Queen (wife of Alfonso VI), 84 (n. 23)
Cordoba, ix, 117; Christian conquest of (1236), xi
Corneille (author of *Le Cid*), xiv
Corpes, Oakgrove of, 65, 77–78, 80, 83, 88, 91
court of justice (convened by Alfonso), 84, 88
Covadonga, Battle of, 198
crow, flight of, as omen, 3–4
Cuenca (Spanish town and province), 193, 196
Cullera, 34–35, 50, 193
Curiel (province), 116

Daniel, in lion's den, 12
Daroca, 26
Denia, xi, 34, 119
Diego (son of Arias Gonzalo), 157
Diego González, 32, 54, 94, 102–103
Diego Laínez (father of Cid), 116, 166–170, 198
Diego Ordóñez, 148, 149, 157
Diego Pérez, 117, 162
Diego Téllez, 80
direct address of *EC* poet to audience, xii
Dozy, Reinhart (Dutch Arabist), 109
duel, judicial, 65 (n. 19)
Duero River, 14, 80, 143, 149, 153, 171

Ebro River, 124, 128
Egypt, 184
El Cid, film (1963), xiv
electrum (alloy of gold and silver), 126
Elpha, 77
Elvira (daughter of epic Cid), 176
Elvira (younger daughter of Fernando I), xi, 128, 142, 146

Elvira Gómez (in *YDR*, eldest daughter of Count Gómez de Gormaz), 167
Enzón, Count, 137
Epic of the Cid, ix, xxi; date of composition, xiv; importance of the law in, xv; compared to other epics, xviii
epic poetry, defined, xviii; primary, xix; French, xix; Greek, xx; secondary, xix, xxi
epithets, in epic composition, xxi, xxiii
Escarp, castle of, 120
Escobar, Ángel (co-editor of *Carmen Campidoctor*), 123
Esgueva River, 203
Eucharistic Fast, 95 (n. 28)
Extremadurans (allies of Sancho II), 134

Fagib, al-, 126
Fagles, Robert (translator of Homer), xvii
Falque, Emma (editor of *Historia Roderici*), 115
Fáriz (Moorish king), 23, 25
Fariza (place name), 17
Félix Muñoz (nephew of the Cid), 23, 75, 78–79, 86
Ferdinand II of Aragon, 183
Fernán González, Count (founder of independent Castile), 187
Fernán Laínez (ancestor of the Cid; *HR*), 116
Fernando Gómez (son of Count Gómez de Gormaz), 167
Fernando González (one of the Scions of Carrión), 32, 54, 67–68, 91–93, 102
Fernando I (king of Castile and León), xi, 128–131, 142, 145, 156, 158, 168, 171
Fernando III, xi
feudalism, meaning of, 4 (n. 5)

feudum (Latin term), 4 (n. 5)
Fez (Moroccan city), 181
fief, meaning of, 4 (n. 5)
fifth, share of plunder reserved for the king, 16
Figueruela, 14
First General Chronicle (Primera crónica general), 127, 161
Fletcher, Richard, xiii, 109 (n. 2)
folklore and theory of epic composition, xii
formulaic language, xxi
Fortún Sánchez, 117
fosterage, 59 (n. 15)
France, epic tradition of, xx
Frankish realm, 29
Froila, Count, 84
Fuentedueña, 171

Gabriel, the angel, in Cid's dream, 14
Galicia, xi, 74, 128, 130, 136, 142; counts of, 82
Galician (Romance language), 199
Galicians, 56, 84, 141, 158; Muslim designation for Iberian Christians, 110 (n. 4)
Galindo García, 15, 23, 57, 86
Gallaecia (Roman province), 190
Gallocanta Pass, 28
Galve (Moorish king), 23
García de Cabra. *See* García Ordoñez
García IV (king of Navarre), 189
García Ordóñez (archenemy of the Cid), 32, 39, 52–53, 58, 84, 87–88, 92, 100, 117, 125, 132–133, 137, 148, 150, 155–156, 162
García, King (youngest son of Fernando I), xi, 128, 130–132, 134–140, 146
García (king of Pamplona), 117
Gate of the Sandpit, 153–154
Gaul, 190, 203

Genoa, xii
genre, verification of, with regard to *EC*, xvii
Germanic law, 65 (n. 19)
Germany, xviii
Gibraltar, Strait of, xi, 195
gift-giving, 8
Gil, Juan (editor of *HR*), 115
girl, nine-year-old (in Burgos), 5
Golgotha, 12
Golpejera, xi, 116, 140, 141
Gómez de Gormaz, Count, 166, 167
Gómez Peláez (Leonese noble, ally of the Vanigómez), 97
Gomiel (place name), 171
Gonzalo Ansúrez (father of the Scions of Carrión), 65, 70, 103
Google Books, 128
Gormaz, Castle of, 80–81, 166
Goths, 129, 131
Granada, 117, 161, 162, 191; conquest of by Catholic Kings, xi
Grañón (town), 171
Grañón, curly-haired man of. *See* García Ordóñez
Graus (castle), 116
Griza (town), 76
Guadalajara, 15–16, 188, 196, 202
Guadalquivir River, 200

Hagar (concubine of Abraham), 125 (n. 17)
Haro, 166, 169
Hayib, al-, 119–121
Hegira, 192
Hélie de Semur-en-Brionnais (mother of Constance of Burgundy), 187–188
Henares River, 15–17, 84
Henry, Count (Henry of Burgundy), 84–85, 87–88, 98
Herod Agrippa (New Testament character), 200
Heston, Charleton (star of film *El Cid*), xiv

Hicham II, 186
Hijri Calendar (Islamic calendar), 192
Hill of the Cid, 27
Hispanic era, 105 (n. 31)
History of Rodrigo (Historia Roderici), 115
Hita (town), 16
Hobsbawm, Eric, xvi
Holinshed (English chronicler), 128
Holy Trinity, 68
Homer, xvii; and epithets, xxi
Homeric epic, xix
horses, importance of, 24, 26, 39, 51–53, 57, 60–61
Huerta (fertile district near Valencia), 47
Huesa (town), 33
Huesca, 27–28

Ibn Alquama, xiii
Ibn Bassam (Hispano-Arabic chronicler), 109
Ibn Ghaldun (historical personage probably corresponding to *EC*'s Abengalbón), 179
Ibn Tûmart, Muhammad (founder of Almohad movement), 180
Ibn Yasin, Abdallah (Almoravid leader), 181
Iliad (Greek epic), xviii
illiteracy, possible, of Cid poet, xxi
India, xviii
Indian epic, xix
individualist model of epic composition, xx
infante, meaning of, 32
Infantes de Carrión (Spanish name of Scions of Carrión), 32 (n. 12)
infanzón (noble of lowest rank), xi, 95

Íñigo Jiménez (emissary of Prince of Navarre), 95–96
Isabel I of Castile, 183
Ishmael, son of Abraham (traditional ancestor of Arabian peoples), 125 (n. 17)
Isidore, Saint, 39, 85, 88, 130
Italian (Romance language), 199

Jalón River, 18, 20, 25, 44–45, 75–76
James I of Aragon, 115
James, Saint (patron saint of Christian Spain), 200
Japan, xviii
Játiva, 34–36
Jérica, 33, 39
Jerome, Bishop, 38, 43–46, 48–49, 51, 56, 58, 64, 68–69, 72, 86
Jerusalem, 200
Jesus Christ, 47, 135
Jews in Visigothic Spain, 204
Jiloca River, 20
Jimena Díaz (wife of the Cid), xi, xviii, 10–12, 39, 41–42, 46–48, 50–52, 57, 62–63, 72, 82, 85, 117. *See also* Jimena Gómez
Jimena Gómez (youngest daughter of Count Gómez de Gormaz; *YDR*), 165, 168, 170, 176
John, Saint, Gospel of, 193
Júcar River, 36

Keturah (mother of Midian), 126 (n. 18)
King's-Ford, 81
knight, meaning of, xii
knighthood, xxiii

La Rioja (Spanish province), 196
La Torre, 80
Laín Calvo (ancestor of Cid), 116, 166
Laín Fernández, 116
Laín Núñez, 116

language, of *EC*, xvii; repetitious, in *EC*, xxi
Lattimore, Richmond (translator of Homer), xvii
law, importance of, in *EC*, xv–xvi
Lazarus, 12
Le Cid (play by Corneille), xiv
left-hand side, significance of, 4 (n. 4)
León, x–xi, 74, 82, 84, 128–129, 134, 142, 187
Leonese, 56, 134, 141
Lérida, xi, 126
Lerma, 171
Libya, 181, 194
Limousin (Occitanian language), 199
linguists and theory of epic composition, xii
lion, incident of, 66, 93–94
literacy, of Cid poet, xxi
litigation, 86
Llantada, 140
Logroño, 196
Longinus (New Testament character), 13
Lope Sánchez, 117, 162
Lord, Albert (author of *The Singer of Tales*), xix–xx
Loren, Sophia (co-star of film *El Cid*), xiv
Luna, castle of, 116, 139, 140
Luzón Mountains, 75

Ma'mun, al-, 157
Madrid, 184
Maghreb, 181
Magi (New Testament characters), 12, 182
Mal Anda, 86
Malaga, ix
Mamun, al- (king of Toledo), 142
manuscript of *EC*, missing opening page of, 3

María (daughter of historical Cid), xii, 176 (n. 26), 193
Mark, Saint, Gospel of, 193
Marrakesh, 181–182
marriage of Cid's daughters, arranged by Alfonso, 59–60
Martín Antolínez, 5–11, 23, 43–44, 56, 80, 86, 89, 94, 99, 102–103
Martín Muñoz, 23, 56, 86
Martín River, 27
Mary, mother of Jesus, 9, 11–12, 37, 47–48, 65, 72
Matamoros (Spanish nickname of Saint James the Greater), 200
Matthew, Saint, Gospel of, 193
Mauritania, 194
Maya, Antonio (editor of *Historia Roderici*), 115 (n. 11)
Mecca, 192
Medina (Spanish town), 75, 81
Medina (Arabian city), 192
Medina de Rioseco, 144–145
Medinaceli, 40, 42–43, 45, 194
Melchior (one of the Magi), 12
Menéndez Pidal, Ramón (Spanish philologist), 127–128
Mérida, 189
meter, poetic, xii
Michael, Ian (British Hispanist), 180
Midian (son of Abraham by Keturah), 126 (n. 18)
Midianites, 126 (n. 18)
Miedes Mountains, 14
miller's fees (slanderously associated with Cid), 95
mills, historical association with *infazones*, 95 (n. 27)
Milton, John, xix
Minaya, meaning of, 182
Minaya Álvar Fáñez. *See* Álvar Fáñez, Minaya
Moabites (Christian name for Almoravids), 115

Mocedades de Rodrigo (Spanish title of *Youthful Deeds of Rodrigo*), 165
Molina, 26, 43, 45, 75, 81
Molina de Aragón (modern Spanish town), 179, 94
Monreal, 26, 35
Monreal del Campo (modern Spanish town), 194
Montalbán, 28, 33
Montaner, Alberto, 104 (n. 30), 123
Montemor-o-Velho (modern Portuguese town), 194
Montes Claros (Spanish range), 76
Monzón (town and castle), 27, 119–120
Moor, Spanish-speaking (vassal of Abengalbón), 76
Moorish king (in ballad of "The Cid and the Moorish King") 176–177
Moors, 27, 48
Moradillo (province), 116
Moriscos, 196
Mormojón (province), 116
Morocco, 47–48, 67, 72
Munia Mayor (mother of Fernando I), 189
Muño Gustioz, 42, 43, 44, 56, 62, 82, 83, 86, 95, 99
Muqtadir, al-, 119
Murviedro, 33–35, 39
musical performance, evidence of in *EC,* xxi
Musta'in, al-, 111–112
Mutamid, al-, 117–118, 162
Mutamin, al-, 119, 120, 121

Nájera, 128, 191
names, proper, xxiii
Nava del Grillo, 171
Navapalos, 14
Navarre, 105
Navarese, 134, 158

Navarre, prince of (suitor of Cid's daughters), 95–96
Navas de Tolosa, Battle of, x, 181
Nuño (townsman of Zamora), 147
Nuño Álvarez de Amaya, 166
Nuño de Lara, Count, 137
Nuño Laínez (ancestor of Cid), 116

Occitanian dialects, 199
Odysseus (Homeric character), xxi
Odyssey (Greek epic), xviii
Ojarra (emissary of Prince of Navarre), 95–96
Old Castilian language, ix
Olocau, 33; Pass, 33
omen, flight of crow as, 3; significance of, 4 (n. 4)
Onda, 33, 39
oral-formulaic theory of epic, xix
oral-traditionalist model of epic composition, xx
Ordoño, Count, 148
Osorio, Count, 168, 170
Oviedo, 82

Palencia, 117, 196, 201
Paradise Lost, as secondary epic, xix
parias, 17 (n. 6)
Paris (Greek hero), 124
Parry-Lord theory of oral-formulaic epic composition, xx
Parry, Milman, and oral-formulaic theory, xix
patriarchy, xvi
patronymics (Old Spanish naming system), 182 (n. 2)
Pax Domini ("Peace of the Lord"), 95 (n. 28)
payments in kind (made by Scions of Carrión to Cid), 91
Pedro (son of Arias Gonzalo), 157

Pedro Ansúrez, 146
Pedro Bermúdez (nephew and vassal of Cid), xv–xvi, 19, 21–22, 42, 44, 52–56, 62, 67–68, 80–81, 86, 89, 92–93, 99, 102
Pelagius (Pelayo; semilegendary founder of Asturian kingdom), 183, 198
Peña Falcón, 171
Peñafiel, 171
peón ("foot soldier"), compared to cavallero, xxiii
Per Abbat, 105
performance of epic poetry, xii, xx–xxi
Périgord (French province), 193
Pico d'Aneto (highest peak of Pyrenees range), 197
Pisa, xii
Pisuerga River, 128, 203
place names, English-language versions of, xxiii
Porto (Portuguese city), 189
Portugal, 130, 137, 142
Portuguese, subjects of King Alfonso, 84; Romance language, 199
prayer, Jimena's, 12, 13
Primitive Rebels (Hobsbawm book), xvi
Provençal (Occitanian dialect), 199
Pyrrhus (legendary Greek hero, son of Achilles; also known as Neoptolemus), 124

Quinea Road, 14
quito, meaning of, 104–105 (n. 30)

Raquel and Vidas, xvi, 6–9, 42
Raymond of Burgundy, 84–85, 87–91, 98
Raymond (Count of Barcelona), xii, 28–31, 126

Reconquest, The (Christian campaign of expansion into Al-Andalus), xi
Redecilla, 171
repetition, as indicator of epic performance, xii
Robert I (Duke of Burgundy), 187
Robin Hood, xvi–xvii
Robledo de Corpes (modern Spanish town), 188
Rodrigo (last king of Spanish Visigoths), 113
Rodrigo (son of Arias Gonzalo), 157
Rodrigo Álvarez (maternal grandfather of Cid), 116
Rodrigo Bermúdez (ancestor of Cid), 116
Rodrigo Díaz de Vivar (the Cid), xi–xii, xiv–xviii, 3–4
Abengalbón, friendship with, 44–46, 75–76; accusations against, 7; alférez (constable) of Sancho II, xi; Alfonso, relationship with, 5; altruism of, xvi; ancestry of, in HR, 116; in YDR, 166; banishment of, by Alfonso VI, 3, 12, 119, 125, 164; banishment of, by Sancho II, 147; beard, importance of, 25, 37, 87, 92, 98, 104; biography of, 198–199; bravery and prowess in battle, 24, 51, 69–71, 124, 126, 141, 167; burial of, at monastery of San Pedro de Cardeña, xii; calumny against, 12; campeador, meaning of, xxiii; acquisition of epithet, 116, 162; charismatic leader, xxiii; Christian view of, as ideal warrior and leader, xiii; Cid, meaning of epithetic title, xiii, xvii; clothing, ostentation of his, 86–87; complaint against

Scions of Carrión, 83, 88, 90–91; counselor to Sancho II, 133–134, 141, 156; court of justice, convened on his behalf, 84–85, 88; crusading spirit, his lack of, in *EC*, xiv; daughters of, 11, 39, 42, 46–48, 50–52, 57, 59, 62–64, 72–83, 85, 89, 91, 94–96, 105; death of, xii, 105; deference toward him, expressed by hand-kissing, 9, 12, 22; deference shown by him to Alfonso, 58–59; 85; divine favor, beneficiary of, 34, 51; economic incentives, offered by him as recruiting incentive, 8; emissary, his role as, of Sancho II to Urraca, 143–145, 147; Everyman, his folkloric role as, xvi; fatherhood, his embodiment of, 4, 12, 14; forbearance toward Scions of Carrión, 67–68, 70, 72; Gabriel, the Angel, his dream of, 14–15; García Ordóñez, rivalry with, 40, 53–54, 84, 87, 92, 125; generosity of, 61–62, 65, 167; generosity toward his men, 12, 25–26, 34, 52; generosity toward abbot of San Pedro, 11; generosity toward church of Santa María in Burgos, 26; generosity toward Count of Barcelona, 31–32; generosity toward Alfonso, 98–99; generosity toward Moors, 18, 20; generosity toward foes, 172–173; generosity toward Scions of Carrión, 73–74, 96; honor of, in relation to law, xvi; hospitality of, 59; family man, exemplary, 47, 48, 49, 51–52, 63; ideology, absence of as motive in, 198; infamy, his

charge of, leveled against Scions of Carrión, 92; *infanzón*, his status as, x, 94; jealousy of and accusations against him, 12, 118–119, 125, 163; jousting, skill at, 65; kinship, his, with royal houses of Spain, 105; leadership in war, 22–23, 30, 35, 37, 49–50, 68, 117, 121, 139–140, 162, 169, 171; legend of, xiv; lion, his confrontation of, 66; literary characterization of, contrasted with historical man, xiv, xvi; little girl of Burgos, his encounter with, 6; lordship, his embodiment of, 15, 38; loyalty to Alfonso, 17, 25, 27, 38, 40, 52–54, 62; loyalty to Sancho II, 139; marriage to Jimena, xi, 168–170; marriage of daughters to Scions of Carrión, 55–56, 60–64; marriage of daughters to princes of Navarre and Aragon, 95–96, 105; marriage of ladies-in-waiting to his vassals, 52; milling, his association with, imputed by Ansur González, 94–95; moneylenders, Cid contrasted with, xvi; Muslim view of, xiii; My Cid, meaning and usage of, as epithetic title, 4 (n. 3); negative view of, in Ibn Bassam, 111–113; oath, his taking of King Alfonso's in Santa Gadea, 158–159; omens, his reading of, 4–5, 74; outlaw status of, xvii; Outrage of Corpes, his reaction to, 80; piety of, xviii; 86; expressed in prayer, 10; in establishment of Valencian diocese, 39; promise to protect heirs of Fernando I, 129; raiding and plundering, organizer of, 4, 28–29, 118; reconciliation with Alfonso, 56–59; reconciliation with Sancho II, 148–149; recruiting of followers, 8, 34, 36, 42; redistributor of plunder, xvii, 17, 25–26, 35, 37–38, 51, 52, 71–72, 172; Robin Hood, comparison to, xvii; Ruy, as short form of Rodrigo, 199; Saragossa, his service to emir of, xi, xvi, 119–121; Seville, his defense of, against Granada and allies, 162; social bandit, similarity to, xvi; strategist, 16, 18–20, 22; *taifa* states, relationship with, 202; tribute, levier of, 19, 27; upbringing of, in household of Sancho II (*HR*), 116; Valencia, his conquest and occupation of, xii, 203; vassalage, his personification of, 5; Vellid Adolfo, his pursuit of, 154; vengeance, declaration of, against Scions of Carrión, 82; warlord, concept of, applied to him, xvi, xxiii; as possible translation of "campeador," xxiv; wedding of daughters, 64–65

Roman Empire, 203
romance (Spanish word for ballad), 175
Romance languages, xix
Romanian (Romance language), 199
Rome, 200
Roncevaux, Battle of, 186
Rosellón, lord of, 120
Ruy Jiménez, 135
Ruy Laínez (uncle of Cid in *YDR*), 166, 169

saddles, Galician, 29
Safar (Arabic month), 109–110

Sagrajas, Battle of, xi, 111 (n. 7), 181
Saguntum (ancient Roman name of medieval Murviedro; modern Sagunto), 195
Sahagún, 38, 82, 134, 142–143
Sahara Desert, 184
Saint James the Greater, 22, 34, 49
Saint John the Evangelist, Feast of, 130
Saint Peter (apostle), 10, 13, 41
Saint Sebastian, 12
Saint Susanna, 12
San Esteban, 14, 77, 80–81, 163
San Pedro de Cardeña (Benedictine monastery), xii, 9, 10, 11, 12, 41–42, 171
San Salvador (plaza in Zamora), 146, 147
San Salvador de Oña (monastery), 157
San Servando (castle and monastery in Toledo), 85–87
Sancha, Queen (wife of Fernando I), 189
Sancho, Don (abbot of San Pedro de Cardeña), 10, 13, 41
Sancho II (eldest son of Fernando I), xi–xi, 116, 125, 128–141, 143–147, 149–150, 152–153, 155–159
Sancho III (king of Navarre, father of Fernando I), 189, 196
Sancho (king of Aragon), 119–120
Santa Aren, 137
Santa Gadea (church in Burgos), 159
Santa María, cathedral of Burgos, 5, 25; cathedral of Valencia, 48, 64; church in Carrión, 141
Santa María de Albarracín, 75
Santander (Spanish town and province), 196

Santerem (town in Portugal; birthplace of Ibn Bassam), 109
Santiago (Christian battle cry), 22
Santiago de Compostela, 82, 84
Santiago's Field (outside Zamora), 157
Saragossa, ix, xi–xii, xxiii, 27, 33, 112, 116, 119, 121, 124, 126
Sarah (wife of biblical Abraham), 126 (n. 18)
Sardinian (Romance language), 199
Scions of Carrión, xvi, 32–33, 40, 52, 54–56, 58–68, 70–80, 82, 83–92, 96–97, 100–101, 104
Segorbe, 20
Segovia, 196
Segre River, 120
Sepúlveda, 188
Seville, ix, xi, 117–118, 124, 161–162; king of, 36
Shakespeare, 128
Sierra de Tragacete, 193
Sierra Miedes, 76
Siete Partidas (Spanish law code), 127
Singer of Tales (book by Albert Lord), xix–xx
singing and epic performance, xxi
Smith, Colin (British Hispanist), 175
social bandits, xvi
society, traditional, xii
Sol (daughter of epic Cid), 176
Song of Roland (old French epic), xviii–xix
Song of the Campeador (Carmen Campidoctoris), 123
Soria, 191, 194, 202
Spain, 15, 143, 145; epic tradition of, xx
Spanish March, 29
Spanish National Library, ix
Spinaz de Can, 14

spoils, division of, 24, 30
style, epic, xvii; oral-formulaic, xx

Tagus River, 56
taifas, xi, 17
Tajuña River, 17
Tamarite, castle of, 120–121
Tamín (fictitional Moorish king), 20
Tangiers, 185
Taranz, 45; plain of, 17; Thickets of, 43
Teresa (wife of Henry of Burgundy), 191
Terrer, 18–19, 20, 23, 25–26
Teruel, 26–27
Tévar, Battle of, xii
Tévar, pine forest of, 28
thieves, crucified with Christ, 12
Third Crusade (1187–1192), xiv
Tiedra (castle), 144–145
titles, of EC in English, ix; selection of, in English, xvii
Tizón, 70, 74, 78, 88–90, 100, 102
Tlemcen (Algerian city), 181
Toledo, ix, xi, 84–86, 88, 101, 110, 142, 146, 148, 157
tonsure, meaning of, 38
Toro (town), xi, 142, 146
Tortosa, xi
Tosios (sheik of Olmedo), 171
Toubkal Mountain (Moroccan peak), 184
tournaments, 64 (n. 18)
Treasury of the Excellencies of the Spaniards, xiii, 109
Tudela de Duero, 171–172
Tunisia, 183, 194

Ubierna River, 95
Umayyads (Spanish Muslim dynasty), 185
Urgel, count of, 120
Urraca (daughter of Fernando I), xi, 128, 131–132, 142–148, 150–151, 154–157

Urraca Hernando (daughter of Cid in ballad of "The Cid and the Moorish King") 176

Valencia, ix, xi–xii, xvii, 32–35, 37–39, 40–43, 45–47, 49–52, 54, 57, 60, 62, 64, 65, 67, 71–75, 79–81, 83, 88, 90–91, 93, 97–99, 109–110, 112–113, 115, 176; Cid's entry into, 36
Valencia, king of, 19
Valencians, reaction to Cid's attack, 35
Valladolid, 52, 144, 145
Vanigómez, 96
vassalage, meaning of, 4 (n. 5)
Vellid Adofo, xi, 125 (n. 16), 151–155, 159
Villafranca de Valcárcel, 137
Villalpando, 144–145
Virgil (author of Aeneid), xix
Visigothic law, 65 (n. 19)
Visigothic Spain, ix
Visigoths, 65 (n. 19)
Vivar, xi, 3, 167, 169, 171

warlord, as possible translation of campeador, xxiv

warlords, concept of, xxiii–xxiv; in Mexico, China, Africa, xxiv
Way of Saint James ("Camino de Santiago"; pilgrimage route), xii, 199
wedding of Cid's daughters to Scions of Carrión, 64

Yoda (place name), 171
Youthful Deeds of Rodrigo (Mocedades de Rodrigo), 165
Yugoslavia, traditional oral-formulaic poetry of, xix
Yusuf (King of Morroco [Yusuf ibn Tashfin], leader of Almoravids), 47, 50, 51, 53, 111, 181
Yusuf al-Mu'tamin (Muslim ruler of Saragossa), xi

Zamora, xi, 128, 142–147, 149–155, 157–158, 168–169, 171
Zebedee (father of Saint James the Greater), 200
Zorita, 182